Best Family Adventures:
Santa Barbara County

IMPORTANT LEGAL NOTICE AND DISCLAIMER

Many activities listed, described or otherwise implied in this book are potentially dangerous. Users of this book should take necessary precautions to protect themselves and their families if they choose to participate in any of the activities listed, suggested or implied by this publication.

All information in this book is subject to change including, but not limited to, locations, contact information, prices and hours of operation. Call ahead for most current information including closures, price changes, new location and rules that may affect the use of any given facility.

The author, editors, contributors, publishers and distributors accept no liability for any errors or omissions in this book or for any injuries or losses incurred while using it as a resource.

Pen & Pad Publishing
P.O. Box 2995
Orcutt, CA 93457
(805) 938-1307
www.bestfamilyadventures.com
JBest@BestFamilyAdventures.com

Printed in the United States of America

ISBN-10   0-9769050-2-7
ISBN-13   978-0-9769050-2-8

Library of Congress Control Number: 2009944184

Researchers: Jennifer Best, Erica Best, Valerie Best, Stephen Best, Julia Cabreros
Editors: Lynn Peterson, Julia Cabreros, Emily Slater
Design: Jennifer Best

Acknowledgements

This book would not be in your hands were it not for the following people: the fans of *Best Family Adventures: San Luis Obispo County* who supported that first dip into the publishing pool, and asked for more; my exceedingly patient husband, Steve; our daughters and research assistants, Erica and Valerie; my mom, Lynn Peterson, for her editing skills and ongoing support of all my hair-brained ideas; and my dad, Randy Peterson, for proudly sharing my books, and my life; my dear friend, researcher and editor, Julia Cabreros, whose gentle editing saved me from a lot of embarassment; and Emily Slater, whose professional editing eye and enthusiasm for the project were priceless. I would also like to thank: Jim Hill for encouraging me to finish my original title, and being first to carry it in a bookstore; Marc Canigiula for inspiring me to go for it; Wayne Agner for not allowing me to leave behind my pen and pad; and Jim Sparks, whose energetic support, local insight and ideas have been greatly appreciated.

For my mom,
Lynn P. Peterson
whose support has helped turn
so many of my wild ideas into
real-life success stories.

Contents

Introduction

This adventure guide is meant to be tossed in your backpack, left on the coffee table, spilled on, marked up, dog-eared and otherwise abused. My dream for this book is that you'll explore its pages in which you'll discover new places and perhaps be reminded of old favorites. My hope is that you'll explore with your children or spouse, best friends or new friends, go it alone or get a group together. The point of it all is to get out and explore all that Santa Barbara County has to offer.

This book was born out of my obsessive need to write, a genetic predisposition to explore, one editor's refusal to let me retire, and readers who kept asking for more. The week before our first child was born in 2000, I resigned from my job as education reporter at *Santa Maria Times* in favor of full-time parenthood. My editor, Wayne Agner, had other plans for me. Within months of leaving my desk, Wayne and I settled on an assignment that fit the paper's needs and those of my family – I'd write weekly features on family-friendly activities anywhere within 150 miles of Santa Maria. We would work around the baby's schedule. Here was an opportunity to hit the trail with my child while continuing my career and adding a little something to the college fund. How could I refuse? The stories ran almost weekly for more than two years.

Readers wanted more. Where did I find out about these places? Was there some guide to which they could turn for reference? Turns out, there wasn't. I'd learned about many of these places as a Central Coast native, or by talking to friends and random strangers. Regular readers told me they were putting the articles together in binders, compiling their own reference books. So *Best Family Adventures* was born.

Why *Best Family Adventures*? I've written my fair share of travel articles, as well as travel guides sponsored by different organizations. The sponsored guides are fun and informative, but their first purpose is to serve the association members, not to provide a comprehensive guide for readers. And while there are wonderful books (see Resources, p. 234) dedicated to the area's hiking or mountain biking, wining or dining, all had a heavy bent toward the city of Santa Barbara, and none presented the myriad family-friendly venues and activities available throughout the rest of the county.

When *Best Family Adventures: San Luis Obispo County* was released in 2006, I quickly learned that many potential readers misunderstood the title. "I don't have kids, so that book's not for me," they said. But families come in a variety of configurations from the nuclear to the childless, newlywed to empty nesters. Then there are the family-like groups – support groups, teams, scouts and musicians, college students and co-workers. This is a guide to all things family-friendly – it's not a guide to nightlife or the club scene, fine dining establishments or local watering holes. You can take your children or your pastor, your conservative grandmother or your future in-laws to any of these venues and have a perfectly wonderful time.

HOW TO USE THIS BOOK

Best Family Adventures: Santa Barbara County is divided into chapters by community, with the vast Los Padres National Forest earning its own dedicated chapter, and all unincorporated areas gathered in another chapter. For quick reference, turn to the community you're most interested in researching. If you have more time, grab a highlight marker, a drink and a snack, curl up in your favorite reading chair and have at it.

Each chapter is divided into five subject areas: Letters for libraries and the like; Arts for galleries and other artistic venues; History for venues of particular historical interest; Nature for venues and activities with a bent toward science and nature; and Other Adventures for those things that were tough to pigeonhole. Golf may be a good walk spoiled, but does it really belong in the Nature category? And if a farm is organic, it's natural, right? Still, it offers more than a walk in the trees.

Each entry includes its address, phone number and Web site address where available, driving directions and a description. You'll also find symbols representing the cost of admission. All of this information is subject to change, but was accurate at press time, including price ranges:

FREE! = Free of charge

$ = $10 or less per person

$$ = $11 to $20 per person

$$$ = $21 or more per person

☞ = Best Bets when time's too short to hit them all

TERMINOLOGY & TECHNICAL DETAILS

You'll find some repeated phrases here that had my editors in fits. Rather than repeat their explanation at each listing, let's cover the basics here.

Adventure Pass is a day-use pass required for motorists using high-impact recreation areas in the Los Padres National Forest, including Upper Santa Ynez River, Figueroa Mountain and the maintained campsites east of Santa Maria. To be on the safe side, carry a day pass in your vehicle every time you venture into the forest, or pick up the annual pass to cover your bases. The passes only are required for visitors traveling by motorized vehicle. Hikers and cyclists are exempt. Depending on the site, there may be additional fees required for camping. Check the forest service Web site (www.fs.fed.us/r5/lospadres) for detailed information about the program, including sales locations.

The **Black Gold library system** (blackgold.org) connects libraries throughout the Central Coast for resource sharing. Anyone with a library card (free) has access to books, recorded books, movies and other resources loaned by libraries from Piru in eastern Ventura County to Templeton in northern San Luis Obispo County. Titles can be ordered online and delivered to your local library, which may charge a nominal fee for the delivery service.

Disc golf, also known as Frisbee golf, is an outdoor activity related somewhat to traditional golf. Take a good old flying disc, fling it toward a target basket, then repeat and you have yourself a short game of disc golf.

Avid disc golfers carry their own bags of specialized discs, but a backpack-friendly flying disc works just as well.

"Skinned infield" refers to baseball or softball diamonds where grass has been removed from the infield, making them safer for competitive play.

The Central Coast's wild places are home to potentially dangerous wild animals, including **bears, mountain lions, coyotes** and **rattlesnakes**. Chances are you'll come across the occasional rattlesnake, but you're unlikely to see the larger animals of concern. They typically avoid people but can be surprised by quiet explorers. Before heading out, acquaint yourself with the proper procedures for avoiding these dangers, and steps to take in the unlikely event you meet one of the creatures. Educate any children who may be exploring with you, and keep them close at hand. The California Department of Fish and Game (www.dfg.ca.gov/news/issues/lion) is a great resource for detailed information. Essentially, make noise while you explore, and don't stick your hands into holes or other potential dens.

Ticks love the Central Coast's natural areas. They most often hitch rides

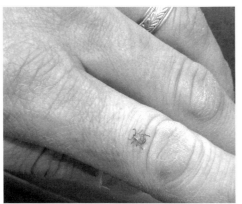

with passersby who rub against brush or tall grass where ticks lay in wait for any warm body. To protect yourself, wear long-sleeved shirts, long trousers, long socks, close-toed shoes and a brimmed hat. Periodically check yourself and your hiking buddies throughout your adventures. No need to panic if you see one. Just flick it off with your finger or a safe object like a leaf.

Poison oak is the common name for the bush scientists like to call toxicodendron diversilobum — poisonous branching plant with opposing leaves. That about sums it up. The plant flourishes along the Central Coast and is a serious issue for many people. Like its relatives, poison sumac and poison ivy, this coastal shrub emits oil that serves as an irritant when it comes in contact with skin. Within a week to 10 days, the oil causes a rash that bubbles, itches and oozes. Did the leaves, or even dormant branches, rub on your boots? Then the oil is there and will continue to cause issues until you clean them. Did you get it on your clothes? Backpack? The dog? Ditto.

Though this rule doesn't hold true for its cousins, poison ivy and poison sumac, it does seem to ring true most of the time: leaves of three, let it be. Poison oak presents leaves in sets of three. They are a vibrant green in early spring and turn to a rich, dark, glossy green before turning sunset red and finally dropping from the plant completely for winter. The bushes can grow to 25 feet, though tend to top out at 6-8 feet in these parts. It's most difficult to identify in winter when the leafless branches look much like those of any number of other deciduous plants.

The best way to prevent irritation from poison oak is to avoid contact with any part of the plant. Even the sticks of overwintering bushes carry the oil.

Just stay out of areas where it is known to exist. Then again, that doesn't sound like fun, so here are some other options:

— Wear long-sleeved shirts, long pants, long socks and boots to cover as much skin as possible

— Prior to exposure, use products like EnviroDerm's Ivy Block, or Tecnu's Poison Oak-n-Ivy Armor

— Wash every stitch of clothing used to remove any residual oils, which can affect anyone who comes in contact with them for weeks to come.

— Immediately upon return to civilization, use cool water and a grease-cutting soap, such as TecNu, though Dawn and other grease-cutting dishwashing soaps have been known to do the trick. Be sure to scrub under your nails, as the oil can hide here and cause problems later. The FDA suggests beginning the entire cleaning process with a complete rubdown in rubbing alcohol. Others add that suds (and rinse) should be done with cold water. The idea is that the oil won't be able to spread deeper into the pores

— Wash the dog. Man's best friend can be poison oak's best carrier. Unless you wash the dog thoroughly, it doesn't matter how much you wash your own belongings and exposed skin. One good scratch of an oily Fido means lots of scratching for you in the near future.

I did all that and got it anyway. Now what?

It probably took up to a week for the rash to show, but now it's there in all its itching, oozing glory. You can try to tough it out, or resort to a variety of anti-itch treatments including over-the-counter hydrocortisone, calamine lotion or poison oak itch treatments available at your local pharmacy. It'll take about a week for the thing to begin to subside and up to three weeks for the damage to disappear completely.

If images of scratching off your own arm (or leg or whatever's affected) are invading your dreams, or the rash appears anywhere near your eyes, it's time to see your doctor. She can provide prescription treatment ranging from prednisone to a fantastic topical called fluocinonide.

The web is full of useful resources about Poison Oak, including the National Institutes of Health, U.S. Food and Drug Administration and poisonivy.aesir.com.

COME OUT AND PLAY

All these warnings aside, we live in a pretty great place full of family-friendly activities. Do your teens doubt it? Toss this book their way, let them pick a few places to explore, then help them find their way.

Happy trails!

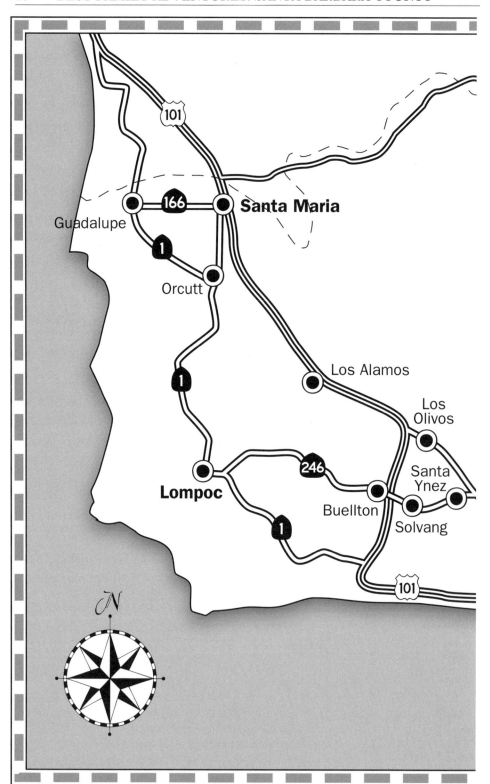

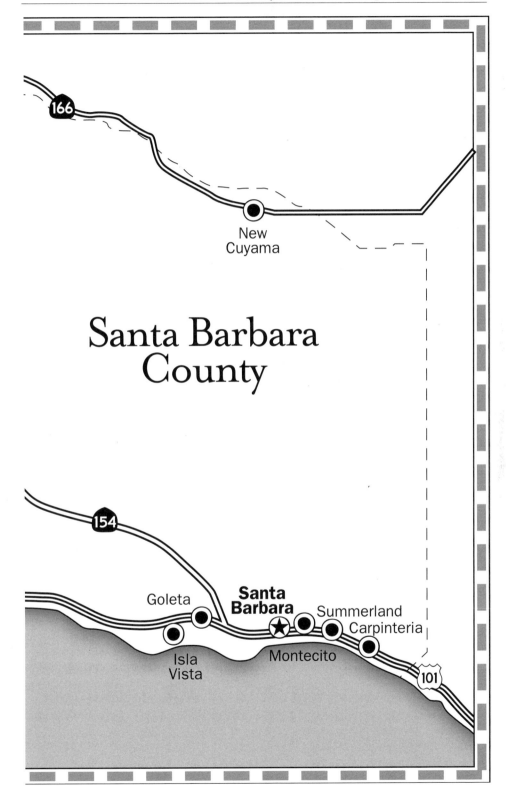

Chapter 1

Santa Barbara

The county's namesake has long attracted visitors, and for good reason. It's easy to lose yourself among the miles of beaches, acres of gardens, dozens of art galleries, and a variety of museums and historic sites. State Street alone is lined with wonderful restaurants and unusual shops, museums and galleries. The waterfront affords plenty of space for sunning yourself, building castles, flying kites and spiking volleyballs. There are sailing lessons, catamaran rides, cigar cruises, and festivals galore. Venture into the neighborhoods and you'll find treasure there, too.

This land of plenty was home to the Chumash people for thousands of years before Europeans discovered its rich resources, not the least of which was a plentiful supply of fresh water flowing from hot and cold springs throughout the coastal mountain range. In 1782, the Spanish established El Presidio de Santa Barbara. Four years later, Mission Santa Barbara, the 10th in the California chain, was established on a hill that overlooked a wide valley, and across the Santa Barbara Channel to the Channel Islands and beyond.

The community continued to thrive as modern forms of agriculture and support industries took hold. Establishment of the state's longest deep-water pier along the naturally protected, south-facing waterfront allowed ships to tie up for easy transfer of freight and passengers beginning in 1872. The completion of the rail link between Los Angeles and Santa Barbara in August of 1887 made the community even more accessible, and the movie industry propelled Santa Barbara to international fame. Its proximity to Hollywood allows Santa Barbara to serve as both movie setting and getaway for the rich and famous, but remains friendly and accessible to the rest of us, too.

All this popularity comes at a price. The city is the most crowded in the county, and parking in the heart of town can be a bear, particularly during summer months and holidays. Instead of driving to your destination, park in the outlying areas along the waterfront shuttle route, then grab the electric shuttle for just a quarter per ride. The shuttle runs along Cabrillo Boulevard from Santa Barbara Zoo (page 58) to Leadbetter Beach (page 44) and along State Street from Stearns Wharf (p. 31) to Alameda Park (page 32). For transit options serving other areas throughout the region, check www.sbmtd.gov.

Want a quick overview of Santa Barbara's history? Hit the mission (p. 28), then take the Red Tile Walking Tour, an easy, 12-block, self-guided journey through historic downtown. Maps are available at the Santa Barbara County Courthouse (p. 29) and from the Santa Barbara Conference & Visitors Bureau (www.santabarbaraca.com/maps).

ARTS

Arlington Theatre

1317 State St.

(805) 963-4408

www.thearlingtontheatre.com

$-$$$

From Highway 101, take the Carrillo Street exit and turn toward the mountains. Turn left onto Chapala Street, right onto Sola Street, then right onto State Street.

This historic theater in the city's center offers an eclectic array of live stage performances varying from internationally acclaimed bands to comedians, from lecturers to film premieres. Movie stars and film buffs, film critics and everyday audience members mingle here during the annual Santa Barbara International Film Festival. The nearest public parking is available less than half a block toward the beach, off Chapala Street.

Art from Scrap

302 E. Cota St.

(805) 884-0459

artfromscrap.org

$

From Highway 101, take the Garden Street exit, turn away from the beach and turn right onto Cota Street.

If you never believed recycling would work, head down to the Art from Scrap Reuse Store. Area businesses donate literally tons of clean materials from paperclips to tiles, Styrofoam packing peanuts to burlap bags. The materials are sorted, stored and sold at this shop that also includes a gallery of work by artists who specialize in building from recycled goods. Art from Scrap also offers drop-in Saturday art projects for all ages (10 a.m. to noon) and summer art camps, environmental education, birthday parties and field trips. The store and gallery are open Tuesdays, Wednesdays and Fridays from 10 a.m. to 2 p.m., Thursdays 10 a.m. to 6 p.m. and Saturdays from 10 a.m. to 3 p.m.

Arts Fund Gallery

205-C Santa Barbara St.

(805) 965-7321

www.artsfundsb.org

FREE

From southbound Highway 101, take the Garden Street exit and turn right onto Santa Barbara Street. From northbound 101, take the Garden Street exit; turn left onto Garden Street at the end of the ramp, right onto Yanonali Street and right onto Santa Barbara Street.

The nonprofit Arts Fund maintains this gallery that features revolving exhibits of works by local artists. This organization also offers the High

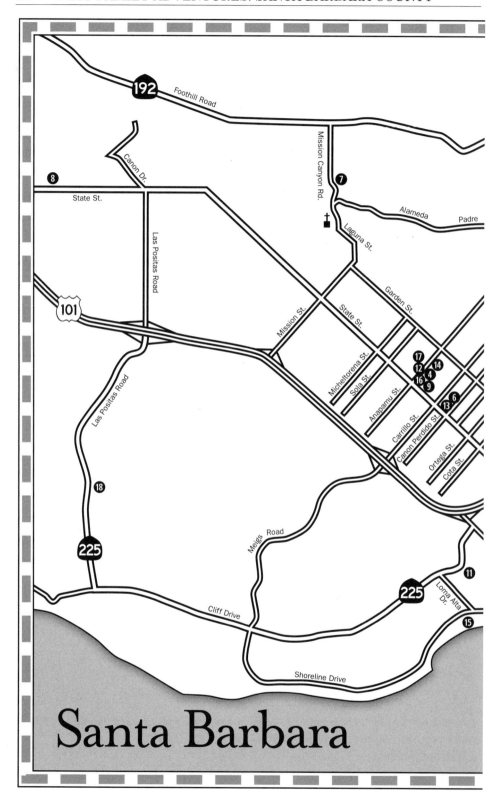

Santa Barbara

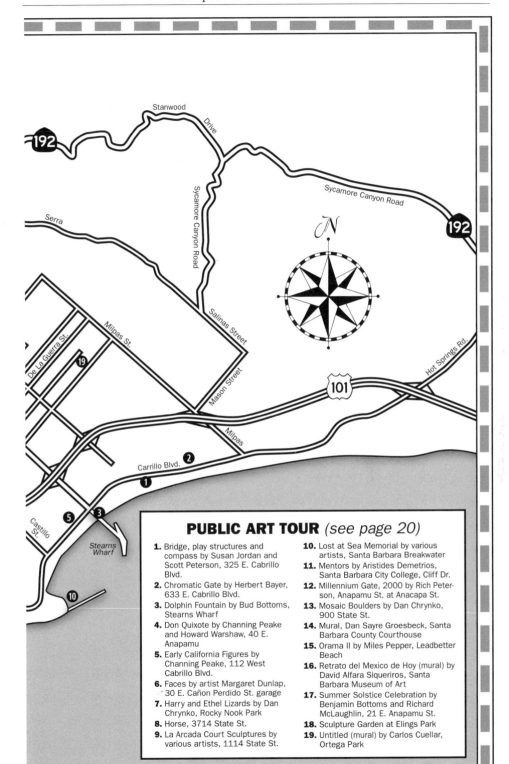

PUBLIC ART TOUR *(see page 20)*

1. Bridge, play structures and compass by Susan Jordan and Scott Peterson, 325 E. Cabrillo Blvd.
2. Chromatic Gate by Herbert Bayer, 633 E. Cabrillo Blvd.
3. Dolphin Fountain by Bud Bottoms, Stearns Wharf
4. Don Quixote by Channing Peake and Howard Warshaw, 40 E. Anapamu
5. Early California Figures by Channing Peake, 112 West Cabrillo Blvd.
6. Faces by artist Margaret Dunlap, 30 E. Cañon Perdido St. garage
7. Harry and Ethel Lizards by Dan Chrynko, Rocky Nook Park
8. Horse, 3714 State St.
9. La Arcada Court Sculptures by various artists, 1114 State St.
10. Lost at Sea Memorial by various artists, Santa Barbara Breakwater
11. Mentors by Aristides Demetrios, Santa Barbara City College, Cliff Dr.
12. Millennium Gate, 2000 by Rich Peterson, Anapamu St. at Anacapa St.
13. Mosaic Boulders by Dan Chrynko, 900 State St.
14. Mural, Dan Sayre Groesbeck, Santa Barbara County Courthouse
15. Orama II by Miles Pepper, Leadbetter Beach
16. Retrato del Mexico de Hoy (mural) by David Alfara Siqueriros, Santa Barbara Museum of Art
17. Summer Solstice Celebration by Benjamin Bottoms and Richard McLaughlin, 21 E. Anapamu St.
18. Sculpture Garden at Elings Park
19. Untitled (mural) by Carlos Cuellar, Ortega Park

School Arts Mentorship Program, which matches promising teen artists with professional master artists. The gallery is open Tuesdays through Saturdays from 1 p.m. to 5 p.m. Stop in for information about other program offerings.

Atkinson Gallery
Santa Barbara City College
721 Cliff Drive
(805) 965-0581, ext.3484
gallery.sbcc.edu
FREE

From southbound 101, take the Castillo Street exit; turn right at the end of the offramp, then right onto Montecito Street, which becomes Cliff Drive. Turn left onto Loma Alta Drive to access campus parking. From northbound 101, take the Bath Street exit, turn immediately left onto Haley Street, then left onto Castillo Street, then proceed as above.

Half a dozen times per year, this gallery changes its exhibits to feature contemporary artists from around the world. If you're looking for student works, check in each spring for the Annual Student Exhibition. The gallery is open Mondays through Thursdays from 10 a.m. to 7 p.m., Fridays and Saturdays from 10 a.m. to 4 p.m. all year round, except college holidays.

☞ Brooks Institute of Photography Gallery 27
27 E. Cota St.
(888) 304-3456
www.brooks.edu/aboutus/cota.asp
FREE

From Highway 101, take the Garden Street exit, turn away from the beach and turn left onto Cota Street.

Since 1945, Brooks Institute has trained photographers and filmmakers whose works have been featured in books and magazines, and on the Internet and the big screen. In 2008, the private college opened this wondrous exhibit space that may feature works by faculty, students or international artists. Even the space itself is artistic with its visually captivating angles, unique lighting — both natural and artificial — and mysterious sliding metal doors. The galleries are open to the public Monday through Friday 8 a.m. to 9 p.m. and weekends 10 a.m. to 9 p.m.

Channing Peake Gallery
County Administration Building
105 E. Anapamu St.
(805) 568-3994
www.sbartscommission.org/exhibitions
FREE

From Highway 101, take Carrillo Street toward the mountains; turn left onto State Street, then right onto Anapamu Street.

This government building provides public space for rotating art exhibits. Open during regular government hours, typically 8 a.m. to 5 p.m. weekdays.

Elizabeth Gallery Mosaic Showroom
1125 E. Ortega St.
(805) 963-2878
FREE
From Highway 101, take Milpas Street exit, turn away from the beach, then right onto Ortega Street.
Santa Barbara mosaic artist Elizabeth Gallery opens her doors by appointment to anyone interested in the art of mosaic. Her studio-gallery features her own works, and she frequently works with groups to demonstrate her process, discuss the art form or teach her techniques. Call ahead to arrange a visit.

Faulkner Galleries
Santa Barbara Central Library
40 E. Anapamu St.
(805) 564-5608
www.spblibrary.org
FREE
From Highway 101, take Carrillo Street toward the mountains, turn left onto Chapala Street and then right onto Anapamu Street.
Three adjacent wheelchair-accessible galleries, located immediately inside the front doors of the Central Library (page 25), provide ever-changing exhibits of locally produced arts and artifacts. The galleries are open Mondays through Thursdays from 10 a.m. to 8 p.m., Fridays and Saturdays 10 a.m. to 5:30 p.m. and Sundays from 1 p.m. to 5 p.m.

Fiesta Five Theatre
916 State St.
(877) 789-MOVIE
metrotheatres.com
$
From Highway 101, take the Carrillo Street exit and turn toward the mountains, then turn right onto State Street.
This theater offers first-run movies, a typical snack bar and, of course, restrooms. Public parking is available in the structure immediately adjacent to the theater.

☞ Granada Theater
(805) 899-2222
1214 State St.
www.granadasb.org

$-$$$

From Highway 101, take the Carrillo Street exit and turn toward the mountains. Turn left onto Chapala Street, right onto Victoria Street, then right onto State Street.

This beautifully appointed historic theater serves as center stage for a variety of local organizations offering opera, symphonic music and dance, as well as a busy schedule of traveling performing arts groups. In addition to a busy evening and weekend performance schedule, the theater offers a performance series for school-age children, associated arts conservatory program, teen program and classes, workshops and other opportunities to interact with performing artists. Public parking is available nearby, off Chapala Street.

Marcia Burtt Studio
517 Laguna St.
(805) 962-5588
www.artlacuna.com
FREE

From Highway 101, take Garden Street away from the beach, turn right onto Haley Street and then left onto Laguna Street.

This commercial gallery offers a heavy emphasis on landscapes, both American and international, by local artists, including Marcia Burtt, Patricia Doyle, Robert Abbott and Meg Torbert. The gallery is open from 11 a.m. to 5 p.m. weekends and by appointment.

Metro 4 Theatre
618 State St.
(877) 789-MOVIE
metrotheatres.com
$

From Highway 101, take the Carrillo Street exit and turn toward the mountains, then turn right onto State Street.

This four-screen theater offers first-run movies and stadium seating, snack bar and, of course, restrooms. Public parking is available less than a block away, off Anacapa Street between East Cota and East Haley streets.

Paseo Nuevo Cinemas
8 West De la Guerra Place
(877) 789-MOVIE
metrotheatres.com
$

From Highway 101, take the Carrillo exit and turn toward the mountains, then right onto De La Vina Street, left onto Ortega Street and left onto Chapala Street for parking.

This four-screen theater located in the Paseo Nuevo shopping center offers first-run movies, a snack bar and restrooms. Public parking is available nearby, off Chapala Street.

Patty Look Lewis Gallery
25 E. De La Guerra St.
(805) 965-2525
www.pattylooklewis.com
FREE

From northbound Highway 101, take Garden Street toward the mountains and then turn left onto De La Guerra Street. From southbound 101, take Carrillo Street toward the mountains; turn right onto Anacapa Street and then right onto De La Guerra Street.

Across the street from historic City Hall is a private, commercial gallery that specializes in works by midcentury Santa Barbara icons such as William Dole, Channing Peake and Selden Spaulding. The gallery is open from noon to 5 p.m. Tuesdays through Saturdays.

Plaza de Oro Theatre
371 South Hitchcock Way
(877) 789-MOVIE (789-6684)
metrotheatres.com
$

From northbound Highway 101, take Hope Avenue, turn right onto Calle Real and then left onto Hitchcock Way. From southbound Highway 101, take La Cumbre Road; turn left at the end of the ramp, right onto Calle Real, then left onto Hitchcock Way.

This two-screen movie theater offers first-run movies, a snack bar and restrooms. Public parking also is available immediately adjacent to the theater.

Public Art Tour
(805) 568-3990
www.sbartscommission.org/exhibitions/public_art.html
FREE

Santa Barbara's abundant art resources include fine art galleries, student venues, retail outlets and education programs. For quick and easy art that's always child friendly, check out these public arts works. (Numbers refer to points mapped on pages 14 and 15.)

1. Bridge, play structures and compass by Susan Jordan and Scott Peterson, 325 E. Cabrillo Blvd.
2. Chromatic Gate by Herbert Bayer, 633 E. Cabrillo Blvd.
3. Dolphin Fountain by Bud Bottoms, Stearns Wharf (page 31)
4. Don Quixote by Channing Peake and Howard Warshaw, 40 E. Anapamu
5. Early California Figures by Channing Peake, 112 West Cabrillo Blvd.
6. Faces by artist Margaret Dunlap, 30 E. Cañon Perdido St. garage

La Arcada, a narrow alley in the 1100 block of State Street, includes lovely kid-friendly sculptures. Art lovers are invited to take a seat with Benjamin Franklin, enjoy the fountain and pose these musicians just so.

7. Harry and Ethel Lizards by Dan Chrynko, Rocky Nook Park (p. 54)

8. Horse, 3714 State St.

9. La Arcada Court Sculptures by various artists, 1114 State St.

10. Lost at Sea Memorial by various artists, Santa Barbara Breakwater

11. Mentors by Aristides Demetrios, Santa Barbara City College, Cliff Drive

12. Millennium Gate, 2000 by Rich Peterson, Anapamu Street at Anacapa Street

13. Mosaic Boulders by Dan Chrynko, 900 State St.

14. Mural, Dan Sayre Groesbeck, Santa Barbara County Courthouse (p. 29)

15. Orama II by Miles Pepper, Leadbetter Beach (p. 44)

16. Retrato del Mexico de Hoy (mural) by David Alfara Siqueriros, Santa Barbara Museum of Art (p. 22)

17. Summer Solstice Celebration by Benjamin Bottoms and Richard McLaughlin, 21 E. Anapamu St.

18. Sculpture Garden at Elings Park (page 39)

19. Untitled (mural) by Carlos Cuellar, Ortega Park (page 50)

Ridley-Tree Education Center at McCormick House

1600 Santa Barbara St. (entrance on Arrellaga Street)
(805) 962-1661
sbmuseart.org/programs/education/artclass.asp
$$-$$$

From northbound 101, take Arrellaga Street toward the mountains. From southbound 101, take Mission Street toward the mountains; turn right onto De La Vina, then left onto Arrellaga.

The Santa Barbara Museum of Art (page 22) offers this facility for hands-on art education for children and adults. The center is available to families, schools and other groups. It offers programs throughout the year, including art classes, camps, studio art practice, parent/child classes and after-school programs, among others. Some scholarships are available. See Web site for current offerings.

Riviera Theatre

2044 Alameda Padre Serra

(877) 789-MOVIE (789-6684)

metrotheatres.com

$

From Highway 101, take the Mission Street exit and proceed toward the mountains. Turn right onto Garden Street, left onto Pedregosa Street, then left onto Alameda Padre Serra.

This neighborhood one-screen theater offers a steady stream of independent films, documentaries and other film festival favorites. Other facilities include a snack bar and restrooms. The theater is tucked away inside the Riviera commercial park, which provides parking adjacent to the theater.

☞ Santa Barbara Arts

1114 State St., No. 26

(805) 884-1938

www.sbarts.net

FREE

From Highway 101, take Carrillo Street toward the mountain, then turn left onto State Street.

This privately owned gallery tucked in art-centric La Arcada off State Street features works by artists and artisans from throughout the United States. Local artists receive special attention in this eclectic collection that varies from children's books to fine jewelry to fiber arts. Works may be entirely creative endeavors or works designed for utilitarian purposes. Children supervised by responsible adults are warmly welcomed to explore the gallery. The gallery also is a good spot for learning about local art classes, workshops and special events.

Santa Barbara Arts and Crafts Show

Cabrillo Pavilion Arts Center

1118 East Cabrillo Blvd.

Santa Barbara, CA 93103

(805) 897-1982

www.sbaacs.com
FREE
From Highway 101, take Garden Street toward the beach.
Come rain or shine, some 200 artists and artisans display their creations along Cabrillo Boulevard every Sunday from 10 a.m. to dusk. Start your walk at Stearns Wharf (p. 31) or Cabrillo Pavilion (p. 39), bring plenty of water and sunscreen, and maybe even a picnic blanket and snacks to share. Many of the artists welcome questions.

Santa Barbara Bowl

900 Block Lowena Drive
(805) 962-7411
www.sbbowl.com
$$$

From Highway 101, take Milpas Street toward the mountains; turn right onto Lowena or park on Milpas Street.
Santa Barbara's premier outdoor performance venue was built in 1936 to serve as the performance home of the annual Fiesta, the city's annual celebration of history, customs, and traditions of the American Indian, Spanish, Mexican, and early American settlers. Today, the renovated facility plays host to a variety of performing artists from around the world. With a seating capacity of 4,562 patrons, the amphitheater is the largest in Santa Barbara County. Expect to get very friendly with your neighbors if you're in the upper sections where bench seats provide very close quarters.

Parking here is limited, so arrive very early and hope for a spot, but plan on a considerable walk. Security is very strict. (We saw an old man who'd brought his own stadium chair turned away.) No bottles or cans are allowed, and plastic water bottles are only allowed if they are sealed and less than 1.5 liters. Don't even think about bringing a backpack, diaper bag, stroller, camera or digital recording device. No ice chests, clearly no knives (leave the Leatherman at home, Tough Guy) or wallet chains. Come to think of it, it's easier to just say: bring a jacket, your ticket and your friends. Leave everything else at home. Oh, cigarettes are OK, but only in the main concession area.

☞ Santa Barbara Museum of Art

1130 State St.
(805) 963-4364
sbmuseart.org
$

From Highway 101, take Carrillo Street toward the mountain, then turn left onto State Street.
The county's largest art museum offers regularly shifting traveling exhibits, as well as works from the museum's collection. The spacious, wheelchair-friendly galleries provide ample room for wiggly bodies to coexist

with more patient souls. For best results with children, follow them through the museum rather than attempt to lead them. You may be amazed by what they see.

The wheelchair-accessible museum is open Tuesdays through Sundays from 11 a.m. to 5 p.m. No admission is charged on Sundays and children ages 5 and under always get in free.

This museum's Fearing Library includes videos, dictionaries, artist files, clippings, exhibit catalogs, auction house catalogs, encyclopedias and more related to art criticism and art history. The library's special focus includes Asian, Latin American, American, European and contemporary art, as well as fine art photography. Though intended for staff, docents and members, the library is open for public use Tuesdays through Thursdays from 1 p.m. to 5 p.m.

For hands-on art education, head to the museum's offsite Ridley-Tree Education Center (page 21).

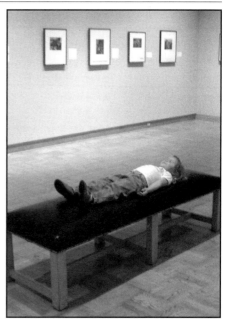

Santa Barbara Museum of Art offers an array of rotating and permanent exhibits, room for groups, strollers or wheelchairs, and resting spots for exhausted visitors.

Santa Barbara Contemporary Arts Forum
653 Paseo Nuevo (Upstairs)
(805) 966-5373
sbcaf.org
FREE

From Highway 101, take Carrillo Street toward the mountains, turn right onto Chapala Street then left into the Paseo Nuevo parking structure.

This spacious gallery bent toward modern works of local and international artists offers rotating exhibits that may include current works, political exhibits or shows emphasizing local current events. Open Tuesdays through Saturdays from 11 a.m. to 5 p.m. and Sundays from noon until 5 p.m.

☞ Sullivan Goss - An American Gallery
7 E. Anapamu St.
(805) 730-1460
www.sullivangoss.com
FREE

From Highway 101, take Carrillo Street toward the mountains, turn left onto Chapala Street and then right onto Anapamu Street.

Thanks to owner Frank Goss and energetic, outgoing, helpful employees like Operations Manager Nathan Vonk, this is, by far, our girls' favorite gallery in Santa Barbara County. Though privately held and commercial in nature, the gallery offers a constantly rotating collection of works by 19th, 20th, and 21st Century American artists with a special emphasis on California artists. The gallery includes three exhibit halls each of which is rotated quarterly to provide fresh art for all seasons.

Mr. Goss and his employees welcome young visitors in particular and enjoy helping foster youngsters' interest in the various styles and media. During your visit, tell them the "child-friendly museum" mom sent you. If they have time, they may walk your family through and discuss the current works, share their highlights and ask your kids for theirs. For a preview of current exhibits, visit the Web site for a video preview.

Open daily 10 a.m. to 5:30 p.m.

Townley Room Gallery
Cabrillo Pavilion Arts Center & Bath House
1118 East Cabrillo Blvd.
(805) 897-1982
ci.santa-barbara.ca.us
FREE

From Highway 101, take Milpas Street toward the beach, then turn left onto Cabrillo Boulevard.

At publication time, the center's hours were reduced due to budget shortfalls. But generally the gallery is open to the public whenever the hall is not rented. The exhibits change monthly, so call ahead for information about current exhibits and opening hours.

This neighborhood is a great one-stop, all-day adventure. Arrive early for a zoo visit just up the street, then run free, play volleyball or in the playground at East Beach after either a picnic lunch or a quick grab at the pavilion's beachfront café. Get out of the sun with a walk through the gallery, then run out the last of that energy on the sand before loading up for the trip home.

Waterhouse Gallery
1114 State St., No. 9
(805) 962-8885
www.waterhousegallery.com
FREE

From Highway 101, take Carrillo Street toward the mountain, then turn left onto State Street.

This compact gallery located deep in La Arcada art court houses volumes of work emphasizing plein-air landscapes, still life painting and figurative works. Younger children may enjoy the fountain outside with an adult close at hand while older siblings, friends and relatives join their adult caretakers in the gallery. There is no stroller access, and the museum is entirely hands-off.

Open Mondays through Saturdays from 11 a.m. to 5 p.m. and Sundays from noon until 4:30 p.m.

LETTERS

Central Library
40 East Anapamu St.
(805) 962-7653
www.sbplibrary.org
FREE

From Highway 101, take Carrillo Street toward the mountains, turn left onto Chapala Street and then right onto Anapamu Street.

This cozy library offers a wonderful collection of books, magazines, movies and music CDs for all ages, access to the Black Gold Library System and the Internet. The Faulkner Gallery (p. 25) provides rotating exhibits of works by local artists and the library also offers several public events and programs, including story time, guest lectures and the system-wide book club for adults, Santa Barbara Reads. Story time offered Tuesdays and Thursdays at 10:30 a.m. (3- to 5-year-olds) and Spanish-language story time Saturdays at 10:30 a.m.

Randall House
835 Laguna St.
(805) 963-1909
randallhouserarebooks.com
FREE

From Highway 101, take Garden Street away from the beach; turn right onto Cañon Perdido and then right onto Laguna Street.

This commercial venture specializing in rare, fine, antique and first-edition books welcomes the public to browse its library and fine art collection in the historical Gonzalez-Ramirez Adobe, a national landmark constructed in 1825. While this may be just a passing stop for the smallest of children, older children and adults who share a particular interest in the printed word find the collection alluring.

When considering whether to take children to view the collection, keep in mind the antiques include the likes of a rare, autographed, first-edition copy of William Faulkner's Go Down Moses and Other Stories offered at $25,000.

The shop is open Mondays through Fridays from 10 a.m. to 5 p.m. and Saturdays from 10 a.m. to 2 p.m.

Santa Barbara East Side Library
1102 E. Montecito St.
(805) 963-3727
www.sbplibrary.org

FREE

From Highway 101, take Milpas Street toward the mountains, then turn right onto Montecito Street.

This public library offers special events, story times and participates in the community-wide Santa Barbara Reads book adult reading program. Open Mondays through Saturdays from 10 a.m. Closing times vary. Story time for 3 to 5 year olds is offered Wednesdays at 10:30 a.m., and bilingual story times are held Fridays at 10 a.m. and 10:30 a.m.

HISTORY

Casa de la Guerra Historic House Museum

15 E. De la Guerra St.

(805) 965-0093

www.sbthp.org/casa.htm

$

From Highway 101, take the Carrillo Street exit and turn toward the mountains, turn right onto Anacapa Street, then right onto De La Guerra Street.

Hands-on history lessons in Santa Barbara are more often than not just around the corner. Such is the case with Casa de la Guerra, located spitting distance from busy State Street.

Built from 1819 to 1927 by the fifth Presidio commander, Jose de la Guerra, Casa de la Guerra is a city landmark, a California landmark and is listed on the National Register of Historic Places. The city held its first official meeting in this home, which stands today as a monument to the community's Hispanic heritage.

Today, the Santa Barbara Trust for Historic Preservation operates the adobe home as a museum featuring original furnishings, family history and rotating art exhibits. The home is open weekends from noon to 4 p.m., though guided tours are available by reservation and may be arranged on alternate days.

El Presidio de Santa Barbara State Historic Park

123 E. Cañon Perdido St.

(805) 965-0093

www.sbthp.org/presidio.htm

$

From southbound Highway 101, take Carrillo Street toward the mountains; turn right onto Anacapa, then left onto Cañon Perdido Street. From northbound 101, take Garden Street toward the mountains, then turn left onto Cañon Perdido Street.

The oldest building in Santa Barbara, El Presidio, still stands as a reminder of the early mission years, the soldiers charged with guarding the territory and the lives forever changed by religious expansion. Since 1966, the park has grown to include the reconstructed and refurbished El Cuartel, soldiers' residence and padre's quarters, chapel and bell tower, the original quadrangle and the commander's quarters.

With the help of docents, recent renovations and museum exhibits, the park provides an easily accessible step back in time.

Open daily from 10:30 a.m. to 4:30 p.m. Closed major holidays.

Fernald Mansion and Trussell-Winchester Adobe

414 W. Montecito St.

(805) 966-1601

www.santabarbaramuseum.com

$

From southbound Highway 101, take Castillo Street toward the beach, then turn right onto Montecito Street. From northbound 101, take Bath Street exit; turn left onto Haley, left again onto Castillo Street, then right onto Montecito Street.

Docents welcome visitors for guided tours of this Queen Anne-style Victorian home divided from the busy street by a white picket fence. The Fernald Mission, circa 1860, was built by Judge Fernald as a gift to his bride. Generations of the family lived here until the 1950s, and many of their belongings are still on display.

The site also is home to the Trussell-Winchester Adobe (1854) built by Captain Horatio Gates Trussell. The construction materials are a particularly interesting combination. Trussell incorporated both the ubiquitous adobe brick, as well as wreckage from the steamer Winfield Scott that foundered in 1853 off Anacapa Island.

Docent-led tours are typically offered on weekends, but call for the current schedule or to make special arrangements.

Karpeles Manuscript Library

21 W. Anapamu St.

(805) 962-5322

www.karpeles.com

FREE

From Highway 101, take Carrillo Street toward the mountains, turn left onto Chapala Street and then right onto Anapamu Street.

The museum is often missed by potential visitors who imagine it filled with ancient books and maps. In fact, David Karpeles hoped to motivate a new generation of youngsters by sharing great works from the past: outstanding writings, earth-shaking innovations and inspiring inventions. Today, this library is one of eight throughout the United States. It's a good place to take the kids for a quick view of history presented in no particular order. A copy of a historical document relating to a given war may be located in one room while a model of a ship from that era is located in another. Let the kids find the connections.

Open Wednesdays through Sundays from noon to 4 p.m.

Old Mission Santa Barbara
2200 Laguna St.
(806) 682-4713
www.santabarbaramission.org
$

From Highway 101, take Mission Street toward the mountains, then turn left onto Laguna Street.

Among the 21 mission locations throughout California, there may be none as lovely as Santa Barbara's. Though surrounded by homes today, it's not difficult to imagine the serenity and view mission founders enjoyed from this foothill location. Year-round springs provided ample water. The nearby mountains and the ocean provided ample hunting and fishing opportunities.

The mission continues to provide Catholic services, and visitors and locals alike are drawn to enjoy the grounds and adjacent A.C. Postell Rose Garden (p. 47) for photo opportunities or family picnics. A self-guided tour may include the interior garden, cemetery, museum and chapel and can take anywhere from half an hour to 90 minutes to complete. The grounds are open Mondays through Saturdays from 9 a.m. to 5 p.m., except during mass, which is held noon to 1 p.m. Fridays, 4 p.m. to 5 p.m. Saturdays and Sundays from 7 a.m. to 1 p.m.

Santa Barbara Carriage & Western Arts Museum
129 Castillo St.
(805) 962-2353
www.carriagemuseum.org
FREE

From southbound Highway 101, take Castillo Street toward the beach. From northbound 101, take Bath Street exit, turn left onto Haley, then left again onto Castillo Street.

Hidden in the back of Pershing Park (p. 52) is an 11,000-square-foot museum filled with horse-drawn vehicles and clothing, tack and art related to the Western horse tradition. Little cowboys and cowgirls, history buffs and carriage fanatics may enjoy a walk through surreys and steam pumpers, bridles, saddles, vests, spurs, chaps and headstalls. There's also a collection of saddles, some of which were used by Clark Gable, Jimmy Stewart and Will Rogers. The collection spiffs up and hits the streets during Santa Barbara's Old Spanish Days Fiesta held each August.

The museum is open Monday through Friday from 9 a.m. to 3 p.m. and for docent-led tours the third Sunday of each month from 1 p.m. to 4 p.m. Private group tours are also available by reservation.

☞ Santa Barbara County Courthouse
1100 Anacapa St.
(805) 962-6464
santabarbaracourthouse.org

FREE

From Highway 101, take the Carrillo Street toward the mountains, turn left onto Chapala Street, right onto Anapamu Street, then right onto Anacapa Street.

Since 1929, this palatial Spanish-Moorish public building has provided some of the most fantastic views of the Santa Barbara coastline and Santa Ynez Mountains. The lawns and tropical gardens are among our favorite local spots for games of hide-and-seek. While this National Historic Landmark continues to serve as home to government offices and court proceedings, much of it is available for public viewing. Take the wide stairs or elevator its top level, then a short, narrow flight of stairs to the rooftop clock tower for a 360-degree view of Santa Barbara. Open weekdays from 8:30 a.m. to 4:30 p.m. and weekends from 10 a.m. to 4:30 p.m. Free guided tours are offered Mondays through Saturdays at 2 p.m. and at 10:30 a.m. on Mondays, Tuesdays and Fridays.

Art is displayed throughout the Santa Barbara County Courthouse.

☞ Santa Barbara Historical Museum & Gledhill Library

136 E. De La Guerra St.

(805) 966-1601

www.santabarbaramuseum.com

FREE

From Highway 101, take the Carrillo Street exit and turn toward the mountains, turn right onto Anacapa Street, then left onto De La Guerra Street.

Docents at this museum seem particularly accommodating to families with an interest in viewing an array of local artifacts. The museum's primary focus is The Story of Santa Barbara, a permanent collection designed to show the region's cultural history from the days when the Chumash ruled through modern times. This collection fills three of the museum's four galleries, leaving room for rotating exhibits that vary from Western art to local history.

The grounds also include two open courtyards ideal for letting rambunctious little ones run off some steam between galleries or simply to explore the native and exotic landscaping. The museum is open Tuesdays through Saturdays from 10 a.m. to 5 p.m. and Sundays from noon until 5 p.m.

The Santa Barbara Historical Society, which runs the museum, also owns and operates Fernald Mansion and Trussell-Winchester Adobe (p. 27).

☞ Santa Barbara Maritime Museum
113 Harbor Way, Suite 190
(805) 962-8404
sbmm.org
$

From southbound Highway 101, take Castillo Street toward the beach, turn right onto Cabrillo Boulevard/Shoreline Drive, then right onto Harbor Lane. From northbound 101, take Bath Street, turn left onto Haley Street, left onto Castillo Street, right onto Cabrillo Boulevard/Shoreline Drive, then right onto Harbor Lane.

This deceptively compact museum located in the Old Naval Reserve Center houses a nice display of local artifacts and hands-on activities. A surfing exhibit covers local heroes, board shapers and surfing lore. An interactive fishing exhibit gives landlubbers the opportunity to hook a big one, and preschoolers will be particularly entertained at the children's area where hands-on is de rigueur.

Santa Barbara Maritime Museum offers lots of hands-on activities.

The museum is open Thursdays through Tuesdays from 10 a.m. to 6 p.m., though closed on major holidays. Check the schedule for guided tours, sing-alongs and other special events.

☞ Santa Barbara Museum of Natural History
2559 Puesta del Sol
(805) 682-4711
sbnature.org

$

From Highway 101, take Mission Street toward the mountains, turn left onto Santa Barbara Street, right onto Los Olivos Street, which becomes Mission Canyon Road, then turn left onto Puesta del Sol.

Tucked away on a side street up Mission Canyon is one of the city's many nearly hidden treasures. This natural history museum fits a lot of information, plenty of fun learning opportunities and room to run all in a rather compact setting.

The Dennis M. Power Bird Hall is without a doubt Santa Barbara County's most spectacular public display of preserved birds. Female and male specimens of dozens of species are displayed side by side. Some displays also demonstrate the difference between winter and summer markings.

Other halls are dedicated to mammals, geology and paleontology, marine life, minerals and gems, Chumash people and more. The museum houses a wondrous display of dozens of butterflies and moths. With help from local astronomy buffs, the observatory offers special programs, including star parties the second Saturday of every month. Maximus Gallery features works of art that emphasize the natural world. The museum also houses Gladwin Planetarium, the only publically accessible planetarium between Los Angeles and San Francisco. The dome features regular presentations with special offerings for the youngest astronomers.

In recent years, the museum has developed the property straddling Mission Creek to include the Sukinanik'oy Garden of Chumash Plants, amphitheater, nature trails and picnic area. A reconstructed whale skeleton also is on display.

Open daily from 10 a.m. to 5 p.m.

☞ Stearns Wharf

South end of State Street
(805) 564-5531
www.stearnswharf.org
FREE
From northbound Highway 101, take Garden Street toward the beach, then turn right onto Cabrillo Boulevard. From southbound Highway 101, take Castillo Street toward the beach, then turn left onto Cabrillo Boulevard.

The oldest working pier on the West Coast juts south into the Pacific here at the end of State Street. Once a bustling freight port complete with railroad spur, today the pier is home to attractions such as Ty Warner Sea Center (page 32), restaurants, an ice cream shop, gift shops and charter boat companies. Begin your whale watching or fishing expedition here or just come to watch wildlife and enjoy a picnic. Fishing off the pier also is legal and no license is required, though no overhead casting is allowed due to potential safety hazards to fellow pier walkers.

☞ Ty Warner Sea Center

211 Stearns Wharf
(805) 962-2526

www.sbnature.org/seacenter
$

From northbound Highway 101, take Garden Street toward the beach, then turn right onto Cabrillo Boulevard. From southbound Highway 101, take Castillo Street toward the beach, then turn left onto Cabrillo Boulevard.

This family-focused marine science center located on Stearns Wharf specializes in hands-on activities with a focus on local marine life. Pull up a sample of water from directly under the pier and analyze its contents. Work side by side with marine scientists to examine sea life, or touch tidepool favorites in easily accessible tanks. Ty Warner Sea Center is overseen by the Santa Barbara Museum of Natural History, which offers annual memberships that provide access to both sites.

Open daily 10 a.m. to 5 p.m., but closed on major holidays.

NATURE

☞ Alameda Park

1400 Santa Barbara St.

(805) 564-5418

www.santabarbaraca.gov/Parks

FREE

From southbound Highway 101, take Mission Street toward the mountains, then turn right onto Anacapa Street. From northbound 101, take Carrillo Street toward the mountains, then turn left onto Santa Barbara Street.

Children will immediately spot Kid's World, an 8,000-square-foot playground designed and built by local residents in the center of this park, among the city's oldest. The play area also includes a giant concrete shark, pirate ship and eel-shaped slide, grassy play areas, ample dappled shade provided by a grove of trees, and group picnic areas available by reservation. The park also includes restrooms and is wheelchair accessible.

Hop across the street to Alice Keck Memorial Garden Park (page 32) for a twofer. Both parks are open sunrise to 10 p.m.

☞ Alice Keck Park Memorial Gardens

1500 Santa Barbara St.

(805) 564-5418

www.santabarbaraca.gov/Parks

FREE

From southbound Highway 101, take Mission Street toward the mountains; turn right onto Anacapa Street and left onto Micheltorena Street. From northbound 101, take Carrillo Street toward the mountains, then turn left onto Santa Barbara Street.

Once the site of El Mirasol Hotel, this park now boasts one of the city's most fantastically landscaped parks. Children are drawn to the koi pond where turtles sun themselves on rocks and friends and lovers share moments in the gazebo. It's not unusual to see people practicing their yoga or tai chi in the shade of a wide variety of trees, or playing Frisbee on the grass. The park offers ample shade, benches, and trails of varying materials and terrain through a vast array of flora. For restrooms, head across the street to Alameda Park (p. 32). Open sunrise to 10 p.m.

Ambassador Park
100 West Cabrillo Blvd.
(805) 564-5418
www.santabarbaraca.gov/
Parks
FREE

From northbound Highway 101, take Garden Street toward the beach, then turn right onto Cabrillo Boulevard. From southbound Highway 101, take Castillo Street toward the beach, then turn left onto Cabrillo Boulevard.

According to a plaque displayed prominently on the north end of this park, this now quiet, open, palm-studded, grassy parcel was once the site of Syujtan, a Chumash village. Burton Mound, as it is now called, is California Registered Historical Landmark No. 306 and has "yielded some of the most important archaeological evidence in California." The site was recorded nearly half a millennia ago in the journals of Cabrillo (1542) and again in 1769 by Crespi and Portola. The park is named for Don Luis Burton, who acquired the property in 1860. No facilities. Open sunrise to 10 p.m.

Andree Clark Bird Refuge
1400 E. Cabrillo Blvd.
(805) 564-5418
www.santabarbaraca.gov/Parks
FREE

From southbound Highway 101, take Cabrillo Boulevard toward the beach. From northbound 101, take the Hermosillo Road exit, turn left at the end of the ramp onto Coast Village Road, then follow the road as it curves under the freeway and becomes Cabrillo Boulevard.

This 32-acre estuary immediately adjacent to Santa Barbara Zoo (p. 58) features a brackish lake and saltwater marsh home to a vast array of native and migratory birds. Walking trails include a level, paved pathway that extends to East Beach (p. 38). Open sunrise to 10 p.m. No restrooms.

☞ Arroyo Burro Beach County Park

(aka Hendry's Beach)
2950 Cliff Drive
(805) 687-3714
www.sbparks.org
FREE

From Highway 101, take Las Positas Road toward the beach, then turn right onto Cliff Drive.

Parking can be a challenge at this hugely popular beach on innumerable gorgeous weekends and holidays. The beach is protected from winds most days and offers whale watching, surf fishing and mild waves. There are barbecue grills, picnic table, group picnic areas and restrooms. The leash law is strictly enforced in the park, but cross Arroyo Burro Creek onto city-owned Shoreline Beach and all leashes come off. The county park also houses a coin-operated, self-service dog bath.

Open 8 a.m. to sunset. During periods of heavy runoff, check water quality first at www.sbcphd.org/ehs/oceanmn.htm.

Arroyo Burro Estuary

2940 Cliff Drive
(805) 564-5418
www.santabarbaraca.gov/Parks
FREE

Parking is limited at Arroyo Burro Beach and Estuary, particularly during holidays and warm weekends. Consider biking, carpooling or taking the bus.

From Highway 101, take Las Positas Road toward the beach, then turn right onto Cliff Drive.

This estuary located between Arroyo Burro Beach and Douglas Family Preserve provides a prime setting for teaching about the importance of estuarine life. The reclaimed estuary includes interpretive signs that explain the roles native plants, birds and animals serve in this crossroads between the Pacific Ocean and the 6,311-acre Arroyo Burro watershed, which includes 11 miles of creek including its namesake and San Roque and Las Positas creeks.

Bohnett Neighborhood Park

1200 San Pascual St.

(805) 564-5418

www.santabarbaraca.gov/Parks

FREE

From Highway 101, take Carrillo Street and turn away from the mountains, turn right onto San Andres Street, right on Anapamu Street, then left onto San Pascual Street.

This very popular neighborhood park adjacent to the Westside Boys & Girls Club offers play structures, swings, baby swings, basketball courts, picnic tables, raised barbecues, grassy play fields, two handball walls and restrooms. Open sunrise to 10 p.m.

Cabrillo Ball Field

800 E. Cabrillo Blvd.

(805) 564-5422

www.santabarbaraca.gov/Parks

$$

From Highway 101, take Milpas Street toward the beach.

This softball field scored a spot on prime real estate just across the street from the beach. It also is home to the Chromatic Gate modern art piece by Herbert Bayer. The field is available by reservation only from sunrise to half an hour after sunset. Restrooms are available.

☞ Cabrillo Bike Path

Start at Leadbetter Beach (p. 44) or Butterfly Beach (p. 72)

(805) 963-7283

www.trafficsolutions.info

FREE

This dedicated 3.2-mile bike route provides riders an opportunity to enjoy the coast without much interference with auto traffic. Though there are some undulations, the paved trail is wide, largely flat and very child friendly. Bikes, in-line skates and surreys are all available for rent at multiple locations near the path.

Free Santa Barbara County bike maps are available. Just call the Traffic Solutions office and request a copy. You also can view it online.

Carrillo Street Gym
102 E. Carrillo St.
(805) 897-2519
www.santabarbaraca.gov/Parks
FREE-$$
From Highway 101, take Carrillo Street toward the mountains.

Tucked amidst the shops, restaurants, offices and tourist magnet that are downtown Santa Barbara is a historic landmark that has played host to pickup games of basketball and private events for more than 70 years.

The original gym, completed in 1918, was destroyed by a 1925 earthquake. Architect Julia Morgan, of Hearst Castle fame, designed this replacement gym that still features wooden floors, high windows and rooftop court.

The compact building houses the city's youth and adult basketball leagues, winter open volleyball, dance classes and aerobic programs, self-defense classes, lunchtime pickup games, weight rooms, locker room and showers. Other programs here have included indoor soccer, yoga, Pilates, even hula hoop. See the city's recreation catalog for current offerings.

The gym offers walk-in play Mondays, Wednesdays and Fridays from noon until 2 p.m. and Tuesdays and Thursdays from 11:30 a.m. to 1:30 p.m.

☞ Chase Palm Park
Straddling East Cabrillo Boulevard from Stearns Wharf to East Beach
(805) 564-5418
www.santabarbaraca.gov/Parks
FREE
From Highway 101, take Garden Street toward the beach, then turn left onto Cabrillo Boulevard.

Ask a local for a park in Santa Barbara and chances are really good she'll send you to this one. This long, 25-acre, wheelchair-accessible beachfront park features everything a little kid could want, including an antique carousel, bike/skate paths and soccer fields. For the younger set, the piece de resistance may be Shipwreck Playground while the older kids may tend toward Skater's Point. The free, 14,600-square-foot, cement skate park offers half pipes, rails, fun boxes and more. Helmets, elbow and knee pads are required, and less experienced skaters should hit the park before lunchtime on weekends to avoid the bustling afternoon crowd.

While big kids hit the skate park, the rest of the family can climb aboard the model of the Winfield Scott — a schooner that sank off the Channel Islands Dec. 2, 1853 — or play in the mist of the whale-shaped climbing sculpture. Take in the weekly arts and crafts show on the beach side or stretch out in the shade of the palm trees. The park also plays host to a summer concert series traditionally held Thursday evenings.

Group areas are available by reservation. The park is open sunrise to 10 p.m. Skate park open sunrise to half an hour after sunset. Restrooms are also available.

De La Guerra Plaza

De La Guerra Street just east of State Street

(805) 564-5418

www.santabarbaraca.gov/Parks

FREE

From Highway 101, take the Carrillo Street exit and turn toward the mountains, turn right onto Anacapa Street, then right onto De La Guerra Street.

This half-acre open grassy area provides a place for downtown visitors to run the kids, stretch their legs during meal breaks or find a shady spot to read while lounging on the lawn. No restrooms.

☞ Douglas Family Preserve

2551 Medcliff Road

(805) 564-5418

www.santabarbaraca.gov/Parks

FREE

For a longer, more difficult walk but ample parking: from Highway 101, take Las Positas Road toward the beach, then turn right onto Cliff Drive. For easier access, limited parking: Take Las Positas Road toward the beach, turn left onto Cliff Drive, right onto Mesa Lane, then right onto Medcliff Road.

This 69.8-acre open space preserve with expansive coastal views is particularly popular among dog owners. Unlike many public areas throughout the county, this preserve welcomes dogs off leash. Pet owners should clean up after their canine companions, and bags are often available for that purpose at park entrances.

Douglas Family Preserve offers relatively accessible trails with stunning coastal views.

The most popular approach to the reserve is via the Oak Grove Trail, which begins at the pedestrian bridge across the creek at adjacent Arroyo Burro Estuary. From there, the poorly maintained path climbs steeply. Even sturdy jogging strollers are not recommended. Poison oak encroaches on this trail, so keep track of dogs and kids. The five-minute hike (longer with small children) leads to a trail system that features expansive views, native plants, a home site and plenty of room to run.

For those wishing to avoid the climb, unable to find parking in the oft-packed Arroyo Burro parking lot, or in durable, off-pavement-style wheelchairs, gain access with very limited on-street parking at the end of Borton Drive, Mesa School Lane or Medcliff Street at Selrose Lane.

While exploring the property, visitors are often confounded by unmarked ruins. An old stone wall, a garage foundation, portions of access road and fire hydrants are all that remain of the commercial nursery that once stood here and a retirement community that was begun but never completed. Open sunrise to 10 p.m. No restrooms.

Dwight Murphy Field
Niños Drive at Por La Mar
(805) 564-5422
www.santabarbaraca.gov/Parks
FREE-$$

From Highway 101, take Milpas Street toward the beach; turn left onto Calle Puerto Vallarta, which becomes Niños Drive.

This 10.5-acre, tree-shaded athletic complex across the street from the Santa Barbara Zoo (page 58) offers one softball field available by reservation, a soccer field, bleachers, a fitness training course, play structure and restrooms. The field is available from sunrise to half an hour after sunset.

☞ East Beach
1400 Cabrillo Blvd.
(805) 564-5418
www.santabarbaraca.gov/Parks
FREE

From southbound Highway 101, take Cabrillo Boulevard toward the beach. From northbound 101, take the Hermosillo Road exit, turn left at the end of the ramp onto Coast Village Road, then follow the road as it curves under the freeway and becomes Cabrillo Boulevard.

This well-protected beach is equally popular for swimming, fishing, sand play, castle building and volleyball alike. The park includes play structures, more than a dozen volleyball courts, seasonal lifeguards and restrooms. Open sunrise to 10 p.m. No dogs allowed.

Since 1927, this beach's Cabrillo Pavilion Bathhouse (805-897-2519) has provided East Beach visitors with showers and changing rooms. The facility also offers lockers, a weight room, and beach wheelchair and volleyball rental. No membership required. Purchase a day pass or punch card at the pavilion. The pavilion is open weekdays from 8 a.m. to 5 p.m. and weekends and holidays from 11 a.m. to 4 p.m.

During periods of heavy runoff, check water quality first at www.sbcphd.org/ehs/oceanmn.htm.

☞ Elings Park
1298 Las Positas Road
(805) 569-5611
elingspark.org
FREE

From Highway 101, take Las Positas Road toward the beach.

Once the home of the Las Positas Landfill, this 230-acre, nonprofit park now plays host to weddings, bicycle motocross (BMX) races, soccer games, softball tournaments, cross country meets and myriad other public and private events. This very popular hilltop park is home to Elings International Raceway (a dirt track for remote controlled trucks), Santa Barbara BMX, the three-field Castagnola Softball/Baseball Complex, Santa Barbara County Veterans Memorial Walk, soccer fields, playgrounds, sculpture garden, amphitheatre, restrooms, picnic areas, nature trails, basketball standards in the upper parking lot, mountain bike trails and jumping off points for hang gliders. Practice or play on these soccer fields is allowed by permit only. Call the park for reservations and permits. Large, unimproved natural areas are also accessible via multiuse trails and dedicated footpaths. Dogs welcome to run off leash through much of the park with $90 annual permit. Open 7 a.m. to sunset.

Eastside Neighborhood Park
Yanonali Street at Soledad Street
(805) 564-5418
www.santabarbaraca.gov/Parks
FREE

From Highway 101, take Milpas Street toward the mountains, turn right onto Mason, then left onto Soledad.

Though surrounded by city, homes and concrete, one of the most impressive aspects of this wheelchair-accessible neighborhood park is its symphony of birdsong. The 2-acre park offers oak-shaded play structures and baby swings, picnic tables, restrooms and raised barbecues. The park also is home to Yanonali Garden, a community garden (see p. 64).

Escondido Neighborhood Park
1306 Flora Vista Drive
(805) 564-5418
www.santabarbaraca.gov/Parks
FREE

From Highway 101, take Carrillo Street toward the beach, turn right onto

Mountain View Road, left onto Fellowship Road, right onto Kenwood Road, right onto Skyline Circle, right onto Skyline Way, then right onto Flora Vista Drive.

This heavily wooded, 2-acre city park provides ample shade for lounging on the grass or kicking back while the kids play in the playground. Grab a pickup game of basketball on the half-court or simply take in the views. Open sunrise to 10 p.m. No restrooms.

☞ Franceschi Park

1501 Franceschi Road
(805) 564-5418
www.santabarbaraca.gov/Parks
FREE

From Highway 101, take Mission Street toward the mountains; turn right onto Garden Street, then left onto Pedregosa Street. Follow Pedregosa as it crosses Alameda Padre Serra and curves around Orpet Park, then turn left onto Alvarado Place, right onto Mission Ridge Road and finally left onto Franceschi Road.

The sound of bells tolling and the general hum of the city below float on the wind to Montarioso, Francesco Franceschi's once-private botanical garden on the east side. Today, this 17-acre park continues to provide among the best publicly accessible views across Santa Barbara and beyond the Channel Islands. The park is an ideal spot for a sunset retreat. Take in the views and fresh breeze while meandering along the paths, some of which are paved, or while enjoying a picnic at one of the patio tables. Restrooms are

Franceschi Park offers picturesque picnic spots away from crowds and sand.

available, but they are not wheelchair accessible. At press time, the house was closed for restoration.

Open sunrise to half an hour past sunset.

☞ Gould Park

Mountain Drive west of Cold Spring Road
(805) 564-5418

www.santabarbaraca.gov/Parks

FREE

From Highway 101, take Old Mill Road/Hot Spring Road exit and turn toward the mountain, then turn left onto Mountain Drive.

This 368-acre open space preserve serves as the trailhead for Cold Spring Trail, a very popular, scenic, strenuous trail along Cold Spring Creek. The trail includes a spur to Montecito Peak, but continues to East Camino Cielo and farther into the Los Padres National Forest trail system. The trailhead is open from sunrise to 10 p.m. No restrooms.

Hale Park

Camino Viejo at El Rancho Road

(805) 564-5418

www.santabarbaraca.gov/Parks

FREE

From southbound Highway 101, take East Village Road, turn toward the mountains, turn left onto Hot Springs Road, then turn left onto Summit Road, which becomes Camino Viejo. From northbound 101, take the Hermosillo Road exit and continue straight off the ramp. Turn right onto Hot Springs Road, then proceed as above.

This 14-acre undeveloped eucalyptus grove offers plentiful shade and well-worn, unmaintained walking paths. It's a popular spot for dog walkers and those seeking some rugged, natural peace and quiet. There are no facilities, it is not wheelchair accessible and parking is extremely limited. Open sunrise to 10 p.m.

☞ Hidden Valley Neighborhood Park

Calle de Los Amigos at Torino Drive

(805) 564-5418

www.santabarbaraca.gov/Parks

FREE

From Highway 101, take Las Positas Road, turn toward the beach, turn right onto Modoc Road, left onto Veronica Springs Road, and right onto Torino Drive.

This 18-acre park is among the best-kept secrets of the west side. The tree-lined, wheelchair-accessible park initially appears to be just a grassy corner lot, but follow the paved trail into the dale and you'll find a fantastic playground, swings and grassy park tucked away between Arroyo Burro Creek and Calle de Los Amigos. The peaceful park also includes picnic benches and room to run on well-maintained lawn. There is no creek access from the playground portion of the park, but a dirt path suitable for rugged jog strollers and foot traffic leads from Torino Avenue into 15 acres of riparian habitat. Though tempting, the area is not suitable for creek walks due to heavy debris. No restrooms. Open sunrise to half an hour after sunset.

☞ Hilda McIntyre Ray Neighborhood Park

1420 Kenwood Road

(805) 564-5418

www.santabarbaraca.gov/Parks

FREE

From Highway 101, take Carrillo Street, turn toward the beach, turn right onto Mountain View Road, left onto Fellowship Road, and right onto Kenwood Road.

This passive, neighborhood park is the west side's answer to Franceschi Park (page 40). The 1.5-acre hilltop reserve offers expansive views south and east beyond Santa Barbara to the Santa Ynez Mountain Range. The park includes a playground, grassy play fields, restrooms, picnic tables and group areas that are available by reservation. Open from sunrise to half an hour after sunset.

Hillside Park/Honda Valley Park

Carrillo Street at Kenwood Road

(805) 564-5418

www.santabarbaraca.gov/Parks

FREE

From Highway 101, take Carrillo Street toward the beach.

This 50-acre open space along Arroyo Hondo Creek provides ample space for exploration. At one time, the Honda Valley Trail extended from Harbor Hills Road through the park, but the upper access has been closed indefinitely due to erosion. The undeveloped parcel is wooded with oaks, sycamores and eucalyptus, shrubs, wildflowers and grasses. Unmaintained trails crisscross the property that is most easily accessed at the east end of Highland with limited on-street parking on Miracañon. Open sunrise to half an hour after sunset.

La Coronilla Park

740 Dolores Drive

(805) 564-5418

www.santabarbaraca.gov/Parks

FREE

From Highway 101, take Carrillo Street exit and turn away from the mountains, then turn left onto La Coronilla Drive, which curves and becomes Dolores Avenue.

This undeveloped park in a residential neighborhood currently provides nothing more than an occasionally mowed, small patch of grass atop a steep incline. It is not wheelchair accessible and there were no facilities at publication time, but keep an eye on it.

La Cumbre School Fields
2255 Modoc Road
(805) 687-0761
FREE
From Highway 101, take Mission Street, turn away from the mountains, then turn right onto Modoc Road.
Multiple soccer fields, basketball courts and baseball diamonds with backstops are available on weekends. Stop here for a pickup game of ball, but use the restroom at home first. There are no facilities here, and it is not wheelchair accessible. No dogs allowed.

☞ La Mesa Neighborhood Park
295 Meigs Road
(or via footbridge at east end of Camino de la Luz)
(805) 564-5418
www.santabarbaraca.gov/Parks
FREE
From Highway 101, take Carrillo Street toward the beach. Carrillo Street becomes Meigs Road.
All kids really need to keep themselves entertained are sticks, perhaps some stones, and plenty of space. The eucalyptus grove here provides those basics while the nearly 9-acre park provides grassy lawn, benches, a play structure, horseshoe pits, restrooms and picnic areas, including a group barbecue area with its own small stage and room for up to 100 guests. The wheelchair-accessible park also is home to the Men's Garden Club of Santa Barbara, which maintains a memorial grove.
The downward slope to the creek is enticing but not advised as the culvert is deep and, when running, is potentially treacherous to all ages due to its misleading width. When flowing, the current can be torrential. When dry, the bed is often full of trash.
No bikes or skateboards are allowed in the park. Dogs allowed on leashes only. Open sunrise to 10 p.m.

☞ La Playa Track
Shoreline at Castillo
(805) 965-0581, ext. 2277
www.sbcc.edu/trackandfield
FREE
From southbound Highway 101, take Castillo Street toward the beach; turn right onto Shoreline Drive/Cabrillo Boulevard. From northbound 101, take the Bath Street exit; turn left onto Haley, left onto Castillo, then right onto Cabrillo Boulevard.
Santa Barbara City College makes this track and bleachers available to the general public from 6 a.m. to 10 p.m. daily, except when reserved for special

events. Run laps, sprints or bleacher stairs. See posted rules regarding spike use and other specifics. Paid parking is available in adjacent lot.

Las Positas Tennis Courts
1002 Las Positas Road
(805) 564-5573
www.santabarbaraca.gov/Parks
FREE

From Highway 101, take Las Positas Road toward the beach. Driveway is immediately across from Stone Creek.

This 3-acre city park includes six hard courts with bleachers, backboards, restrooms, and shower and locker facilities. Court use is available by city permit (805-564-5573) from sunrise until half an hour after sunset, though lighted play is available by permit until 9 p.m. Mondays through Fridays.

Laurel Canyon Park
3300 block Laurel Canyon Road
(805) 564-5418
www.santabarbaraca.gov/Parks
FREE

From Highway 101, take Las Positas Road and turn toward the mountains; turn right onto Foothill Road, then left onto Laurel Canyon Road.

This open, grassy, sometimes-mowed field at the base of a hill provides a quiet spot for running the kids or the family dog in this 6-acre park. A makeshift backstop with homemade benches provides an old-school feel. No restrooms. Open sunrise to 10 p.m.

+ Leadbetter Beach
Shoreline Drive at Loma Alta
(805) 564-5418
www.santabarbaraca.gov/Parks
FREE

From southbound Highway 101, take Castillo Street toward the beach; turn right onto Shoreline Drive/Cabrillo Boulevard. From northbound 101, take the Bath Street exit; turn left onto Haley, left onto Castillo, then right onto Shoreline Drive/Cabrillo Boulevard.

This inviting stretch of sand across the street from Santa Barbara City College stadium is particularly popular with students, though windsurfers and kayakers appreciate the easy access to the ocean, and beginning surfers appreciate the gentler waves. This is a great spot to enjoy a family picnic while watching beginning sailors learn basic skills. The adjacent 17-acre Leadbetter Beach Park also offers restrooms, showers and a gazebo. Group picnic areas and volleyball courts are also available by reservation. Open sunrise to 10 p.m.

There is no free parking nearby. Expect to pay at least $2 for three hours or

$5 for a full-day pass at the college parking lot across the street, head east to the city's 90-minute lot where the 90 minutes are strictly enforced, or carry on farther east to the city's attended lot for $1.50 per hour, up to $9 per day. Those willing to take a long walk may find a free spot in the busy Shoreline Park parking lot.

During periods of heavy runoff, check water quality first at www.sbcphd.org/ehs/oceanmn.htm.

☞ Lifescape Garden & Chumash Point Ethnobotanical Preserve

Santa Barbara City College
721 Cliff Drive
(805) 965-0581
sbcceh.org
FREE

From southbound 101, take the Castillo Street exit; turn right at the end of the offramp, then right onto Montecito Street, which becomes Cliff Drive. Turn left onto Loma Alta Drive to access campus parking. From northbound 101, take the Bath Street exit, turn immediately left onto Haley Street, then left onto Castillo Street, then proceed as above.

Santa Barbara City College offers not only one of the state's finest community college programs, but also one of the most spectacular campus settings in the system. With expansive views and cool coastal breezes, the campus is a nice place for a picnic or a stroll, and the student gardens provide inspiration for coastal gardeners looking to put a little more native flora back in their gardens.

If you're interested in learning more about the propagation of medicinal herbs, edible ornamentals or fruits, or you're curious about garden water conservation, irrigation systems and hardscapes, the Lifescapes Garden is your answer. Are the kids studying Chumash history? Take a peek at the neighboring Chumash Point Ethnobotanical Preserve. The preserve project aims to focus entirely on plants the area's indigenous people experienced throughout their lands including the greater Santa Barbara area and Channel Islands.

Students throughout campus use the gardens overlooking La Playa Stadium to expand on their studies, or simply to relax. The public is invited not only to meander the campus' native garden, but to participate in its maintenance while taking an informal tour and learning side by side with students in the Environmental Horticulture Program. Pull on your garden gloves any Wednesday morning during regular school terms and you're in.

Parking on campus can be both pricey and crowded, so consider other means of transportation. A paved path out of Pershing Park, for example, leads directly onto campus and is stroller friendly. Consider using the city's bus system; the inexpensive Waterfront Shuttle (p. 244) provides a stop nearby.

Los Baños del Mar Pool & West Beach Wading Pool
401 Shoreline Drive
(805) 966-6110
www.santabarbaraca.gov/Parks
$

From southbound Highway 101, take Castillo Street toward the beach. From northbound 101, take the Bath Street exit, turn left onto Haley, then left onto Castillo.

This public swimming complex spitting distance from Santa Barbara Harbor and adjacent to West Beach (p. 63) offers year-round, outdoor swimming in a heated, 50-meter pool with starting blocks, springboard, changing rooms and lockers. The pool is open daily for lap swimming and open swimming under the supervision of lifeguards. The complex also is home to Santa Barbara Swim Club (page 255) for athletes ages 5 to 18 and a U.S.A. Swimming Masters Program for adults, while nearby West Beach Wading Pool is available to children ages 7 and younger. The 18-inch-deep wading pool is open daily May through September from noon to 5 p.m., weather permitting.

Los Robles Neighborhood Park
4010 Via Diego
(805) 564-5418
www.santabarbaraca.gov/Parks
FREE

From Highway 101, follow the Cachuma Lake / San Marcos Pass Road / Highway 154 exit toward the mountains; turn right onto La Colina Road, then left onto Via Diego.

This wheelchair-accessible, grassy open space with paved paths and picnic tables offers a quiet retreat or a quick getaway from home or work. No restrooms.

MacKenzie Park
Las Positas Road across from McCaw Avenue
(805) 564-5418
www.santabarbaraca.gov/Parks
FREE

From Highway 101, take Las Positas Road toward the mountains.

This expansive, two-level park offers something for all ages. The lower portion of the 9.5-acre park bounded by State Street and Las Positas Road includes play structures, group barbecue areas, restrooms and wide-open lawn areas, Pony League baseball/softball diamonds with skinned infields and a batting cage. The park is open from sunrise to 10 p.m.

The upper portion of the park, also accessible via Samarkand Drive at Hermosa Road, is home to MacKenzie Park Lawn Bowling Club. The club is open to players of all ages and ability levels. Free lessons are available (563-5494).

Mesa Lane Steps
Southern end of Mesa Lane
(805) 564-5418
www.santabarbaraca.gov/Parks
FREE
From Highway 101, take Carrillo Street toward the beach; turn right onto Cliff Drive then left onto Mesa Lane.
Limited on-street parking provides relatively quick access to the heart of Shoreline Beach (see page 60) via a 400-foot footpath that leads to a long set of more than 200 stairs. This is the only access for one mile in either direction. No facilities. No lifeguards.

☞ Mission Historical Park & A.C. Postel Garden
Los Olivos and Laguna streets
(805) 564-5418
www.Santabarbaraca.gov/Parks
FREE
From Highway 101, take Mission Street toward the mountains, then turn left onto Laguna Street.
This 8-acre parcel across the street from Mission Santa Barbara was once owned by the Franciscan fathers. Today, the largely unimproved park features rugged trails among the mission's waterworks and tannery vats. Another 2 acres north of Alameda Padre Serra contains the filter house, grist mill, reservoir and additional portions of the aqueduct.
The lower portion of the park also is home to A.C. Postel Garden known for its more than 1,500 All-American roses and a large grassy area. This portion of the park is a popular spot for photographers of all abilities.
Open sunrise to half an hour after sunset. For best viewing, visit before the annual January pruning, or volunteer for the massive pruning project and get involved. No restrooms.

More Mesa
1100 block Orchid Drive
(805) 966-4520
www.sblandtrust.org/openspaces.html
FREE
From Highway 101, take Patterson Avenue south and continue as it becomes Shoreline Drive. Turn right onto Orchid Drive.
Developers, local government agencies and environmentalists have battled long and hard for this parcel of prime real estate. Today, 36 acres of the mesa are public. The remaining nearly 300 acres are privately held, but locals wander the entire piece, some for bird watching on the bluffs, others to access More Mesa Beach.
The walk to the beach from the legal access point on Orchid Drive is a long haul for little legs, so plan accordingly. Unofficial, unmaintained trails

crisscross the property and run along the bluff's top to a grove that shelters a wooden stairway leading to the beach. At the bottom of the steep set of stairs, a long, sandy beach welcomes visitors to the surf. Those who may be offended by the site of nudists should tend west, or avoid this beach altogether.

☞ Moreton Bay Fig Tree

Montecito Street at Chapala Street
(805) 564-5418
www.santabarbaraca.gov/Parks
FREE

From southbound Highway 101, take Castillo Street toward the beach, then turn left onto Montecito. From northbound 101, take Bath Street, turn left onto Haley, left onto Castillo, then left onto Montecito.

This unique specimen once served as a shady respite for weary travelers making their way along the coast wagon route, later the highway and, until the turn of the century, just a short jog off U.S. Highway 101. Today, motorists speed past the oldest tree of its kind in the United States.

The tree was planted in 1877. In 1970, it was labeled the city's first "tree of notable historic interest." Today, the trunk measures more than 38 feet in circumference and its beautiful, expansive canopy provides more than 21,000 square feet of shade. Its photogenic buttress roots stretch into adjacent grassy park space and once served as prime hiding spots for children and beds for homeless people. The roots are now cordoned off for their protection.

While no climbing is allowed, still isn't she grand? Lay under her boughs. Look up into her branches. Tell stories of local history, family history or your own whimsical works of fiction. No restrooms.

Municipal Tennis Center

1414 Park Place
(805) 564-5573

www.santabarbaraca.gov/Parks

$

From northbound 101, take Salinas Street, turn right onto Pitos Street then right onto Park Place. From southbound 101, take the Milpas Street exit, cross under the freeway, at the roundabout turn right onto Carpinteria Street, turn right onto Canada Street, which becomes Pitos Street, then turn right onto Park Place.

The city's largest public tennis facility includes a dozen hard courts, one of which is in an enclosed stadium that can seat up to 1,000 fans. Three of the courts are lighted until 9 p.m. Monday through Friday.

Unlike the city's other courts, this 8-acre, wheelchair-accessible facility includes full services, including lessons, a tennis shop for rentals or racket stringing, showers, lockers and restrooms.

The courts are available from sunrise to half an hour after sunset except by permit available at the center's office.

☞ Oak Park

600 block West Junipero St.

(805) 564-5418

www.santabarbaraca.gov/Parks

FREE

From northbound Highway 101, take the Pueblo Street exit and continue straight onto Calle Real, then turn right onto Junipero Street. From southbound 101, take Las Positas Road, turn toward the mountains, right onto Calle Real, then left onto Junipero Street.

The 17-acre, wheelchair-accessible, sycamore- and oak-studded park is particularly popular among adventurous souls with a penchant for creekbed exploring and rock hopping. The park includes grassy play areas, picnic tables, play structures, raised wooden dance floor, group barbecue areas and restrooms also houses one of the city's neighborhood wading pools. The 18-inch-deep pool is open May through September.

Dogs on leash are welcome in this park that also is home to the Santa

The creekbed, which can run dry late in the year, is a popular feature at Oak Park.

Barbara Horseshoe Club, a bridge over Mission Creek and one of the city's four tennis facilities. Courts are, however, only available to those holding a permit. Call (805) 564-5573 for permit information. Open sunrise to 10 p.m.

Orpet Park
Alameda Padre Serra at Pedregosa Street
(805) 564-5418
www.santabarbaraca.gov/Parks
FREE

From Highway 101, take Mission Street toward the mountains, turn right onto Anacapa Street, then left onto Pedregosa and right onto Alameda Padre Serra.

There are no facilities beyond picnic benches on this steep, grassy hillside, yet the park provides ample room to run. The 4.2-acre park is largely historic in nature; it was established in 1921 by Park Superintendent E.O. Orpet as a horticultural showplace. In 2001, the original streetcar stop at the western corner of the park was rebuilt and declared a historic landmark.

Open sunrise to 10 p.m. No restrooms. Not wheelchair accessible.

Ortega Park
Salsipuedes Street at Cota Street
(805) 564-5418
www.santabarbaraca.gov/Parks
FREE

From Highway 101, take the Garden Street exit, turn away from the beach and turn right onto Cota Street.

A tiny wading pool for the little folk is the highlight of this wheelchair-

Ortega Park's mural provides an artistic backdrop to the popular playground.

accessible 9.5-acre neighborhood park adjacent to Santa Barbara Junior High School. The Ortega Wading Pool, 4 feet at its deepest, offers splash opportunities for up to 40 people at a time from May to September. The park also includes play structures, picnic tables, raised barbecues, basketball court, a softball diamond, big kid swings and restrooms. A community building also is available by reservation. The park is open sunrise to 10 p.m. Call for pool hours.

☞ Outdoors Santa Barbara Visitor Center
Santa Barbara Harbor
outdoorsb.noaa.gov
FREE

From southbound Highway 101, take Castillo Street toward the beach, turn right onto Cabrillo Boulevard/Shoreline Drive, then right onto Harbor Lane. From northbound 101, take Bath Street, turn left onto Haley Street, left onto Castillo Street, right onto Cabrillo Boulevard/Shoreline Drive, then right onto Harbor Lane.

This unusual upstairs office space offers an uninterrupted, 360-degree, uninterrupted view that includes Santa Barbara Harbor, Santa Barbara Channel, Channel Islands and the Santa Ynez Mountain Range. Friendly volunteer staff also can provide information about local activities and brochures, maps and other printed information are also available. Open daily from 11 a.m. to 5 p.m. Restrooms nearby.

☞ Paddle Sports of Santa Barbara
117B Harbor Way
(805) 899-4925
kayaksb.com
$$$

From southbound Highway 101, take Castillo Street toward the beach, turn right onto Cabrillo Boulevard/Shoreline Drive, then right onto Harbor Lane. From northbound 101, take Bath Street, turn left onto Haley Street, left onto Castillo Street, right onto Cabrillo Boulevard/Shoreline Drive, then right onto Harbor Lane.

This paddle-focused aquatic center offers lessons, tours and simple rentals of kayaks. The company specializes in family-friendly kayak programs, including tours of Santa Cruz, Anacapa and Santa Barbara Islands. Instructors also offer classes for all kayak types and surf kayaking. Ever wonder how those kayakers right themselves without ever getting out of their boats? Sign up for the Eskimo roll class to learn the trick.

Boat rentals and classes are offered in the Santa Barbara Harbor, as well as off West Beach (p. 63) and Leadbetter Beach (p. 44). Bike rentals are also available. Call for current offerings, hours and details.

☞ Parma Park

2000 Stanwood Drive

(805) 564-5418

www.santabarbaraca.gov/Parks

FREE

From Highway 101, take Milpas Street toward the mountains, turn right onto Mason Street, left onto Salinas Street, right onto Sycamore Canyon Road, then left at the fork onto Stanwood Drive/Highway 192.

Though heavily damaged by the 2008 Tea Fire, this 200-acre unimproved park continues to provide some 5 miles of trails through native trees, shrubs, grasslands and wildflowers for hikers and horseback riders.

The Parma family, which had owned this property since the 1890s, donated the land to the city in 1973. The move preserved, in perpetuity, the scenic views, creek and wild, open spaces.

Dogs are allowed on leash and on trail. Bicycle use is limited to the Ridge Trail and fire roads. Open sunrise to 10 p.m. No restrooms.

Parque de Los Niños & Children's Orchard

520 Wentworth Ave.

(805) 564-5418

www.santabarbaraca.gov/Parks

FREE

From southbound Highway 101, take Carrillo Street toward the beach, turn left onto San Pascual Street, left onto Cañon Perdido, then right onto Wentworth Avenue. From northbound 101, take Bath Street, turn left onto Haley Street, left onto Castillo, right onto Montecito, then right onto Rancheria, which curves before the final right-hand turn onto Wentworth Avenue.

This half-acre park offers play structures, benches, shade and swings, but no restrooms. An associated Children's Orchard is fenced and often locked.

Pershing Park

100 Castillo St.

(805) 564-5418

www.santabarbaraca.gov/Parks

FREE

From southbound Highway 101, take Castillo Street toward the beach. From northbound 101, take Bath Street, turn left onto Haley, then left onto Castillo Street.

This 6-acre sports facility adjacent to Plaza del Mar Park (page 53) includes two baseball fields and one softball field all with a shared outfield and skinned infields, warm-up/batting cages, bleachers and restrooms. Two of the fields are available by reservation. Eight tennis courts are home to the Santa Barbara City College tennis program, but are open for public use (by permit, 564-5573) on weekends, after 5 p.m. weekdays and any other time the college isn't using them. Four of the courts are lighted until 9 p.m. weekdays.

Pilgrim Terrace Park & Community Garden
Modoc Road at Pilgrim Terrace Drive
(805) 564-5418
www.santabarbaraca.gov/Parks
FREE

From Highway 101, take Mission Street, turn away from the mountains, then turn right onto Modoc Road.

This small, passive park offers tree-shaded picnic tables and a large, grassy field, but is not particularly wheelchair friendly. It also is home to one of the city's three community gardens. Call (805) 963-7567 to reserve one of this setting's 50 garden plots.

Plaza del Mar Park
23 Castillo St.
(805) 564-5418
www.santabarbaraca.gov/Parks
FREE

From southbound Highway 101, take Castillo Street toward the beach. From northbound 101, take Bath Street, turn left onto Haley, then left onto Castillo Street.

This 4.5-acre, shaded, grassy park is just across the street from Los Baños del Mar Pool (page 46), beaches and the marina. The park's amenities include a stage with band shell, ample running room and restrooms. It also is immediately adjacent to Pershing Park (page 52). Open sunrise to 10 p.m.

Plaza Vera Cruz Neighborhood Park
130 E. Cota St.
(805) 564-5418
www.santabarbaraca.gov/Parks
FREE

From Highway 101, take the Garden Street exit, turn away from the beach and turn left onto Cota Street.

The oldest city park in Santa Barbara provides ample space for running on the lawn, a play structure and benches. Nearby parking is time-limited, and a significant number of homeless people tend to hang out here. No restrooms.

Rancheria Community Garden
300 block Rancheria Street
(805) 564-5418
www.santabarbaraca.gov/Parks
FREE

From southbound Highway 101, take Castillo Street toward the beach, turn right onto Montecito Street and right again onto Rancheria Street. From northbound 101, take Bath Street, turn left onto Haley Street, left onto Castillo Street, then right onto Montecito Street and right onto Rancheria Street.

This organized and fenced community garden in a residential neighborhood is one of three such efforts by the city to provide anyone with a few bucks and some spare time a patch of dirt to tend. The fee includes access to tools and water for growing ornamentals or vegetables. Call for plot availability.

☞ Rattlesnake Canyon Wilderness Area
1800 block Las Canoas Road
(805) 564-5418
www.santabarbaraca.gov/Parks
FREE

From Highway 101, take Milpas Street toward the mountains, turn right onto Mason Street, left onto Salinas Street, right onto Sycamore Canyon Road then continue straight onto Stanwood Road/Highway 192. Turn right onto El Cielito Road, then right onto Las Canoas Road.

This 451-acre, unimproved open space park along Mission Creek adjacent to Skofield Park (page 61) is particularly popular for its Rattlesnake Trail, but also provides access to other hiking and horseback riding trails, spurs to small waterfalls and creekside pools. The heavily wooded canyon provides shade and running water when other canyons have run out of both. The trails are largely single-track, involve creek crossings or are otherwise too rugged for strollers and many toddlers.

Trailhead open sunrise to 10 p.m. No restrooms.

☞ Rocky Nook
Mission Canyon Road
(805) 568-2461
Countyofsb.org/parks
FREE

From Highway 101, take Mission Street toward the mountains, turn left onto Laguna Street, then right onto Los Olivos Street, which becomes Mission Canyon Road.

This quiet, heavily wooded park is fantastic for beginning hikes with toddlers, exploring the woods with small children and creek play. Those seeking wide open grassy areas will be disappointed in this park, but those seeking a more natural setting are sure to enjoy it. For an added treat, watch for the giant mosaic lizards on the south side of the creek. Facilities include a small play structure, picnic tables, barbecues and restrooms. A group area is available by reservation.

San Roque Park
Cañon Road
(805) 564-5418
santabarbaraca.gov/parks
FREE

From Highway 101, take Las Positas Road toward the mountains, turn left onto Calle Noguera, then left onto Cañon Drive.

This grassy area in a traffic triangle is often confused with nearby Stevens Park. There are no facilities and it is not wheelchair accessible, but it's an easy public meeting spot for an outdoor gathering, to walk the dog or feel grass between your toes when nearby parks are too crowded.

Sand Spit Beach
Santa Barbara Harbor
(805) 564-5531
www.santabarbaraca.gov/Government/Departments/
Waterfront
FREE

From southbound Highway 101, take Castillo Street toward the beach, turn right onto Cabrillo Boulevard/Shoreline Drive, then right onto Harbor Lane. From northbound 101, take Bath Street, turn left onto Haley Street, left onto Castillo Street, right onto Cabrillo Boulevard/Shoreline Drive, then right onto Harbor Lane.

While tourists crowd Stearns Wharf (p. 31), Leadbetter Beach (p. 44) and West Beach (p. 63), follow the path to this more solitary beach in the midst of harbor activity. Sand Spit Beach is located at the eastern end of the Santa Barbara Harbor wall. It's an excellent spot for aspiring sailors to watch the comings and goings at the harbor and for sun worshippers to find a less-crowded bit of sand.

From the harbor, follow the stroller-friendly path around the harbor. You'll have to leave the strollers at the walkway, then walk carefully over the boulders to this less-crowded stretch of sand. Be particularly aware of tidal changes, and do not attempt during heavy surf or ultra-high tides. No facilities and certainly not wheelchair accessible.

During periods of heavy runoff, check water quality first at www.sbcphd.org/ehs/oceanmn.htm.

☞ Santa Barbara Botanic Garden
1212 Mission Canyon Road
(805) 682-4726
sbbg.org
$

From Highway 101, take Mission Street toward the mountains, turn left

Santa Barbara Botanic Garden invites exploration and hands-on learning.

onto Garden Street, right onto Los Olivos and proceed past the mission. At Foothill Road, turn right, then turn left onto Mission Canyon Road.

This 65-acre garden is one of Santa Barbara's best-kept secrets. Small children especially enjoy the hidden treasures in the entirely hands-on Discovery Garden. Take a picnic, a good book or meander along a variety of paths and trails through landscaped gardens or a native oak forest. One such trail leads to a historic dam built for Mission Santa Barbara in 1806 by the Chumash. For a more natural setting, try the wooded Pritchett Path. Near the garden's gift shop is a nursery that specializes in California native plants, propagated in the nursery, which also is available for public exploration. Though severely damaged in the 2009 Jesusita Fire, the well-established garden is bound to recover.

The garden offers a vast array of special events related to botanical arts and culture, including gardening and horticulture classes, field courses, garden tours, seasonal nature walks, summer nature camps, family workshops and campouts.

Open daily from 9 a.m. to 5 p.m. (winter) and 9 a.m. to 6 p.m. (summer). Closed Thanksgiving Day, Christmas Eve, Christmas Day, New Year's Day and during some special events. The Blaksley Library, which houses some 15,000 volumes dedicated to plants, animals, and geology, is free but available by appointment only.

Santa Barbara Municipal Golf Club
3500 McCaw Ave.
(805) 687-7087

www.sbgolf.com

$$$

From Highway 101, take Las Positas Road toward the mountains, then turn left onto McCaw Avenue.

This 18-hole, par-70 public course is one of the longest short courses in Southern California at 6,037 yards. The course offers discounts for city residents and play time runs from dawn to dusk with reservations available up to a month in advance. The facility also includes a driving range and golf shop. Programs include lessons, leagues, a junior golf program designed for golfers from 7 to 17 years old and junior golf camp for golfers ages 8 to 15.

Santa Barbara Orchid Estate

1250 Orchid Drive

(805) 967-1284

santabarbaraorchidestate.com

FREE

From Highway 101, take Patterson Road toward the beach and continue as it becomes Shoreline Drive and, finally, Orchid Drive.

Visitors are welcome to drop in and explore the growing grounds for some 2,000 varieties of orchids that are nurtured in the 5-acre greenhouse. The grounds are open from 8 a.m. to 4:30 p.m. Mondays through Saturdays and 11 a.m. to 4 p.m. Sundays.

☞ Santa Barbara Sailing Center

133 Harbor Way

(805) 962-2826

sbsail.com

$$$

From southbound Highway 101, take Castillo Street toward the beach, turn right onto Cabrillo Boulevard/Shoreline Drive, then right onto Harbor Lane. From northbound 101, take Bath Street, turn left onto Haley Street, left onto Castillo Street, right onto Cabrillo Boulevard/Shoreline Drive, then right onto Harbor Lane.

Since 1967, the Santa Barbara Sailing Center has provided affordable sailing instruction and public access to boats of varying descriptions. Today, services include lessons in kayaking, sailing and boater safety, summer sailing camps and kayaking camps for kids, power boat rentals, kayak rentals and guided tours. The center also offers public and charter cruises, as well as boat rentals varying from pedal boats and rowing sculls to 50-foot yachts. A sailing club provides members unlimited daily access to boats.

Open daily from 9 a.m. to 5 p.m.

The Santa Barbara Zoo's Forest's Edge lowland gorilla exhibits provides super close-ups.

☞ Santa Barbara Zoological Gardens

500 Niños Drive
(805) 962-6310
santabarbarazoo.org
$

From southbound Highway 101, take Cabrillo Boulevard toward the beach, then turn left onto Niños Drive. From northbound 101, take the Hermosillo Road exit, turn left at the end of the ramp onto Coast Village Road, then follow the road as it curves under the freeway and becomes Cabrillo Boulevard and turn left onto Niños Drive.

Most zoos are kid friendly, but the Santa Barbara Zoo also is enticing to adults keen on a good walk in a beautiful setting. The zoo is set on 16 acres of prime real estate with wonderful views of the coast and the adjacent Andree Clark Bird Refuge (page 33). More than 500 animals are housed in this 30-acre park that also features a miniature train, carousel, snack bars, playground, gift shops and a dedicated picnic area. A grassy hill invites kids to run, and, more often than not, hosts rolling children and their child-like adults. Near the playground, friendly goats are particularly happy with guests who purchase the specialty feed in the neighboring gift store to give the animals a snack.

The zoo is open from 10 a.m. to 5 p.m. daily, except Thanksgiving and

Christmas days. Special seasonal events include Boo at the Zoo, Zoo Camps, Breakfast with the Butterflies and more.

☞ Seven Falls Trail
End of Tunnel Road
(805) 967-3481
www.fs.fed.us/r5/lospadres
FREE

From Highway 101, take Mission Street toward the mountains, turn left onto Laguna Street and then right onto Los Olivos Street, which becomes Mission Canyon Road. Turn right onto Foothill Road, then left onto Mission Canyon Road and bear left at the fork onto Tunnel Road.

This tough hike up a route that only loosely fits the definition of "trail" offers multiple rewards, not the least of which is a dip in the cold, clear water of one of the Santa Ynez Mountains' multiple hidden springs. Be sure to pack plenty of water, snacks, even a picnic and, of course, the camera.

From your parking spot off the pavement, walk up the gentle grade of the paved road about three quarters of a mile. At the end of the pavement, continue on the dirt road straight ahead, then watch for a single-track trail about 35 yards ahead on your left. There is a laser-cut steel sign, but it is often overgrown. Follow this trail another 30 yards to the first creek crossing.

Many hikers have been deceived by the often-dry creekbed the Seven Falls Trail follows, but continue on and you'll be rewarded with cold, clear, running water, falls and pools.

This is where things get really interesting. If you cross the creek, which is often dry here, and head upstream, look for a narrow trail on your left. For easiest passage, take this rough trail as it parallels the creekbed for less than a half mile to the first of three ponds.

For a more adventurous route, follow the creekbed directly. This option involves some sandy areas, boulder hopping and even a bit of climbing. Previous adventurers have notched holes in the stone wall next to one of the lower falls to provide an uninterrupted trail along this route, but the notches are spaced too far apart for youngster's legs.

While my girls were only 6 and 8 when we first made it to the ponds, I would not recommend the creek bed route for most young children. Even the trail route will be too difficult for young children who are not used to hiking regularly.

Sheffield Park

2400 block Stanwood Drive
(805) 564-5418
santabarbaraca.gov/parks
FREE

From Highway 101, take Milpas Street toward the mountains, turn right onto Mason Street, left onto Salinas Street, right onto Sycamore Canyon Road, then left at the fork onto Stanwood Drive/Highway 192.

This 23-acre park looks like it's always been here - rolling hills, native plants, well-developed trails. In fact, the park hides two giant water tanks that replaced the above-ground reservoir which served the city into the new millenium. When the old reservoir was filled and replaced with the underground tanks, city officials and local residents worked together to develop this natural open space area now open to all for hiking and nature exploration. There are no additional facilities here, so use the restroom before you leave home, and bring your own picnic blankets, chairs, water and other necessities.

Shoreline Park

Shoreline Drive at La Marina
(805) 564-5418
santabarbaraca.gov/parks
FREE

From southbound Highway 101, take Carrillo Street toward the beach. Carrillo becomes Meigs Road, then Shoreline Drive. From northbound 101, take the Bath Street exit; turn left onto Haley, left onto Castillo, then right onto Shoreline Drive/Cabrillo Boulevard.

This 15-acre blufftop park with its channel views, wheelchair-accessible paths and beach access is among the city's most popular. In addition to ideal sunset picnic dinner locations, the park provides grassy passive play areas, paved paths, raised barbecues, group barbecue area, play structures, restrooms and stairs to a 3-mile stretch of beach that extends past Thousand Stairsteps (page 62) and Mesa Coastal Access to Arroyo Burro County Park (page 34). This park also is the western terminus of the dedicated bike path that extends along the city's beaches beyond the Andree Clark Bird Refuge (page 33) with only a short section near Leadbetter Beach (page 44) shared with motorists. Dogs off leash are welcome along this stretch of beach. Open sunrise to 10 p.m.

Skofield Park
1819 Las Canoas Road
(805) 564-5418
santabarbaraca.gov/parks
FREE

From Highway 101, take Milpas Street toward the mountains, turn right onto Mason Street, left onto Salinas Street, right onto Sycamore Canyon Road, then continue straight onto Stanwood Road / Highway 192. Turn right onto El Cielito Road, then right onto Las Canoas Road.

This 35-acre property adjacent to Rattlesnake Canyon Wilderness Area (page 54) was named for its last private owner, Ray Skofield. The wheelchair-accessible area served as a camp for Los Rancheros Visitadores – an invitation-only horseback riding group for the elite, established in the 1920s. Today, the property hosts nonprofit youth groups by reservation only. The rest of the park is open to the public and includes grassy stretches, native flora, walking and hiking trails, restrooms, picnic areas and group barbecue areas. Open sunrise to half an hour after sunset except by permit.

Spencer Adam Park
1216 De La Vina St.
(805) 564-5418
santabarbaraca.gov/parks
FREE

From Highway 101, take Carrillo Street toward the mountains; turn left onto Bath Street, right onto Victoria Street, then right onto De La Vina Street.

Visitors seeking large grassy play areas or facilities for children will be disappointed, but a segment of the population that seeks relief from boisterous youth is particularly drawn to this downtown facility.

The 1½-acre recreational facility houses Santa Barbara Lawn Bowl (805-965-1773), which offers free lessons and regular league play. The adjacent Louise Lowry Davis Recreation Center (1232 De La Vina St., 897-2568) is here, too. It offers year-round recreational and educational opportunities for seniors 60 and older, including arts, crafts, chess, bridge, board games and a variety of support groups. Restrooms are available.

☞ Stevens Neighborhood Park

258 Cañon Drive

(805) 564-5418

www.santabarbaraca.gov/Parks

FREE

From Highway 101, take Las Positas Road toward the mountains, turn left onto Calle Fresno, then right onto Cañon Drive.

This beautiful, peaceful, 25-acre, neighborhood park offers all that a passive, family park should: oak-shaded grassy playing area, picnic tables, play structure, swings, restrooms and a path along a bubbling creek. The well-maintained, relatively flat trail along the east side of the creek runs about two-thirds of a mile to Jesusita Trail and a network of forest trails, not the least of which is Inspiration Point . Stevens Park trail is wide and well maintained along San Roque Creek, which begs for feet soaking and play. If any trail in the Santa Barbara area could be considered wheelchair accessible, this would be the one.

Sunflower Park

100 block Mason Street

(805) 564-5418

santabarbaraca.gov/parks

FREE

From Highway 101, take Milpas Street toward the mountains, then turn right onto Mason.

This half-acre, wheelchair-accessible park, nearly hidden on a narrow quarter-acre lot across the street from Franklin School, offers swings, play structures, grass, a paved pathway and shade trees. There are no restrooms, but Eastside Park (p. 39) literally around the corner has full facilities. Open sunrise to 10 p.m.

Sylvan Park

Dover Road at Alameda Padre Serra

(805) 564-5418

www.santabarbaraca.gov/Parks

FREE

From Highway 101, take Carrillo Street toward the mountains, turn left onto Santa Barbara Street, right onto Sola Street, left onto curvy Jimeno Road, then right onto Alameda Padre Serra and left onto Dover Road.

This passive park landscaped in bark and wood shavings features pepper trees and other drought-tolerant shade trees. While the corner lot is steep, it offers a quiet place for a short walk, benches and views. There are no restrooms and the park is not wheelchair accessible.

Thousand Steps Coastal Access
Southern end of Santa Cruz Boulevard
(805) 564-5418
santabarbaraca.gov/parks
FREE

From Highway 101, take Carrillo Street toward the beach and continue as it becomes Meigs Road and curves to become Shoreline Drive, then turn right onto Santa Cruz Boulevard.

Though there aren't really 1,000 steps in this long staircase that provides access to Shoreline Park (p. 60), your kids will certainly think otherwise. This set of some 150 concrete stairs has provided access since 1923. A wide landing about halfway along provides a resting spot and easy passing. At low tide, visitors here can walk west beyond Arroyo Burro Beach or east along Shoreline Park, Leadbetter Beach, the harbor and eastern beaches. This section is a great spot for beachcombing with plentiful rocks and shells, as well as splendid views of sailboats and the Channel Islands. No restrooms.

Truth Aquatics
301 W. Cabrillo Blvd.
(805) 962-1127
truthaquatics.com
$$$

From southbound Highway 101, take Castillo Street toward the beach and then turn left onto Cabrillo Boulevard. From northbound 101, take Bath Street, turn left onto Haley Street, left onto Castillo Street, then left onto Cabrillo Boulevard.

This well-established dive and sport-fishing company, named after its first sailing vessel, provides public access to coastal waters with lobstering and spear fishing trips, crab hunting adventures and fishing for bass, lingcod, rock fish, snapper and sole. Charter a boat or join a scheduled cruise for whale watching (May through September), lobstering (October through March), sport fishing, diving or kayaking. The company offers half-day and multi-day outings, as well as daily runs to Channel Islands National Park.

Children ages 4 and younger are permitted free, though obviously they must be accompanied by an adult. Group discounts are also available.

West Beach
Cabrillo Boulevard
(805) 564-5418
www.santabarbaraca.gov/Parks
FREE

From northbound Highway 101, take Garden Street toward the beach, then turn right onto Cabrillo Boulevard. From southbound Highway 101, take Castillo Street toward the beach, then turn left onto Cabrillo Boulevard.

The 11-acre portion of beach sandwiched between Stearns Wharf (p. 32) and Santa Barbara Marina/Harbor offers easy access to the sand along the popular coastal bike/skate path. The marina and jetty protect the beach from pounding surf, so this stretch is popular not only with sunbathers and volleyball players, but also kayakers, swimmers and wind surfers. Home to the West Beach Wading Pool (p. 46) and only a stone's throw from Los Baños del Mar Municipal Pool (page 46).

Open sunrise to 10 p.m. Restrooms nearby at Pershing Park (p. 52). During periods of heavy runoff, check water quality first at www.sbcphd.org/ehs/oceanmn.htm.

Willowglen Neighborhood Park
600 Willowglen Road
(805) 564-5418
www.santabarbaraca.gov/Parks
FREE

From southbound Highway 101, take the State Street/Highway 154 exit and proceed straight onto State Street; turn left onto Hope Avenue, right onto San Ramon Drive, left onto Grove Lane, left onto Callecita, then right onto Willowglen Road. From northbound 101, take Hope Street toward the mountains and proceed as above.

This wooded, 3-acre, wheelchair-accessible, neighborhood park also includes a baseball backstop, grassy passive playing fields, and a paved walkway to a tiny tot play structure, swings and basketball courts. No restrooms. Open sunrise to 10 p.m.

Yanonali Garden
Yanonali Street at Soledad Street
(805) 963-7605
www.santabarbaraca.gov/Parks
$$$

From Highway 101, take Milpas Street toward the mountains, turn right onto Mason and then left onto Soledad.

Located in the back of Eastside Neighborhood Park (p. 39) is a plot of land dedicated to community farming. For a fee, residents may adopt one of the 72 designated 10-by-20-foot plots. Some use the soil for fruits and veggies, others for ornamentals. The garden is surrounded by chain-link fence and a key is required for entry. The park and some of the garden plots are wheelchair accessible. Restrooms are nearby.

OTHER ADVENTURES

Batty's Batting Cages

226 S. Milpas St.

(805) 962-6666

$

From Highway 101, take Milpas Street toward the beach.

These eight batting cages just blocks from the beach include baseball and softball pitches of varying speeds. Groups should call ahead for reservations, but the cages are open to all from 11 a.m. to 9 p.m. Mondays through Fridays, 10 a.m. to 9 p.m. Saturdays and 10 a.m. to 8 p.m. Sundays.

Children's Museum of Santa Barbara

125 State St.

(805) 680-7235

www.childrensmuseumsb.org

From Highway 101, take Garden Street toward the beach, turn right onto Yanonali Street, then left onto State Street.

This promise of a children's museum was still in the works at publication time. The initial vision for the vacant lot beside the railroad tracks included 7,000 square feet of interactive experiences for children in a 14,000-square-foot facility that will also provide job-skill development opportunities for teens, assistance for caregivers and training for educators. The site is slated to include classroom space, an outdoor amphitheater, rooftop garden and a museum store.

Grant House Sewing Machines

128 E. Cañon Perdido St., Unit B

(805) 962-0929

www.granthousesewingmachines.com

$$$

From southbound Highway 101, take Carrillo Street toward the mountains, turn right onto Anacapa Street, then left onto Cañon Perdido. From northbound 101, take Garden Street toward the mountains, then turn left onto Cañon Perdido.

This sewing machine retailer also offers year round sewing classes for all levels and summer sewing camps. See Web site for current offerings. Tuition includes use of a sewing machine.

Land and Sea Tours
Stearns Wharf & Santa Barbara Harbor
(805) 683-7600
out2seesb.com
$$$

From northbound Highway 101, take Garden Street toward the beach, then turn right onto Cabrillo Boulevard. From southbound Highway 101, take Castillo Street toward the beach, then turn left onto Cabrillo Boulevard.

Climb on board a 39-foot Land Shark for a tour of Santa Barbara's roadside and harbor attractions. Have the camera ready to capture your kids' reactions as this street-legal, sea-worthy vehicle drives directly into the harbor. Throughout the tour, guides offer true stories, and perhaps a tall tale or two, about the city.

Tours are offered daily at noon and 2 p.m. year round, weather permitting. A 4 p.m. tour is added during summer months. Charters, educational tours and other services are also available by prior arrangement.

☞ Li'l Toot Water Taxi
Stearns Wharf & Santa Barbara Harbor
(805) 896-6900
www.sbwatertaxi.com
$

From southbound Highway 101, take Castillo Street toward the beach, turn right onto Cabrillo Boulevard/Shoreline Drive, then right onto Harbor Lane. From northbound 101, take Bath Street, turn left onto Haley Street, left onto Castillo Street, right onto Cabrillo Boulevard/Shoreline Drive, then right onto Harbor Lane.

Santa Barbara Harbor's only officially designated water taxi service isn't too tough to spot. She's bright yellow, for starters, and there's a giant grin on her bow. That's Li'l Toot, a 26-foot-long tugboat that ushers customers between Stearns Wharf and the Santa Barbara Harbor every half an hour from noon until sunset daily. Children often are welcomed to the helm to help steer, and the ship's captain offers harbor insights from celebrity yacht sightings to wildlife information.

Li'l Toot also is available for breakfast and dinner cruises during most weekends, as well as private charters by reservation. No restrooms onboard.

Page Youth Center

4540 Hollister Ave.

(805) 967-8778

pageyouthcenter.org

$-$$$

From Highway 101, take Turnpike Road toward the beach, then turn left onto Hollister Avenue.

This nonprofit center focused on providing facilities for young athletes includes a 16,000-square-foot gymnasium. Adult coaches guide children in after-school, summer and school break programs that include football, as well as recreational and club volleyball and basketball. The facility also hosts badminton play, table tennis (aka pingpong) and adult programs, including league basketball, jazzercise and other fitness programs. The gym is available for rent, and adults are welcome for pickup games very early Saturday mornings or between 1 p.m. and 3 p.m. weekdays.

Santa Barbara Outfitters

1200 State St.

(805) 564-1007

www.sboutfitters.com

$

From Highway 101, take Carrillo Street toward the mountains; turn left onto Chapala Street, then right onto Anapamu Street.

This outdoor recreation retailer also houses a small indoor climbing wall that is open to the public every day except major holidays. Visitors of all ages are welcome to try the wall for a small fee after signing a liability waiver. There is no spotting equipment and adults must supervise their children's climbing adventure. The wall is open from 10 a.m. to 5 p.m. daily.

☞ Susan Quinlan Dolls & Teddy Bear Museum

122 W. Cañon Perdido St.

(805) 730-1707

www.quinlanmuseum.com

$

From Highway 101, take Carrillo Street toward the mountains; turn right onto De La Vina Street and left onto Cañon Perdido Street.

Susan Quinlan began collecting dolls in 1979, not as a child but as an adult. Today, more than 3,000 of the toys, art and artifacts she has gathered are artfully displayed behind glass in themed cases: cultural heritage and history; literary characters; and artists and manufacturers with California, and more specifically, Santa Barbara ties. The museum also is thoughtfully designed. It is wheelchair accessible with ample floor space to pass visitors intrigued by details. Glass shelves that allow even the tiniest visitors clear views to the uppermost dolls, and mirrors allow for viewing details on the back side of the most ornately decorated pieces.

You can meander through the museum on your own, but Quinlan's guided tour is engaging and worth the extra time. She joyfully answers questions, points out details and explains the history behind her favorites as she walks visitors from cornhusk dolls of the 19th Century through bisque, cloth and sawdust dolls, then on to purposed dolls, such as the hospital baby used to teach nurses and new mothers how to care for newborns. The tour continues past Civil War topsy-turvy dolls and cultural celebration displays to fairy scenes and modern figures, such as Space Camp Barbie, Harry Potter action figures and Star Trek figures.

The museum is open Fridays through Mondays from 11 a.m. to 5 p.m. Quinlan also welcomes group tours and offers special tea parties by reservation. A shop at the front of the museum includes new and used doll and teddy bear paraphernalia from books on collecting to toys and antiques.

Chapter 2

Montecito

The view of Montecito from Highway 101 does no justice to this peaceful, pristine California coastal community. Like the rich and famous residents who seek peace and privacy here, the community only offers glimpses of itself to passersby, flashes through the trees, peeks over bushes. Slow down here for beautiful drives, an impressive park, unparalleled botanical offerings and warm, sandy beaches.

Montecito is technically an unincorporated area of Santa Barbara County, but it has a strong sense of place, complete with uniform, stylized street signage, its own village, fire department, even a hometown newspaper. It was paradise for the Chumash people who introduced Europeans to area hot springs, most compelling attractions for homesteaders and profiteers who began streaming into the area. Farmers and dairymen, bankers and royalty settled here. When William Randolph Hearst attracted movie stars, moguls and media to his castle in the early 1920s, the visitors invariably passed through Montecito where they found refuge from the frantic life of stardom in Southern California.

Today, the community retains a quiet, private feel while offering intimate glimpses of Montecito's artistic architectural and botanical treasures.

ARTS

Peregrine Galleries
1133 Coast Village Road
(805) 969-9673
FREE

From the north, take Highway 101 south and take the Hot Springs Road exit. At the end of the ramp, turn left onto Cabrillo Boulevard which becomes Coast Village Road. From the south, take Highway 101 north, exit onto Hermosillo, then turn right onto Coast Village Road.

For a quarter century, this private commercial endeavor in the heart of Montecito has offered an eclectic collection of works, including jewelry, coins, old Oriental rugs and paintings. The gallery is open from noon to 5:30 p.m. Mondays through Saturdays and 11 a.m. to 5 p.m. Sundays.

Reynolds Art Gallery
Westmont College
955 La Paz Road

(805) 565-6162
www.westmont.edu/reynolds_gallery
FREE

From the north, take Highway 101 south, exit at Milpas and turn toward the mountains. Turn right onto Mason Street, left onto Salinas Street, right onto Sycamore Canyon Road, left onto Cold Springs Road, and continue straight onto La Paz Road. From the south, take Highway 101 north, exit at Olive Mill Road and proceed straight ahead. Turn right onto Olive Mill Road, left onto Hot Springs Road, right onto Sycamore Canyon Road and right again onto Cold Springs Road before veering left onto La Paz Road.

This lesser-known local gallery is tucked away on the serene campus of Westmont College. The short walk from an uncrowded parking lot to the gallery is, alone, worth the visit. There's room for kids to expend some of that backseat energy before venturing into the gallery. Inside, and sometimes outside, you'll find either the works of international artists or Central Coast favorites, students or faculty. Exhibits change regularly. Generally open Mondays through Fridays from 10 a.m. to 4 p.m. and Saturdays from 11 a.m. to 5 p.m., but call ahead for any unexpected closures. Closed Sundays and holidays.

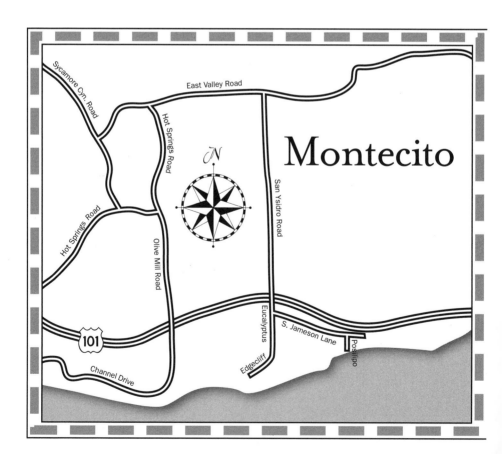

LETTERS

☞ Montecito Branch Library
1469 East Valley Road
(805) 969-5063
www.sbplibrary.org
FREE

From Highway 101, take San Ysidro Road toward the mountains, then turn left onto Valley Road.

This very nice, quiet library is part of the Santa Barbara County Public Library System and even more expansive Black Gold Library System. This branch provides a limited collection, but specializes in local-interest titles. There is also a dedicated children's corner and a comfortable reading room.

The library is open Monday through Saturday from 9 a.m. to 5 p.m. Storytime for 3- to 5-year-old children is offered Thursdays at 10:30 a.m.

HISTORY

Casa del Herrero
1387 East Valley Road
(805) 565-5653
www.casadelherrero.com
$$

From Highway 101, take San Ysidro Road toward the mountains, then turn left onto Valley Road.

It was June 29, 1925. A massive earthquake flattened portions of Santa Barbara in a matter of seconds. The city was in disaster mode, but just a few short miles away in Montecito the Steedman family carried on. After three years of planning and designing and laboring, American industrialist George Fox Steedman and his wife, Carrie Howard Steedman, moved into their new home – Casa del Herrero (House of the Blacksmith).

Today, the property is a National Historic Landmark, a symbol of Montecito's boom days, magnificent estates and its high society. The house remains in its original condition, complete with furnishings, uneven tiles, even tools in Steedman's own blacksmith shop, and the gardens remain immaculately manicured. Public tours of the estate shed light on ties between this property and other Montecito standouts, including Lotusland (p. 72) and Biltmore Gardens (p. 71).

The 90-minute, docent-led tours are offered mid-February to mid-November by reservation only. All tours are limited to visitors ages 10 and older. General tours are offered Wednesdays and Saturdays at 10 a.m. and 2 p.m. Groups of 10 or more may schedule their tours Tuesdays through Saturdays. Holiday tours also are offered. Check the schedule online or call for the latest offerings.

NATURE

☞ Biltmore Gardens

Biltmore Hotel
1260 Channel Drive
(805) 969-2261
www.fourseasons.com/santabarbara
FREE

From the south, take Highway 101 north to Olive Mill Road and proceed straight ahead. Turn left onto Olive Mill Road which becomes Channel Drive. From the north, take Spring Road, turn right onto Olive Mill Road.

When Ty Warner of Beanie Baby fame purchased the historic Biltmore Hotel, he spared no expense in its renovation. Nowhere is that more evident to the public than in the gardens of the 22-acre property. The garden was originally designed by Ralph T. Stevens, whose father owned and designed Lotusland (p. 72). The Biltmore garden includes rare plants and an impressive, picturesque Moreton Bay fig tree. Maps for self-guided tours are available from the concierge.

Butterfly Beach

Channel Drive near Butterfly Lane
(805) 568-2461
sbparks.org
FREE

From the south, take Highway 101 north to Olive Mill Road and proceed straight ahead. Turn left onto Olive Mill Road, which becomes Channel Drive. From the north, take Spring Road, turn right onto Olive Mill Road.

Just across the street from the Biltmore Hotel, this stretch of sand between the Pacific Ocean and the Channel Drive sea wall is the place to see and be seen. At normal high tide there may be just 5 feet of white sand separating seawall from sea, but the south-facing wall reflects heat, making this a preferred spot for sunbathers. At low tide, it is possible to walk to East Beach (p. 38) and other points west without ever leaving the sand.

On-street parking, while free, is limited. No restrooms. During periods of heavy runoff, check water quality first at www.sbcphd.org/ehs/oceanmn.htm.

☞ Ganna Walska Lotusland

695 Ashley Road
(805) 969-9990
Lotusland.org
$$$

From the north, take Highway 101 south and exit onto Hot Springs Road. At the end of the ramp, turn left onto Cabrillo Boulevard, which becomes Coast Village Road. Turn left onto Hot Springs Road, left onto Sycamore Canyon Road, then right onto Ashley Road.

From the south, take Highway 101 north, exit at Olive Mill Road, turn left onto Hot Springs Road, right onto Sycamore Canyon Road and right onto Ashley Road.

This 37-acre estate with winding paths through immaculately landscaped gardens was preserved by its final owner, Ganna Walska, to provide public access to a vast collection of rare and beautiful plants in an unparalleled setting. Though limited by its location in a high-end residential neighborhood, Ganna Walska Lotusland Foundation welcomes up to 15,000 visitors per year, by reservation only.

Ganna Walska, a Polish-born opera star of the early 20th century, made this estate her final home. It was originally built and designed by famed landscape architect Ralph Kinton Stevens in 1882. Stevens was a nurseryman who developed the first tropical and subtropical catalog, and specialized in plants like lemon and palm trees. He enjoyed botanical gifts from around the world, many of which found permanent homes in his gardens and continue to thrive throughout the estate: wine palms with trunks so thick it takes half a dozen children with their arms outstretched to circle them; the giant bunya bunya, or "widowmaker," whose cones weigh up to 18 pounds and crash down from the height of the evergreen tree; a 30-foot-tall bird of paradise; the Dali-esque relaxed euphorbia; prehistoric zamiaceae, forage for dinosaurs.

The garden's tendency toward the unusual includes a bounty of cycads – a family similar in appearance to ferns or, in a sense, palms, but unrelated to either. Some, such as three encephalartos woodii casting shadows on the koi pond, are incredibly rare; the last wild occurrence of this plant was cited in 1895, and there are no females of the species known to remain.

Other attractions include the whimsical garden theater, an extensive cactus garden, a giant clock, topiary creations such as a dinosaur, as well as a butterfly garden, and even a blue garden. The namesake lotus, floating on

Joyful treasures are hidden around each corner at Ganna Walska Lotusland.

one of the garden's many ponds, typically begins blooming in late June and continues through August.

Rumors abound that Lotusland does not welcome children. In fact, docents guide more than 5,000 students per year through the estate's outreach programs, including school tours. Visitors must, however, be capable of remaining on designated paths, listening to and following docents' instructions, and avoiding contact with plants. Some of the plants have sharp edges and points or poisonous seeds so small children should be monitored closely. All tours are adapted to accommodate visitors' needs.

The gardens open each February, with the tour season running until November or whenever it has reached its maximum 15,000 visitors. Call for reservations. Special privileges and events are offered to Friends of Lotusland members.

Hammonds
South end of Eucalyptus Lane
(805) 568-2461
sbparks.org
FREE

From Highway 101, take the San Ysidro exit and proceed south to the road's end.

Differentiating South Coast beaches seems kind of strange, particularly when the stretch of sand from Goleta to Carpinteria could conceivably be walked without interruption at low tide. Hammonds is one of those that really doesn't need its own name. There is no visible man-made marker delineating this stretch of sand from neighboring Butterfly Beach (p. 72).

This stretch of coast is popular for its sand, tidepools and mild surf, but there are no facilities. And while hiking round Fernald Point, to the west, or Hammonds Point, to the east, may seem like a good idea, be sure to take into account tidal changes and watch for sweeper waves. Your best bet is to simply enjoy this beach for what it has to offer, and save the other beaches for another day.

During periods of heavy runoff, check water quality first at www.sbcphd.org/ehs/oceanmn.htm.

☞ Manning Park
449 San Ysidro Road
(805) 568-2461
www.sbparks.org
FREE

From Highway, take San Ysidro Road north.

Manning Park is nothing if not diverse. The 12-acre county park is separated into three different use-type areas, each divided by one of two streets. The parcel adjacent to Montecito Union School offers active play facilities, including skinned Little League baseball diamond, basketball courts, handball courts, swings, a soccer field and an all-weather track.

Cross School House Road and you'll find yourself in an entirely different world. This peaceful, thickly forested portion echoes the serenity Dr. and Mrs. J. Manning experienced here before gifting their estate to the county in 1935. Today, this portion offers public restrooms, group picnic areas and an old, deteriorating trail system. Old stone steps also lead down to the hand-cobbled creekbed, providing access to seasonal runoff that passes through this canyon. The old carriage house, also knows as the Manning Youth Center, is available to area youth groups fee-free by advance reservation.

For wide-open grassy play areas, cross San Ysidro Road at Santa Rosa Road. This park annex includes a play structure and lots of running room, a large parking lot and restrooms. Open 8 a.m. to sunset.

Miramar
Posilipo Lane
(805) 568-2461
sbparks.org
FREE

From Highway 101, take the San Ysidro exit. From the north, this merges into Jameson Lane. From the south, turn left onto San Ysidro, then left onto Jameson. Finally, turn right onto Posilipo Lane.

Another in the chain of south-facing beaches in the South County. Like its neighbors to the west – Hammonds Beach and Butterfly Beach (p. 72) – this stretch of sand is a good stop for sand play and sunbathing, but parking is limited and there are no restrooms. During periods of heavy runoff, check water quality first at www.sbcphd.org/ehs/oceanmn.htm.

Chapter 3

Summerland

Many visitors to Santa Barbara County, indeed many county residents, simply zoom past the Summerland exit never knowing what's behind those tall hedges. In fact, the community built out of the early 20th Century oil industry has become a sleepy, unincorporated community of fewer than 2,000 residents. The oil derricks that once crowded the landscape have all been replaced with homes, parks and roads. Today, the community offers one of the quietest beaches in the county, and one of the best, large rural county parks.

HISTORY

Summerland Memorial Park

2347 Lillie Ave.

FREE

From northbound Highway 101, take the Evans Avenue exit, then turn right onto Lillie Avenue. From southbound Highway 101, take the Wallace Avenue exit, turn left onto Evans Street, then right onto Lillie Avenue.

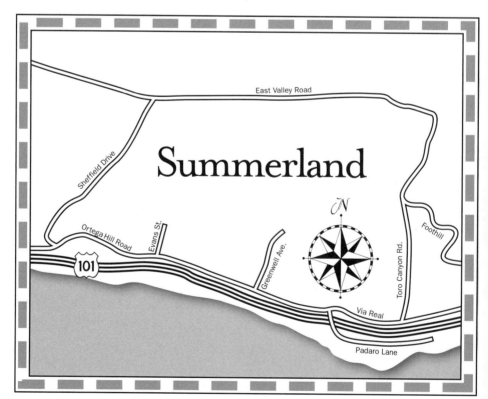

Gravel pathways wind through this tiny park that memorializes the community's fallen World War I soldiers. Picnic tables and benches dot the park, which is separated from the freeway by a chain-link fence. The park also is immediately adjacent to the fire station, which welcomes drop-in visitors. No restrooms.

NATURE

Lookout Park
Evans Avenue
(805) 969-1720
www.sbparks.org
FREE

From southbound Highway 101, take the Wallace Avenue exit, then turn right onto Evans Avenue. From northbound 101, take Evans Avenue, turn left at the end of the ramp, then left onto Evans Avenue.

This county park atop the bluffs is a wonderful spot for picnics, family barbecues or pickup games of volleyball, just a short walk from Summerland Beach. The park includes a play structure, lawn and restrooms, as well as beach access via a wide, sloping trail.

☞ Loon Point Beach
Padaro Lane
(805) 681-5650
www.sbparks.org
FREE

From Highway 101, take Padaro Lane west, then turn left into the parking lot.

A wide, well-maintained path that runs adjacent to the railroad tracks for about 30 yards wends its way down a notable hill to a long, sandy beach. The route is passable on foot or with sturdy jogger-strollers, but don't try it with street strollers.

Walk along this sandy stretch east to Loon Point, where a rocky outcropping protects the bluffs. The beach is best visited at low tide because space between the water and tall, steep bluffs is narrow. The water often is clear at Loon Point.

Although not officially designated as such, Loon Point has historically been known locally as a nude beach. If you're uncomfortable answering toddlers' questions about nudity, head to any number of other area beaches.

There are neither trash cans nor restrooms here, and visitors are asked to carry out anything they carry in to keep the area pristine for everyone.

During periods of heavy runoff, check water quality first at www.sbcphd.org/ehs/oceanmn.htm.

Oceanview Park
Greenwell Avenue at Via Real
(805) 568-2465
sbparks.org
FREE

From Highway 101, take Padaro Lane toward the mountains, turn left onto Via Real, then right onto Greenwell Avenue.

This mid-sized county park parallel to Highway 101 offers a spot to picnic with room to run and views of the ocean. The freeway noise may be off-putting to some, but the park offers easy access to toddler-friendly trails through both the manicured lawn section of the park, and a more rugged, though still landscaped, section that extends to Caspia Lane.

Amenities include picnic tables, benches and restrooms, hiking trails and ample lawn.

Summerland Beach
2500 block Wallace Avenue
(805) 969-1720
www.sbparks.org
FREE

From southbound Highway 101, take the Wallace Avenue exit, turn right onto Evans Avenue, then left onto Wallace Avenue. From northbound 101, take Evans Avenue, turn left at the end of the ramp, then left onto Evans Avenue, then left onto Wallace Avenue.

This sandy stretch from Lookout Park to Loon Point is perhaps most easily accessed from the Wallace Avenue public access, but parking here is tricky and there are no public services. The beach is particularly popular with local dog owners and beach walkers. During periods of heavy runoff, check water quality first at www.sbcphd.org/ehs/oceanmn.htm.

☞ Toro Canyon County Park
Toro Canyon Park Road
(805) 969-3315
www.sbparks.org
FREE

From Highway 101, take Padaro Lane north, turn right onto Via Real, left onto Toro Canyon Road, then right onto Toro Canyon Park Road.

This beautiful, peaceful, fairly remote, 68-acre park minutes from civilization seems to be seriously underutilized. We've seen few other visitors enjoying the park during our play days there, despite the well-maintained facilities that include: swings, play structure, group barbecue areas of varying sizes, restrooms, individual barbecues, volleyball court (not always with a net), oak open spaces, natural bouldering opportunities near the park's Area 4 and a fenced-in dog run. For fantastic ocean views, take the short trail from Area 4 to the viewpoint gazebo.

The park is closed from dusk until 8 a.m., which is a shame because its remote location, wide open spaces and scenery, make it an ideal camping area. Dogs are allowed on leash most hours, though the meadow is available for off-leash use from 8 a.m. to 10 a.m. and 4 p.m. to sunset.

On your way back out of the canyon and just beyond the exit from the park, watch for a pullout with a well-marked trail to the left. The single-track Toro Ridge Trail — part of a trails network maintained by the Montecito Trails Foundation (p. 252) — leads to a gazebo with wonderful 360-degree views.

Chapter 4

Carpinteria

When Gaspar de Portola explored this coast in 1769, he sailed his sea-ravaged ships into the mouth of a creek sandwiched between the rugged Santa Ynez Mountain Range and Pacific Ocean. Tribal residents welcomed Portola and his crew and repaired their ships with the asphalt that flows naturally along area beaches. Portola's soldiers, who witnessed the locals' construction of wooden boats, named the area Carpinteria in honor of those industrious builders.

A century later, shovel-armed miners heated their tools in brick fireplaces to cut into those black masses and pools of goo. The asphalt and its byproducts provided the stuff of road building and medicine, alike. Now, 150 years later, the asphalt mines have long since been obscured by nature and development. The community has grown into a beautiful, peaceful seaside haven for families, best known for its placid shore protected by Carpinteria Reef.

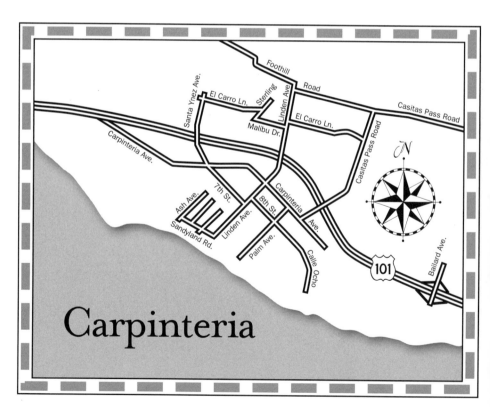

ARTS

Plaza Theatre

4916 Carpinteria Ave.

(877) 789-MOVIE (789-6684)

metrotheatres.com

$

From southbound Highway 101, take the Linden Avenue exit. Turn right onto Linden, then right onto Carpinteria Avenue. From northbound 101, take the Casitas Pass exit; turn left onto Casitas Pass Road, then right onto Carpinteria Avenue.

This single-screen, 1940s-era theater was renovated in 2005 to provide a more comfortable setting to view first-run movies. Now, the theater offers modern sound, but the original 325 seats have been reduced to just over 200 with cup holders. Still, that old movie standard treat, popcorn, is sold at the snack bar.

LETTERS

Carpinteria Branch Library

5141 Carpinteria Ave.

(805) 684-4314

sbplibrary.org

FREE

From southbound 101, take Linden Avenue west to Carpinteria Avenue. Turn left onto Carpinteria Avenue. From northbound 101, take Casitas Pass Road west to Carpinteria Avenue. Turn right onto Carpinteria Avenue.

This branch of the Santa Barbara Public Library system is a local treasure that offers a nice collection of children's books in a fairly relaxed, relatively quiet, well-lit, designated area and friendly, knowledgeable staff. There's also a homework center, frequent family-friendly programs and a variety of special events held in the adjacent Carpinteria Arts & Lecture Center. Storytime is offered at 10:30 a.m. Thursdays. Call for other current hours and schedule.

HISTORY

Carpinteria Valley Museum of History

956 Maple Ave.

(805) 684-3112

carpinteriahistoricalmuseum.org

FREE

From southbound 101, take Linden Avenue west to Carpinteria Avenue. Turn left onto Carpinteria Avenue, then right onto Maple Avenue. From northbound 101, take Casitas Pass Road west to Carpinteria Avenue. Turn right onto Carpinteria Avenue, then left onto Maple Avenue.

This largely volunteer-driven local museum provides a compact collection spanning centuries of area history. Exhibits focus on local Native American culture, Euro-American pioneers and the rancho period. Other exhibits highlight the area's industrial history, including tar mining, aviation and agriculture. There is an old-time school room, dolls, saddles, carriages and myriad antique machinery. The property also includes an enclosed courtyard, picnic tables and dedicated parking. Open Tuesday through Saturday, 1 p.m. to 4 p.m. Closed holidays. Group tours by appointment.

NATURE

Carpinteria Bluff Open Space

Bailard Avenue/Carpinteria Avenue

(805) 684-5405

www.carpinteria.ca.us/parks_rec

FREE

From Highway 101, take Bailard Avenue south to the park.

Nature is left to its own devices throughout this 52-acre open space reserve particularly popular with dog walkers and strollers. Unpaved paths crisscross the property. One of our favorites: Walk toward the southwestern portion of the park to find a tree-lined trail which ultimately leads across the railroad tracks to the Carpinteria Seal Sanctuary (p. 84) and on to Tar Pits Park (p. 88) and Carpinteria State Beach (p. 85).

☞ Carpinteria City Beach

Linden Avenue to Ash Street

(805) 684-5405

www.carpinteria.ca.us/parks_rec

FREE

From northbound 101, take Casitas Pass Road west. Turn right onto Carpinteria Avenue, then left onto Linden Avenue. From southbound 101, take Linden Avenue west to the beach.

This narrow stretch of sand between vacation rentals and the water provides a wonderfully sandy, long stretch for walks, beachcombing or sandcastle building. This is a particularly popular swimming, kayaking and tidepooling beach since a reef protects the shore from heavy surf. The park at Linden Avenue includes volleyball nets, plentiful picnic tables, barbecues and a large, grass play area, all near the state park's restrooms.

Beach access also is available at the ends of Holly and Elm avenues. City park restrooms are located at the Ash Street end of the beach. Lifeguards in summer only. During periods of heavy runoff, check water quality first at www.sbcphd.org/ehs/oceanmn.htm.

Carpinteria Coastal Vista Trail

Rincon Beach County Park to Carpinteria State Beach

(805) 684-5405

www.parks.ca.gov/?page_id=25116
FREE
Access from Viola Fields (p. 89), Rincon Beach County Park (p. 228) or
Carpinteria State Beach (p. 84).
After years of negotiations and fundraising, this 6-mile stretch of coastal
bluff is now accessible to the public. Portions of the trail are passable with
hardy jogger-style strollers, but most of the trail is maintained in a rugged
state. Begin at Linden Avenue for access to the seal rookery, hop on at Viola
Fields for the blufftop view of Channel Islands, or make a day of it and walk
the entire length to Rincon Beach.

Carpinteria Community Pool

5305 Carpinteria Ave.

(805) 566-2417

www.carpinteria.com/activities/CarpPool

$

From northbound 101, take Casitas Pass Road west. Turn right onto
Carpinteria Avenue. From southbound 101, take Linden Avenue west. Turn
left onto Carpinteria Avenue.
This outdoor, 10-lane, 25-yard-by-25-meter pool offers a vast array of
programs, including adult lap swimming, U.S. Masters program, recreational
swimming, lessons for all ages and aqua aerobics. It also is home to
Carpinteria Swim Club, which welcomes swimmers of all abilities ages 6 to
18. Hours vary.

☞ Carpinteria Salt Marsh Nature Park

Ash Avenue west of 3rd Street

(805) 684-5405

carpinteria.ucnrs.org

FREE

From Highway 101, take Linden Avenue west. Turn right onto Third Street,
then left onto Ash.
This interpretive park immediately adjacent to Carpinteria Salt Marsh
Reserve (below) provides educational signs, amphitheater, restrooms and a
well-maintained, stroller-friendly pathway along the marsh. Docents lead
walks each Saturday morning at 10 a.m. Meet at the park sign with good
walking shoes, snacks, camera and binoculars.

Carpinteria Salt Marsh Reserve

Ash Street

(805) 893-7670

carpinteria.ucnrs.org

FREE

*From Highway 101, take Linden Avenue west. Turn right onto Third Street,
then left onto Ash.*

The University of California keeps a portion of this 230-acre reserve
under lock and key to protect habitat for a variety of wildlife, including
more than 250 species of plants and more than 340 species of animals. A
variety of educational programs is hosted on the site, and the reserve is
available by previous arrangement for class use and bona fide research.
Restrooms are available in neighboring Carpinteria Salt Marsh Nature
Park (see above).

☞ Carpinteria Seal Sanctuary
East of Dump Road
www.venocoinc.com/seals-master.html
FREE

*Park or walk into Carpinteria State Beach (next entry). Walk east along
the bluff, past the pier and onward to the rookery. Or park at Carpinteria
Bluffs Open Space (p. 82), walk to the bluff and head west to the rookery.*

Watch nature in action as mother seals birth, nurse and train their
pups. The beach is generally populated by the young families from
January into May. Do not approach wildlife. The bluffs offer the safest
view. Bring binoculars for a closer look.

Carpinteria State Beach
West end of Palm Avenue
(805) 968-1033
www.parks.ca.gov/?page_id=599
FREE-$$$

From Highway 10,1 take the Casitas Pass exit and turn west onto

Casitas Pass Road. Turn right onto Carpinteria Avenue, then left onto Palm Avenue and continue straight to the park's campground entrance.

Sandwiched between an offshore reef and the railroad tracks is a long, narrow state park that provides year-round camping immediately adjacent to the sheltered shore. Think "camping at the drive-in," minus the big screen, with a soundtrack that includes crashing waves, passing trains and reveling campers.

The park, which also may be accessed via neighboring Carpinteria City Beach, offers restrooms with pay showers, free outdoor cold showers and a long stretch of sand where amazing natural treasures can be found. At low tide, the park is a local favorite for exploring tidepools. During periods of heavy runoff, check water quality first at www.sbcphd.org/ehs/oceanmn.htm.

Day use is free and the campground provides some of the most affordable accommodations along the South Coast. It's difficult to be bothered by the regular passage of tooting trains, even the drive-in feel of the parking lot campground, given the proximity to sand and surf, and the starting cost of $20 per campsite per night.

Carpinteria Valley Memorial Park
Santa Ynez Avenue at Aragon Drive
(805) 684-5405
www.carpinteria.ca.us/parks_rec
FREE

From southbound 101, take Reynolds west. Turn right onto Carpinteria Avenue, right onto Santa Ynez Avenue. From northbound 101, take Santa Monica Road and immediately turn right onto Via Real. Turn left onto Santa Ynez Avenue.

This neighborhood park offers a large, grassy play area, play structure, barbecues, picnic tables and a group barbecue area that is available by reservation. No restrooms.

El Carro Park
El Carro Lane across from Namouna Street, or 5300 block Lincoln Road
(805) 684-5405
www.carpinteria.ca.us/parks_rec
FREE

From northbound 101, take Casitas Pass road east, then turn left onto El Carro Lane or Foothill Road. From southbound 101, take Linden Avenue east then turn right onto El Carro Lane or Foothill Road.

This large park neighboring Girls Inc. (p. 249) offers parking lots on both Lincoln Road and El Carro Lane. The El Carro entrance offers immediate access to swings, barbecue pits, play structures and two baseball diamonds with skinned infields. The Lincoln access offers wide-open, grassy play areas. The park also includes three group barbecue areas available by reservation, shade trees and restrooms.

Eucalyptus Park
Between Eucalyptus Street and Chaparral Drive
(805) 684-5405
www.carpinteria.ca.us/parks_rec
FREE
From southbound 101, take Reynolds west. Turn right onto Carpinteria Avenue, right onto Santa Ynez Avenue, then right onto Chaparral Drive. From northbound 101, take Santa Monica Road and immediately turn right onto Via Real. Turn left onto Santa Ynez Avenue, then right onto Chaparral Drive.

A Victorian fountain, adobe ruins and towering eucalyptus trees offer this neighborhood park unique flavor. According to the Carpinteria Valley Historical Society, Russel Heath paid $336 in 1858 for the 52-acre farm that included this site. The sheriff, district attorney and eventual state legislator grew almonds, grapes and distilled brandy here. Today, only the ruins of his adobe home, his fountain and five of the trees that lined his driveway still stand. The park also includes picnic tables, lawn, play structure and a drinking fountain. No bathrooms.

Franklin Park
(805) 684-5405
www.carpinteria.ca.us/parks_rec
FREE
From northbound 101, take Casitas Pass Road west. Turn right onto Carpinteria Avenue, then right onto Linden Avenue, left onto Malibu Drive and right onto Sterling Avenue. From southbound 101, take Linden Avenue east, then proceed as above.

A few trees provide shade in this narrow, long, grassy neighborhood park with swings. No restrooms.

Island View Distinctive Flora
3376 Foothill Road
(805) 684-0324
www.islandviewnursery.com
FREE
From Highway 101 southbound, take the Padaro Lane exit; turn left onto Padaro Lane, right onto Via Real, left on Nidever Road, which becomes Foothill Road.

Visitors are welcome to bring picnic lunches and enjoy a leisurely stroll through this 10-acre commercial nursery that offers succulents, pottery, cacti, natives and arid climate plants.

Monte Vista Park

Bailard Avenue & Pandanes Street

(805) 684-5405

www.carpinteria.ca.us/parks_rec

FREE

From Highway 101, take the Bailard Avenue exit, turn north onto Bailard.
This open, grassy park has plenty of room for pickup soccer matches, flying kites or just plain running wild. Also includes play structure, picnic benches, shade trees and restrooms.

Palm-Linden Trail & Tomol Park

Adjacent to state park along the railroad, extending from Linden Avenue to Palm Avenue

(805) 684-5405

www.carpinteria.ca.us/parks_rec

FREE

From northbound 101, take Casitas Pass Road west. Turn right onto Carpinteria Avenue, then left onto Linden Avenue. From southbound 101, take Linden Avenue west.
When completed, this brand-new park is slated to include a paved segment of the California Coastal Trail, native landscaping, an amphitheater, a Chumash-themed play area, climbing sculptures featuring dolphins, toddler swings, a model tomol (a Chumash plank canoe) and wheelchair-accessible paths.

Santa Claus Lane Beach

Santa Claus Lane

(805) 568-2461

FREE

From Highway 101, take the Padaro Road / Santa Claus Lane exits. Head for the beach.
Locals know this stretch of sand paralleling the freeway as one of the most family-friendly places to build sandcastles or make a splash. The easiest access is about 500 feet south of the Padaro Lane overpass near the public portable outhouse. Beach access requires crossing the railroad tracks, so watch out for frequent trains. During periods of heavy runoff, check water quality first at www.sbcphd.org/ehs/oceanmn.htm.

Seaside Gardens

3700 Via Real

(805) 684-6001

www.seaside-gardens.com

FREE

From Highway 101, take the Padaro Road / Santa Claus Lane exits. Turn away from the beach, then immediately turn right onto Via Real.

Steel sculptures of wild horses greet visitors to this privately owned garden and gift store. The property provides an expansive demonstration garden, which invites visitors to take a botanical world tour. Visit Australia, Asia, South Africa and return to the natives of California all within minutes on family-friendly paths. Beware of potentially dangerous plants and uneven footing. Please maintain control of children to ensure public access for future families. Open daily, except major holidays.

Tar Pits Park
On the bluffs between Calle Ocho and Dump Road
(805) 684-5405
www.carpinteria.ca.us/parks_rec
FREE

Walk south from Carpinteria State Beach (p. 84), which is immediately adjacent to Tar Pits Park. Or from Highway 101, take Casitas Pass Road west; turn left onto Carpinteria Avenue, then right onto Arbol Verde, right onto Concha Loma, then left onto Calle Ocho. Walk across busy railroad tracks (watch for frequent trains and wave to their passengers) and head toward bluff and beach.

This underutilized open space and beach cove harbors some of the state's richest hidden historic treasures. From Carpinteria Creek east to the oil pier parking lot were once exposed tar pits second in size and significance only to the La Brea Tar Pits in Los Angeles, according to Gloria Calamar's 1993 Tar Pits Landmark Proposal. The pits have given up fossils of distinct native cultures — Hunting People, Canalion/ Chumash and Oak Grove People — plants, 55 species of birds and 26

The natural asphaltum mounded on the beach is a potentially messy attraction. Elbow grease and vegetable oil remove it from skin, but fabric is doomed.

animal species, not the least of which was smilodon fatalis, also known as smilodon californicus, the state's official vertebrate fossil.

Native people used the naturally occurring sticky, black goo to seal the joints in their canoes, known as tomols, and to build various tools. On August 17, 1769, Gaspar de Portola and his crew were hosted by local Chumash people who repaired the European ships with tar. Other European explorers noted the "spring of pitch" including Crespi, Bautista de Anza and Sebastian Viscaino.

From 1875 to 1924, the pits were deeply mined for road-paving material and byproducts including varnish, ink, enamel and ichthyol, which has medicinal uses.

From the park, walk northwest along the beach to a thick asphalt seep and the remainder of a sea wall built to keep high tides out of the pits. There you'll find the remains of a red-brick oven that asphalt miners used to heat their shovels to make cutting through the black tar easier.

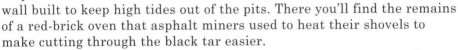

The beach below the bluffs, referred to by locals as Jelly Bowl, offers spectacular beachcombing, particularly during winter low tides.

TeeTime Driving Range
5885 Carpinteria Ave.
(805) 566-9948
$

From Highway 101, take Bailard Avenue west to Carpinteria Avenue, then turn right.

This public driving range offers a pro shop and practice range yards from the Pacific Ocean. Lessons also are available for golfers of all skills and ages. Open 8 a.m. daily. Closed on rainy days.

Viola Fields
6145 Carpinteria Ave.
(805) 684-5405
www.carpinteria.ca.us/parks_rec
FREE

From Highway 101, take Bailard Avenue west to Carpinteria Bluffs Open Space parking.

This public park immediately adjacent to Carpinteria Bluffs Open Space (p. 82) offers two baseball diamonds with skinned infields and shared outfields that can double as soccer fields. Restrooms also are available.

OTHER ADVENTURES

Gallup & Stribling Orchid Farm

3450 Via Real

(805) 684-1998

gallup-stribling.com

FREE

From Highway 101, take Padaro Road/Santa Claus Lane. Head toward the mountains, then turn left onto Via Real.

Never knew the difference between a cymbidium and a dendrobium? Always wondered what laelis, vanda and cattleya had in common? Can't tell your phalaenopsis from your odontoglossum, oncidium from your paphiopedilum? Stop by the visitors' center for up-close-and-personal views of this 48-acre orchid farm's best samples. For a special treat, visit during peak blooming season, generally February and March. Visitors welcome seven days a week. Closed major holidays.

Santa Barbara Polo & Racquet Club

3375 Foothill Road

(805) 684-6683

Sbpoloschool.com

$-$$$

From Highway 101, take Padaro Road/Santa Claus Lane. Head toward the mountains, then turn left onto Via Real.

Since 1911, this polo club has provided playing grounds for the rich and famous, up and comers and unknowns. In 1975, the property was entrusted to the state of California in perpetuity for the purpose of playing polo. Today, the club focuses its efforts on maintaining interest in this action-packed, quick-paced equestrian sport by developing the next generation of players. Tournaments are traditionally held the first and third Sundays from May through mid-October and spectators are welcome. The related Santa Barbara Polo School offers lessons to riders of all experience levels. The club also offers various memberships that provide access to regular polo play, pool and tennis courts.

Chapter 5

Goleta & Isla Vista

The coastal and foothill areas west of Santa Barbara have been home to Chumash villages, Spanish explorers, World War II aviators in training, and pioneers in disciplines from agriculture to aerospace. Leathernecks and rednecks, farmers and engineers, students and retirees have lived in and loved these communities. Today, the newly incorporated City of Goleta, long-time university neighborhood of Isla Vista, and surrounding unincorporated areas provide an astonishing number of outdoor recreation opportunities.

While I was born and raised no further than a neighboring county, I confess I never stepped onto the University of California, Santa Barbara campus until 2000, or visited storied Isla Vista until 2008. What a pleasant surprise it has been to discover the many recreational opportunities the campus and college neighborhood provide the community at large. Amidst the commotion that only a university neighborhood can create are some of the best kid-friendly parks in the county, natural spaces, even a wildlife refuge. Parking is an issue both on campus and in Isla Vista, so build in time for a hunt, or avoid the frustration by traveling any of the well-established, in some cases even off-street, bike paths, or taking mass transit that serves the area.

ARTS

Camino Real Cinemas
7040 Marketplace Drive
(877) 789-MOVIE (789-6684)
metrotheatres.com
$
From Highway 101, take Glen Annie/Storke Road exit. Drive south on Storke Road.
This six-screen movie theater offers first-run, mainstream movies. It is also one of two theaters in the south county offering "Movies & Me," a 10 a.m. matinee designed for parents who always have their children in tow. While the films playing may not be child-friendly, the audience will be. Call for current schedule.

Fairview Theatre
225 N. Fairview Ave.
(877) 789-MOVIE (789-6684)
metrotheatres.com

$

From Highway 101, take Fairview Avenue north.
This three-screen theater with stadium seating offers first-run, mainstream movies.

University Art Museums
UCSB University Center
(805) 893-7564
www.instadv.ucsb.edu/ps/libraries.aspx
FREE
From northbound Highway 101, take the Airport / UCSB exit (Highway

217). From southbound 101, take Storke Road/Glen Annie Road away from the mountains, then turn left on El Colegio Road. Public parking is available in Lot 20, where mandatory permits also are sold.

The University Art Museum is the largest of three on-campus venues for budding and established artists. The UAM features three galleries that exhibit works of local and internationally acclaimed artists. These galleries are open Wednesdays through Sundays, noon until 5 p.m. Docent-led tours also are available by reservation. (In 2009, the UAM was slated to begin earthquake retrofitting. The construction project is estimated to take two years, during which time the galleries will be housed in the Old Gym, located by the bus loop on Ocean Road.)

The university also displays a regular rotation of student artwork in

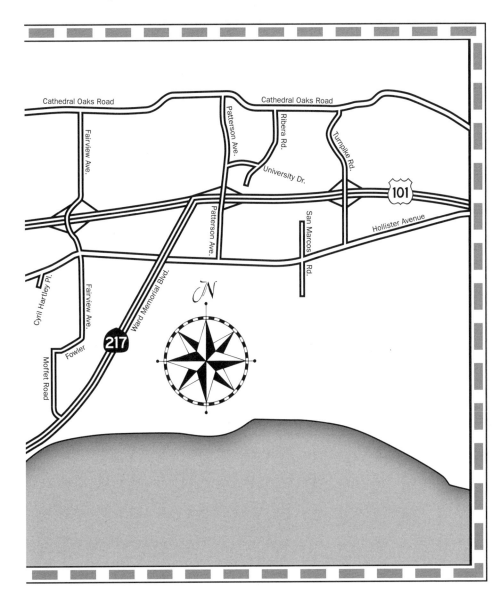

Gallery 1434 (Art Department Room 1434, phone 893-3138) and thematic works in the Women's Center Art Gallery (893-3778) at the Student Resource Center, which is immediately south of Lot 22.

LETTERS

☞ Goleta Branch Library

500 N. Fairview Ave.

(805) 964-7878

www.sbplibrary.org/hourslocations/goleta.html

FREE

From Highway 101, take the Fairview Avenue exit and head toward the mountains.

From a parent's perspective, Goleta's library is a godsend. This branch of the Santa Barbara Public Library System has been divided roughly in half. The collection to the right of the librarians' desk is dedicated to picture books, children's titles, and works aimed at tweens and teens. The collection for more mature readers comprises the left portion of the library.

This branch is unique in that it welcomes patrons to picnic, snack, drink coffee, or simply soak up some sun while reading on any of the enclosed outdoor patios. High walls help contain rambunctious children while older siblings enjoy some quiet time in the stacks. Works by local artists are displayed on nearly every wall, including the multipurpose room and conference rooms, which are available by reservation.

This library is open daily with story times offered for 3 to 5 year olds each Wednesday and Thursday at 10:30 a.m.

HISTORY

Rancho La Patera & Stow House

304 N. Los Carneros Road

(805) 964-4407

www.stowhouse.com

FREE-$

From Highway 101, take the Los Carneros exit and head for the hills.

La Patera Ranch, once the core of Goleta's lemon industry, provides today's visitors a feel for what life in Goleta was like more than a century ago. The property includes the home Sherman Stow built in 1872 — today Goleta's oldest frame house — as well as a working blacksmith shop and the Horace Sexton Memorial Museum. Pack a picnic and let the kids run wild after the tour, or take a quiet walk in neighboring Lake Los Carneros Park (p. 106).

While the grounds are open daily, the Goleta Valley Historical Society opens the Stow House for docent-led tours at 2 p.m. and 3 p.m. on Saturdays and Sundays only. The society also provides educational group tours for area schools and other organizations by reservation (681-7216).

☞ South Coast Railroad Museum

300 N. Los Carneros Road
(805) 964-3540
goletadepot.org
FREE

From Highway 101, take the Los Carneros exit and head for the hills.

It's hard to believe the Goleta Depot was left to ruin. The Victorian-styled Southern Pacific station built in 1901 was once a hub of community activity. By the 1970s, with local passenger rail service defunct, the depot had become an antiquity. Fortunately, local railroad buffs and historians saved the structure and moved it to its current location. Today, the depot is on the National Register of Historic Places, California Register of Historical Resources and is a Santa Barbara County Historical Landmark (No. 22).

The museum and grounds are open from 1 p.m. to 4 p.m. Wednesdays through Sundays, but stop by on the third Saturday of the month for a special treat — rides on the handcar. Visitors are free to walk the grounds, stop in the visitors' center, wander through a caboose, tour the furnished depot and view the HO-scale "Railroading on the South Coast." Docents play along with children as they tour the Freight Office, relax in the passenger area, or observe various artifacts from the days when rail was king before stepping outside for a walk through Southern Pacific Caboose 4023. "Gandy Dancer Theater" offers rail-centered travel films daily with special showings Thursdays and Sundays. Rides on "Goleta Short Line," a miniature train, are offered most Wednesdays, Fridays, Saturdays and Sundays for a nominal fee. Docents provide group tours by reservation at no charge.

The facility hosts several special events. Visiting steam locomotives pull the miniature train during Steaming Summer. Special hands-on activities, exhibits, food and games are included during Depot Day the last Sunday of September. Other special events include the Easter Bunny Express and Candy Cane Train.

The grounds also include a picnic area and a gift shop. All dogs must remain on leash. No skateboards or bikes. Volunteer engineers, conductors, station agents and shopkeepers always are needed, and the museum offers Junior Engineer Club for kids 12 and younger.

NATURE

Andamar Open Space

West end of Andamar Way
(805) 968-6848
www.cityofgoleta.org/index.aspx?page=206
FREE

From Highway 101, take Fairview Avenue north. Turn right onto Cathedral Oaks, right onto Dara Road, then right onto Andamar Way.

This 2.5-acre park hidden midblock behind homes is a nice spot for mellow play dates. The park includes a play structure, picnic table, maintained lawns and unimproved areas. There are no restrooms and the limited parking is all on-street in a residential cul-de-sac.

Anisq'oyo' Park
960 Embarcadero Del Mar
(805) 968-2017
ivparks.org
FREE

From Highway 101, take Storke Road toward the ocean; turn left onto El Colegio Road, then right onto Embarcadero Del Mar.

This 2.65-acre park, which carries the Chumash name for this area, is a surprising find in a neighborhood known more for its college atmosphere than its family-friendly flair. Set the kids loose to waddle behind the ducks that frequent the pond, ramble along the paths, romp on the play structures or wonder at the windmill. The park's wheelchair-accessible amphitheater often plays host to events ranging from political demonstrations to music festivals and is available to rent. Picnic tables, benches and restrooms also are available.

Anisq'oyo' Park is connected to Perfect Park (p. 110) via People's Park (p. 110).

Armitos Park
5551 Armitos Ave.
(805) 968-6848
www.cityofgoleta.org/index.aspx?page=206
FREE

From northbound Highway 101, take the UCSB/Airport/Highway 217 exit west, turn right onto Hollister Avenue, right onto South Kellogg Avenue, then right onto Armitos. From southbound 101, take North Fairview Avenue west; turn left onto Hollister Avenue, left onto South Kellogg, then right onto Armitos.

This splendid little park is the newest in Goleta. A third of the 1.5-acre parcel hosts the play structure, manicured lawn and benches along a paved path. The remainder of the property has been left to nature and neighboring San Jose Creek. No restrooms.

Armstrong Park
7100 block Marymount Way
(805) 968-6848
www.cityofgoleta.org/index.aspx?page=206
FREE

From Highway 101, take Storke Road south; turn right onto Phelps Road, left onto Pacific Oaks Road then right onto Marymount Way.

This half-acre city park is located uniquely midblock, surrounded entirely by private residences. The neighborhood park offers a play structure, picnic benches and manicured lawn for passive play. Although the park is accessible via short paths from both Marymount Way and Armstrong Road, parking is more plentiful along Marymount. No restrooms.

Bella Vista Open Space
100 block Placer Drive
(805) 968-6848
www.cityofgoleta.org/index.aspx?page=206
FREE

From Highway 101, take Glen Annie Road north. Turn left onto Del Norte Drive, then right onto Placer Drive.

This 4-acre neighborhood park includes nearly 3 acres of sloping lawn, paths, two footbridges, shade trees, picnic tables, benches and a grassy hill that begs for a good tumble. No restrooms.

Brandon Park
Brandon Drive near Calle Real
(805) 968-6848
www.cityofgoleta.org/index.aspx?page=206
FREE

From Highway 101, take Hollister Avenue toward the mountains, then turn right onto Calle Real, left onto Winchester Canyon Road, right onto Bradford Drive, right onto Calle Real, then left onto Brandon Drive.

This unimproved city open space provides a dirt path to the residential neighborhood along 7500 block of San Cassino Way, as well as native flora to explore. No restrooms.

Calle Barquero Open Space
5100 block Calle Barquero
(805) 568-2461
countyofsb.org/parks
FREE

From Highway 101, take Patterson Road toward the mountains, then turn right onto University Drive.

This 5.3-acre parcel offers a more secluded setting than many of the city's other parks. Wide, maintained dirt trails are accessible for rugged strollers or wheelchairs and provide access to tree-shaded picnic tables, benches and a playground. You won't find acres of grass or restrooms here, but it's a nice, quiet setting that naturalists will particularly enjoy. For a little extra biology lesson, take a peek at the eucalyptus trees where monarch butterflies perch during their winter stay beginning in October, but peaking from December through February.

This park ties nicely into a chain of adjoining parks, including Patterson Open Space (p.109) across University Drive, and, on the opposite bank of San Ygnacio Creek, Ribera Bikeway (p. 110) which leads to Tabano Hollow Open Space (p. 115).

Camino Corto Open Space & Del Sol Vernal Pool Reserve
721 Camino Corto
(805) 968-2017
ivparks.org
FREE

From Highway 101, take the Storke Road exit and head toward the ocean. Turn left onto El Colegio Road.

The 19-acre unimproved Camino Corto Open Space and neighboring 12-acre Del Sol Vernal Pool Reserve are popular, car-free routes through native grassland and vernal wetlands. The well-traveled, dirt paths are popular with cross-country runners and mountain bikers headed for the hills or to the beach. No restrooms.

Camino Pescadero Park
6605 Del Playa Drive
(805) 968-2017
ivparks.org
FREE

From Highway 101, take the Los Carneros exit and head for the ocean. Turn left on El Colegio road, right onto Camino Pescadero, then right on Del Play Drive.

Half-acre coastal access park provides picnic tables, showers, drinking fountain, bike racks, steep stairs to beach, and no restrooms.

Campus Glen Open Space
Pebble Beach Drive to bluffs
(805) 968-6848
www.cityofgoleta.org/index.aspx?page=206
FREE

From northbound Highway 101, take Storke Road south; turn right onto Hollister Avenue and left onto Pebble Beach Drive. From southbound 101, take Hollister Avenue east; turn right onto Pebble Beach Drive.

This lesser-known eucalyptus grove through a residential neighborhood provides the monarch butterflies a wintering ground and the public access to the beach. The stroller-friendly, maintained dirt trail follows the drainage from Pebble Beach Drive across Santa Barbara Shores Drive and Newport Drive before merging with the Coronado Butterfly Preserve (p. 99) and Ellwood Main Monarch Butterfly Grove (p. 100).

Children's Park
810 Camino Del Sur
(805) 968-2017
ivparks.org
FREE

From Highway 101, take the Los Carneros exit and head for the ocean. Turn left on El Colegio road, then right on Camino Del Sur.

This ¾-acre park with its giant eucalyptus tree includes tree-shaded grass areas, a play structure, benches, picnic tables, a drinking fountain, a gazebo and restrooms. The park is particularly attractive because Picasso Road, which used to run along the north side of the park, has been transformed into a bikeway, leaving only one short side of the parcel exposed to vehicle traffic.

☞ Coal Oil Point Natural Reserve

(805) 893-5092

coaloilpoint.ucnrs.org

FREE

Access from Santa Barbara Shores Park (p. 112) or Del Playa Open Space (p. 100). From Del Playa, continue west along the bluff trail and beach access. From Santa Barbara Shores, follow the trail to the bluff, then head east.

This point adjacent to the western edge of Isla Vista offers another of the South County's great sandy stretches of coastline. The 158-acre reserve includes the Devereaux Slough, Sands Beach, vernal ponds, tidepools, dunes and protected habitats for species including the snowy plover and tidewater goby. No easy access means more protection for wildlife but hassles for families with small children, wheelchair-bound explorers and visitors with limited time. Combine remote access with a lack of restrooms and you're in for some exciting choices for those with smaller bladders.

Estuarine life comes to call in the Devereaux Slough. Some of the most-frequent visitors include various herons, cormorants, pelicans, gulls, sandpipers, avocets, stilts, dowitchers and ducks. The slough opens to the sea just two or three times each year during heavy runoff. The Audubon Society has designated the slough an Important Bird Area. The slough, an ecological study area, is closed to pedestrians.

Self-guided tours of the reserve include 21 interpretive signs posted along a 3-mile loop beginning at Del Playa and Camino Majorca in Isla Vista. The area may also be reached via Ellwood Mesa (see Santa Barbara Shores Park, p. 112).

UCSB (p. 121) offers docent-led tours of the reserve the first Sunday of each month from 2 p.m. to 4:15 p.m. Group tours are also available by request.

☞ Coronado Butterfly Preserve

400 block Coronado Drive

(805) 966-4520

www.sblandtrust.org/coronado.html

FREE

From northbound Highway 101, take Storke Road and head away from the mountains, turn right onto Hollister Avenue and left onto Coronado Drive. From southbound 101, take Hollister Avenue east; turn right onto Coronado Drive.

This 9.3-acre portion of a relatively expansive eucalyptus grove provides visitor information and access to the Ellwood Main Monarch Butterfly Grove (p. 100). While the butterflies begin floating into the grove as early as October, visit between December and February for the highest density. The preserve is most easily accessed from Coronado Street, where a dirt path leads visitors past informational signs, up a gentle rise, then down into Ellwood Main. Informational signs explain the history and science of the area. The reserve also can be reached via a flat, dirt path from Santa Barbara Shores Park (p. 112). There are no restrooms at either entrance.

Del Playa Open Space
6621 & 6850 Del Playa Drive
(805) 968-2017
ivparks.org
FREE

From Highway 101, take the Los Carneros exit and head for the ocean. Turn left on El Colegio road, right on Camino Corto, then right onto Del Playa Drive.

This blufftop, 5-acre parcel provides access to Isla Vista Beach at Camino Majorca. It also provides access to an unimproved trail that stretches east to adjacent Gaffney Park (p. 102), neighboring Sea Lookout Park (p. 113) and west to Coal Oil Point Reserve (p. 99).

☞ Ellwood Main Monarch Butterfly Grove
400 block Coronado Drive
(805) 968-6848
www.cityofgoleta.org/index.aspx?page=206
FREE

From northbound Highway 101, take Storke Road and head away from the mountains, turn right onto Hollister Avenue and left onto Coronado Drive. From southbound 101, take Hollister Avenue east; turn right onto Coronado Drive.

This eucalyptus grove adjacent to the Coronado Butterfly Preserve (p. 99) is a winter playground for monarch butterflies. The frail insects travel thousands of miles annually to reach this protected coastal grove. Visit between December and February for the highest density. Since butterflies tend to venture out for nourishment and companionship on warm days, you're more likely to spot them clumping in the branches on cooler days or during morning and late evening hours.

The flattest, easiest access is just beyond the barricade at the south end of Coronado Drive, but the grove also can be accessed via the Coronado Butterfly Preserve (p. 99) or via easy trails from Santa Barbara Shores (p. 112).

Emerald Terrace Tennis Courts
450 Arundel Road
(805) 968-6848
www.cityofgoleta.org/index.aspx?page=206
FREE

From Highway 101, take Fairview Avenue north; turn right onto Berkeley, then left onto Arundel.

This 4-acre park, previously known as Berkeley Park, offers swings, picnic tables, benches, manicured lawn, and wheelchair-accessible tennis courts that are available on a first-come, first-served basis. Portable restrooms are typically also available. At publication time, planning was under way to transform an acre of this property into a fenced-off dog park.

Estero Park and Community Gardens
889 Camino Del Sur
(805) 968-2017
ivparks.org
FREE

From Highway 101, take the Los Carneros exit and head for the ocean. Turn left on El Colegio road, then right on Camino Del Sur.

At nearly 8 acres, this is among the larger parks offered in Isla Vista. In the spirit of this land's farming heritage, half an acre has been dedicated for use as a community garden, with plots available by reservation for a fee. The park also includes basketball and volleyball courts, a play structure, picnic tables, sports field, restrooms, a drinking fountain and shade provided by a grove of mature oak trees. The last five baskets of the three-park, nine-basket Isla Vista Disc Golf Course (p. 105) are also here, and the Teen Center (p. 121) is next door.

At publication time, plans were in the works to build a 17,000-square-foot skate park here, complete with kidney pool, bowls and a street course.

Evergreen Acres Open Space
Evergreen Drive between Cathedral Oaks and Brandon Drive
(805) 968-6848
www.cityofgoleta.org/index.aspx?page=206
FREE

From Highway 101, take Glen Annie Road toward the mountains, turn left onto Cathedral Oaks Road and left onto Evergreen Drive.

At nearly 29 acres, this is one of the largest neighborhood parks in the city of Goleta. The park includes tennis courts, an 18-basket disc golf course, paved pathways, grassy fields, backstops, bridges, play structures, as well as unimproved areas for nature explorers. Restrooms are limited to those of the portable variety.

Gaffney Park
6805 Del Playa Drive
(805) 968-2017
ivparks.org
FREE

From Highway 101, take the Los Carneros exit and head for the ocean. Turn left on El Colegio road, right onto Camino Corto, then right onto Del Playa Drive.

This unimproved, half-acre, blufftop, open space provides coastal views but no beach access and no restrooms.

☞ Girsch Park
7050 Phelps Road
(805) 968-2773
www.girshpark.org
FREE

From Highway 101, take Storke Road south toward the beach. Turn right onto Phelps Road.

If you're looking for great soccer-playing fields, clean basketball courts or play structures with good old-fashioned metal slides, Girsch Park is the answer.

From 7 a.m. to sunset daily, the wheelchair-accessible, 25-acre park welcomes visitors to pick up a game, pack a picnic, enjoy a barbecue or pound a piñata. Softball and baseball diamonds play host to several local leagues. Camps and other programs are offered throughout the year.

The park is off limits to skateboarders, and dogs must remain on leash. Group picnic areas are available by reservation. Restrooms are on site.

Glen Annie Golf Club
405 Glen Annie Road
(805) 968-6400
www.glenanniegolf.com
$-$$$

From Highway 101, take Glen Annie Road toward the mountains.
This 18-hole golf course offers the public tremendous ocean views, club rentals, a pro shop, lessons and an affordable putting green.

☞ Goleta Beach County Park
Sandspit Road
(805) 967-1300
countyofsb.org/parks
FREE

From Highway 101, take Highway 217/UCSB/Santa Barbara Airport exit, then take the Sandspit Road exit.

It's no wonder this beach is particularly popular, even overcrowded at times. Palm trees line the mile-long, 29-acre park that provides access to glassy water for swimming, floating or paddling. The park offers loads of amenities including grassy picnic areas, a sandy shore, barbecue pits, playgrounds, volleyball courts, horseshoe pits, a restaurant, showers, dressing rooms, restrooms and seasonal lifeguards. Other activities include fishing off Goleta Beach Pier, swimming, kayaking and paddleboarding.

The lagoon connecting what remains of Goleta Slough to the beach occasionally opens to the sea at the east end of the beach. According to a sign posted here, this slough was visited by Cabrillo in 1542 and the Spanish Martinez Expedition in 1782.

Since UCSB is within walking distance and the car-free Coast Bike Route crosses the park, the area is usually quite busy, and parking can be a challenge. Still, it's usually worth braving the crowds. During periods of heavy runoff, check water quality first at www.sbcphd.org/ehs/oceanmn.htm.

Greek Park
820 Embarcadero Del Norte
(805) 968-2017
ivparks.org
FREE
From Highway 101, take the Los Carneros exit and head for the ocean. Turn left on El Colegio road, then right onto Embarcadero Del Norte.

This small park is dominated by its basketball court, but it also includes a volleyball court, picnic tables and barbecue area. No restrooms.

☞ Haskell's Beach
Bacara Entrance Road
(805) 967-1300
countyofsb.org/parks
FREE
From Southbound Highway 101, take Hollister Avenue south, then turn left into the Bacara Golf Course frontage road. Drive 6/10 of a mile to the coastal access parking lot at the tennis courts. From northbound Highway 101, take

the Calle Real offramp, continue west to Hollister Road. Turn left, then proceed as above.

Until the turn of the 21st Century, this rock-strewn beach was shared primarily by surf buddies and other locals in the know. Through an agreement with local government agencies, the Bacara Resort now provides a beautiful entry to, and publicity for, this stretch of coastline. Though this beach specializes in good surf, rock hunting and driftwood rather than smooth, white sand, its ease for strollers, wheelchairs and toddlers alike help make it popular.

A 50-space parking lot near the resort's tennis court provides off-street parking for beach goers. The lot can quickly fill in summer and on weekends and holidays. Follow the wide, flat, well-maintained dirt path about a quarter mile to the long beach, where facilities include restrooms and summer snack bar. At low tide, there's a thin strip of sand, but high tide leaves a slip of beach ideal for driftwood construction projects and rock hounding. Pilings and piers along this stretch of coast also attract a multitude of birds.

During periods of heavy runoff, check water quality first at www.sbcphd.org/ehs/oceanmn.htm.

Hidden Oaks Golf Course
4760 Calle Camarada
(805) 967-3493
hiddenoaksgolfsb.net
$-$$

From Highway 101, take Turnpike south, turn left onto Turnpike, right onto Puente, then right onto Calle Camarada.

This nine-hole, par-27 course caters to juniors and beginning golfers, though many advanced golfers find it a fun course for a quick game between other obligations.

Isla Vista County Beach
Del Playa Drive
(805) 968-2017
ivparks.org
FREE

From Highway 101, take the Los Carneros exit and head for the ocean. Turn left on El Colegio road, then right on Camino Corto.

This kelp-strewn beach sandwiched between the bluffs of Isla Vista and the Pacific Ocean offer neighborhood residents a quick ocean fix, but may pose difficulties for visitors. On-street parking is very limited, and high tide can completely engulf the beach. At times, the beach is packed with party goers or special student events.

The beach is most easily accessed from the south end of Camino Majorca, Camino Del Sur, Camino Pescadero Park, El Embarcadero and Escondido Pass between Camino Corto and Camino Del Sur.

. During periods of heavy runoff, check water quality first at www.sbcphd.org/ehs/oceanmn.htm.

Isla Vista Disc Golf Course
6700 block Sueño Road
(805) 968-2017
ivparks.org/frisbee golf course/frisbeegolf.pdf
FREE

From Highway 101, take the Los Carneros exit and head for the ocean. Turn left on El Colegio road, right onto Camino Del Sur, then right onto Sueño.

Take a good old flying disc — call it a Frisbee if you will — fling it toward a target basket, then repeat and you have yourself a short game of disc golf. Avid disc golfers carry their own bags of specialized discs, but an old-fashioned flippy flier works just as well.

Isla Vista's relatively compact, nine-basket course covers three public open areas through three city blocks. Play begins in the Sueño Orchard (p. 114), crosses through Tipi Village (p. 116), then wraps up in Estero Park (p. 101). A score sheet is available at the Isla Vista Parks Web site.

Kellogg Open Space/North Kellogg Open Space & Tennis Courts
Queen Anne Lane to University Circle Open Space (p. 118)
(805) 681-5650
countyofsb.org/parks
FREE

From Highway 101, take Patterson Road north; turn left onto Cathedral Oaks, then right onto Kellogg, and right onto Queen Anne Lane.

Sometimes it's easier to find a park than it is to explain the convoluted lot lines and property combinations that form it. This is one of those times.

Kellogg Open Space comprises a collection of properties at the confluence of San Jose Creek and Fremont Creek. Venture to the north side of the creek's confluence and you're on Queen Anne Vineyard. Cross to the west side of the creek between Patterson Avenue and Cathedral Oaks Road and you're on North Kellogg Open Space. Venture east on the segment between Patterson Road, south along Calle Alberta and Paseo Cameo to Cathedral Oaks and you're on Town & Country Open Space.

Lot line divisions aside, the open space provides seamless access to unimproved riparian habitat via dirt trails. In other words, this is a spot that provides a bit of nature in an urban setting. Continue south along San Jose Creek to Kellogg Tennis Courts, then carry on to the University Circle Open Space (p. 118) and points south for an extended adventure.

The courts, also accessible by car at the 600 block of North Kellogg, are free and available to the public. There is no shade on the courts, but several trees outside the fence offer respite. These courts also may be reserved (568-2461) for a fee. Portable restrooms are available.

Kids' Trail Park
6998 Pasado Road
(805) 968-2017
ivparks.org
FREE

From Highway 101, take the Los Carneros exit and head for the ocean. Turn left on El Colegio road, right on Camino Corto, then right on Pasado Road.

A small play structure on less than 1/3 acre is designed to provide outdoor play for neighborhood kids. The street-width path connecting Pasado Road with Fortuna Road is part of a popular jogging route that also includes Tierra de Fortuna Park (p. 116), Camino Corto Open Space (p. 98) and Del Sol Vernal Pools (p. 98). No restrooms.

Koarts Open Space
300 block Paseo Del Piñon
(805) 968-6848
www.cityofgoleta.org/index.aspx?page=206
FREE

From northbound Highway 101, take the Winchester Canyon Road/ Hollister Avenue exit and turn right at the end of the ramp onto Winchester Canyon Road, right onto Cathedral Oaks, then left onto Paseo Del Piñon. From southbound 101, take the Hollister Avenue exit, turn left at the end of the ramp, turn right onto Calle Real, left onto Cathedral Oaks, then left onto Paseo Del Piñon.

This 10.5-acre open space behind Koarts Apartments is particularly popular for early morning dog walking. The natural setting includes plenty of long grass, some shade trees, and all the treats and tribulations wild places can afford. No restrooms.

La Goleta Open Space
La Goleta at Paseo Palmilla
(805) 968-6848
www.cityofgoleta.org/index.aspx?page=206
FREE

From Highway 101, take Fairview Avenue north, turn left onto La Goleta.

This unimproved, 6-acre open space along Las Vegas Creek provides a natural setting for children to explore flora and fauna close to home. No restrooms.

Lake Los Carneros Park
304 N. Los Carneros
(805) 968-6848
www.cityofgoleta.org/index.aspx?page=206
FREE

From Highway 101, take Los Carneros Road toward the mountains.

This 140-acre park represents a mere fraction of the Stow family's La Patera Ranch. The once-bustling agricultural endeavor has been left largely to nature, though several attractions share the site, including a historic home, railroad museum, trails and a 22-acre, manmade lake. There is ample room to run, explore, scream into the wind, but don't come looking for manicured lawns or athletic playing fields.

Lake Los Carneros was built by the Stow family for crop irrigation. Today, it is a popular spot for bird watching or simple nature walks. Fishing is allowed, but not swimming. A web of trails offers relatively stroller-friendly passage around the lake. Take the old paved road extending from Stow House (p. 94), then follow the dirt trails in either direction. A boardwalk ensures visitors have a dry route across the potentially wet or marshy northern end of the lake. The southerly route crosses the dam.

It's easy to spend all day in this corner of Goleta. Take small children for a visit to the County Fire Station, get your train fix at South Coast Railroad Museum (p. 95), take a tour of the Stow House (p. 94) for a taste of life here in the late 19th Century, then cruise the trails.

Lassen Open Space

63 Lassen Drive

(805) 568-2461

countyofsb.org/parks

From Highway 101, take Patterson Road south, turn left on Hollister Avenue, then left onto Lassen Drive.

A half-mile, off-street bike path gently curves in dappled shade from a park at Lassen Drive to Hollister Avenue. The area includes a lawn, native riparian habitat, benches, and a footbridge over Maria Ignacio Creek. Stop by in late spring to see the monkey hand tree in bloom.

Little Acorn Park

Sabado Tarde Road at El Embarcadero Road

(805) 968-2017

ivparks.org

FREE

From Highway 101, take the Los Carneros exit and head for the ocean. Turn left on El Colegio road, then right onto Embarcadero Del Mar.

This neighborhood park located on a trapezoidal corner in Isla Vista's deli district offers just over half an acre of lawn with picnic tables, benches and a few shade trees. If you're in the neighborhood and want to grab a quick sandwich or pita, soup or coffee, then have a seat; the park's proximity to multiple delis and cafes may make this just the spot for you. There is no barrier between the busy street and park, so keep an eye out for wandering toddlers. Restrooms are available at nearby Anisq'oyo' Park (p. 96).

Mathilda Park

300 block Mathilda Drive

(805) 968-6848

www.cityofgoleta.org/index.aspx?page=206

FREE

From Highway 101, take Stork Road south; turn right onto Hollister Road, left onto Entrance Road, then right onto Mathilda Drive.

While this neighborhood park is among Goleta's smallest, it is also among its most beautifully landscaped. A paved path winds through manicured bedding to a play structure, picnic bench and small lawn area. No restrooms.

Nectarine Park

Nectarine Avenue at Mandarin Drive

(805) 968-6848

www.cityofgoleta.org/index.aspx?page=206

FREE

From Highway 101, take Fairview Avenue south; turn left onto Hollister Avenue, then left onto Nectarine Avenue.

The city's smallest park is the closest thing to a sandlot I've seen in years. The .14-acre lot includes play structures, benches and plenty of dirt, but no shade, restrooms or other amenities.

Ocean Meadows Golf Course

6925 Whittier Drive

(805) 968-6814

www.oceanmeadowsgolfclub.com

$-$$$

From Highway 101, take Storke Road south, then turn right onto Whittier Drive.

This affordable, 3,241-yard, nine-hole golf course located along Devereaux Creek and just off UCSB is particularly popular. The facility's practice areas include a putting green, chipping greens and sand bunker. Lessons and camps also are available, and a public path around the perimeter of the course provides a nice route for cyclists, joggers and walkers.

Oro Verde Open Space

Via Salerno

(805) 968-6848

www.cityofgoleta.org/index.aspx?page=206

FREE

From Highway 101, take Patterson north, turn left onto Cathedral Oaks, right onto Cambridge, then left onto Via Salerno.

This 7-acre public open space behind Cathedral Oaks Athletic Club provides local residents space to roam. Single track trails, undefined trails and a variety of trees dot the landscape. No restrooms.

Pardall Gardens
6514 Pardall Road
(805) 968-2017
ivparks.org
FREE

From Highway 101, take the Los Carneros exit and head for the ocean. Turn left on El Colegio road, right onto Embarcadero Del Norte, and then left onto Pardall Road.

At less than ¼ acre, Pardall Gardens is the smallest of the Isla Vista parks, but its shade trees and additional landscaping invite picnickers to enjoy the shade on lawn or picnic tables. No restrooms.

Patterson Open Space
5100 block University Drive
(805) 681-5650
countyofsb.org/parks
FREE

From Highway 101, take Patterson Road toward the mountains, then turn right onto University Drive.

Goleta includes several serial parks and open spaces, which makes delineating them difficult. Patterson Open Space, located just across the road from Barquero Open Space and Ribera Bikeway (p. 110), extends from University Drive north to the 500 block of Calle Aparejo and the 500 block of Ribera Drive.

With more than 1.5 acres to explore, this tree-shaded park divided in two by Maria Ygnacio Creek includes a play structure on the west side of the creek and paved path along the east side. No restrooms.

☞ Pelican Park
6543 Del Playa Drive
(805) 968-2017
ivparks.org
FREE

From Highway 101, take the Los Carneros exit and head for the ocean. Turn left on El Colegio road, right onto Camino Pescadero, then left onto Del Playa Drive.

This 1-acre park is a jewel on the bluffs of Isla Vista. Want to lure prospective students? Show them the terrazzo pingpong table in this 1-acre whimsically landscaped park with breathtaking views of the Santa Barbara Channel. That should do the trick.

Wheelchair-accessible dirt paths and terrazzo benches top off this neighborhood park. No restrooms.

People's Park
967 Embarcadero Del Norte
(805) 968-2017
ivparks.org
FREE

From Highway 101, take the Los Carneros exit and head for the ocean. Turn left on El Colegio road, then right onto Embarcadero Del Norte.

This half-acre park that offers lawn, picnic tables and shade trees links Perfect Park (p. 110) with Anisq'oyo' Park (p. 96). It is also home to the People's Park Peace Monument — Isla Vista's take on Speaker's Corner. Head to Anisq'oyo' Park for restrooms.

Perfect Park
977 Embarcadero Del Norte
(805) 968-2017
ivparks.org
FREE

From Highway 101, take the Los Carneros exit and head for the ocean. Turn left on El Colegio road, then right onto Embarcadero Del Norte.

A passive park designed and landscaped by Isla Vista residents offers maintained trails that lead to neighboring People's Park (p. 110) and Anisq'oyo' Park (p. 96). Perfect Park amenities include lawn, shade trees and picnic tables. Head to Anisq'oyo' Park for restrooms.

Rhoads Open Space
600 block S. San Marcos Road
(805) 568-2461
countyofsb.org/parks
FREE

From northbound Highway 101, take Turnpike and head toward the beach. Turn right onto Hollister Avenue, then left onto South San Marcos Road. From southbound 101, take Patterson Road toward the beach; turn left onto Hollister Avenue, then right onto South San Marcos Road.

This nearly 2.5-acre lot has evolved into a neighborhood park complete with play structures, swings, benches, picnic areas, a drinking fountain and a large lawn area. The park lawn is immediately adjacent to San Marcos Road, but the tot lot is tucked deeper into the block. For wheelchair access, look for the paved path from the 700 block of Via Miguel. No restrooms.

Ribera Bikeway
Ribera Drive at Pintura Drive
(805) 568-2461
sbparks.org
FREE
From Highway 101, take Patterson Road toward the mountains, then turn right onto University Drive and left onto Ribera Drive.

This paved, off-street bike path parallel to Ribera Drive meanders under sprawling oaks and towering eucalyptus trees along San Ygnacio Creek. The flat trail between Pintura and University is ideal for a toddler ride, but the gentle dip toward the creek south of University and related climb back out may pose a challenge to the least-experienced riders.

This route dovetails into the San Marcos Bike Route through Tabano Hollow Open Space (p. 115), the North Goleta Route Bikeway leading to Calle Real and the Maria Ignacio Route through Lassen Open Space (p. 107). Continue south along this off-street trail to the Coast Bike Route which provides a dedicated bike route east to Goleta Beach County Park (p. 102) and UCSB (p. 121) or west to Arroyo Road.

Rottappel Park
6751 Del Playa Drive
(805) 968-2017
ivparks.org
FREE
From Highway 101, take the Los Carneros exit and head for the ocean. Turn left on El Colegio road, right onto Camino Corto, then left onto Del Playa Drive.

This long, narrow open slot between apartment buildings provides public access to the priceless views of the Santa Barbara Channel and south coast. No amenities.

San Marcos Foothill Preserve
Via Gaitero
(805) 681-5650
countyofsb.org/parks
FREE
From Highway 101, take San Marcos Pass to the Cathedral Oaks exit. Turn west onto Cathedral Oaks, right onto Via Chaparral, right onto Salvar Road and left onto Via Gaitero.

This newly acquired, 200-acre open space preserve provides adventurers expansive views across Santa Barbara and on to Channel Islands National Park. Plans still are in the works for this park's development, which may include interpretive signs, manmade wetlands, benches, a native plant garden and dedicated hanggliding and paragliding landing space. The park may eventually include portable toilets.

At publication time, none of the 6 miles of established trails were particularly stroller-friendly, and given that mountain bikes are not currently allowed in the park, strollers are unlikely to be welcomed. Dogs are allowed only on leash and there is no horseback riding, mountain bike riding, camping, firearms or alcohol allowed.

San Miguel Open Space
Winchester Canyon Road
(805) 968-6848
www.cityofgoleta.org/index.aspx?page=206
FREE

From northbound Highway 101, take the Winchester Canyon Road/ Hollister Avenue exit and turn right at the end of the ramp. From southbound 101, take the Hollister Avenue exit, turn left at the end of the ramp, turn right onto Calle Real, left onto Cathedral Oaks, then left onto Winchester Canyon Road.

Some visitors first approach this park from its access on Rio Vista Drive, where the park offers little more than a fire hydrant, paved pathway and mowed weeds. What a surprise, then, to follow the path across a footbridge to an irrigated, mowed lawn surrounding a large play structure. This particularly quiet section of the 6-acre park includes benches, shade trees, a picnic table and drinking fountain. No restrooms.

Sandpiper Golf Course
7925 Hollister Ave.
(805) 968-1541
www.sandpipergolf.com
$$$

From southbound Highway 101, take Hollister Avenue exit, then turn right at the end of the ramp onto Hollister. From northbound 101, take the Winchester Canyon Road/Hollister Avenue exit and proceed straight onto Calle Real, then turn right onto Hollister Avenue.

This 18-hole, oceanfront golf course offers peerless views from its six blufftop holes. The championship, 7,000-foot course also offers a grass driving range, pro shop, practice putting and chipping greens, rental clubs and instruction.

Golfers must adhere to a dress code that includes collared, long-sleeve shirts and mid-thigh-length shorts for men, collared shirts that cover the shoulder or long-sleeved shirts without a collar and shorts or skirts that reach to mid-thigh for women. No denim is allowed and players must wear soft spikes.

☞ Santa Barbara Shores Park
7700 block Hollister Ave.
(805) 968-6848
www.cityofgoleta.org/index.aspx?page=206

FREE

From southbound Highway 101, take Hollister Avenue. From northbound 101, take the Hollister Road/Winchester Canyon Road exit. Proceed straight at the end of the ramp, then turn left onto Hollister Avenue.

Bring your kids, your dogs, your horses, cameras, binoculars, sunscreen, picnic lunch and chairs to this city park that provides access to bluffs, beaches and monarch butterfly groves. After parking in the off-street lot, follow the wide, dirt path toward the ocean. The noise of the freeway soon gives way to the rumble of the ocean, bird song, wind in the trees, creaking eucalyptus and occasional aircraft.

This very large public parcel provides access to the wildly popular Ellwood Mesa. Walks along the relatively flat, easy trails in the Ellwood Main Monarch Grove (p. 100) eventually lead to the Coronado Butterfly Preserve (p. 99). Other easy paths lead to the bluff, where you can turn left and continue on to Coal Oil Point Reserve (p. 99) and Sands Beach or turn west to explore adjacent Sperling Preserve (p. 113).

While dogs and horses are welcome in the park, horses are not allowed in the butterfly groves, and owners are asked to pick up their animals' waste. Doggy Doo bags are provided at the trailhead. There is no trailer parking allowed in the lot, so plan your equestrian visits accordingly. Paintballing, smoking, campfires, motorized vehicles and firearms also are banned from the park.

Sea Lookout Park
6785 Del Playa Drive
(805) 968-2017
ivparks.org
FREE

From Highway 101, take the Los Carneros exit and head for the ocean. Turn left onto El Colegio road, right onto Camino Corto, then left onto Del Playa.

While there are several blufftop parks along the coast, this is by far the most serene offered in Isla Vista. Though less than half an acre, the landscaped park is generally well maintained and offers room to run, and a seat on a knoll overlooking the Pacific. No restrooms.

Sperling Preserve
Accessible from Santa Barbara Shores Park (p. 112)
(805) 968-6848
www.cityofgoleta.org/index.aspx?page=206
FREE

From southbound Highway 101, take Hollister Avenue. From northbound 101, take the Hollister Road/Winchester Canyon Road exit. Proceed straight to the end of the ramp, then turn left onto Hollister Avenue.

This 191-acre preserve adjacent to Santa Barbara Shores Park provides ample open space in its natural state for hikers, bikers and dog-walkers. The property boasts beautiful blufftop views of south coast beaches. The property is basically flat, making the trails hugely toddler-friendly. Just watch out for the edges. No restrooms.

Stonebridge Walkway
6200 block Cathedral Oaks Road to 6200 block Stow Canyon Road
(805) 968-6848
www.cityofgoleta.org/index.aspx?page=206
FREE
From Highway 101, take Fairview Avenue north, then turn left onto Cathedral Oaks.

An unimproved, rough, single-track trail leads through this fairly densely wooded parcel straddling San Pedro Creek. The trail ends just across the street from Stow Open Space (p. 114). No restrooms.

Stow Grove Park
400-600 blocks La Patera Lane
(805) 968-6848
www.cityofgoleta.org/index.aspx?page=206
FREE
From Highway 101, take Los Carneros Road north; turn right onto Cathedral Oaks, then right onto La Patera Lane.

In 1876, William Whitney Stow and family planted a grove of redwoods in the heart of their immense La Patera Ranch. The grove was intended as their own private picnic grounds. Generations later, the grove plays host to small family picnics and large barbecue events alike. The 11-acre park includes the original grove, as well as newer developments: a soccer field, ball diamond, volleyball courts, horseshoe pits, swing, play structure, restrooms and three group picnic areas, the largest of which accommodates up to 200 guests.

Stow Tennis Courts & Open Space
6200 block Muirfield Drive or 6200 block Stow Canyon Road
(805) 968-6848
www.cityofgoleta.org/index.aspx?page=206
FREE
From Highway 101, take Fairview Avenue north, turn left onto Cathedral Oaks, left onto Carlo Drive, then right on Stow Canyon Road.

This 2½-acre park along San Pedro Creek provides ample room to run or pick up a game of soccer on maintained lawns. The park also includes two tennis courts that are available on a first-come, first-served basis. There is no legal access to the creek here, and there are no restrooms.

Sueño Orchard
6723 Sueño Road
(805) 968-2017

ivparks.org

FREE

From Highway 101, take the Los Carneros exit and head for the ocean. Turn left on El Colegio road, right onto Camino Del Sur, then right onto Sueño.

This less-than-half-acre, tree-studded park is home to the first two holes in the nine-hole, three-park Isla Vista Disc Golf Course (p. 105).

Sueño Park

6650 Sueño Road

(805) 968-2017

ivparks.org

FREE

From Highway 101, take the Los Carneros exit and head for the ocean. Turn left on El Colegio road, right onto Camino Del Sur, then right onto Sueño.

At less than half an acre, this park includes a playground, barbecues, a drinking fountain, lawn and wheelchair-accessible picnic benches. The park also houses two baskets in the nine-basket, three-park Isla Vista Disc Golf Course (p. 105). No restrooms.

Tabano Hollow Open Space

5100 block University to 5100 block Tabano Way

(805) 681-5650

www.sbparks.com

FREE

From Highway 101, take Patterson Road north, turn right onto University Drive, then right onto Tabano Way.

This 1-acre open space neighborhood park provides a grassy lawn area for passive play, shade trees and, Mondays through Fridays from 4 p.m. to sunset, a legal, off-leash dog area. No restrooms.

Tarragona Open Space

500 block North San Marcos Road

(805) 568-2461

countyofsb.org/parks

FREE

From Highway 101, take Turnpike Road north; turn left onto La Ramada Drive, then right onto San Marcos Road.

This neighborhood, passive park offers a paved path through a tree-studded parcel that is largely unimproved. The lower portion of the park includes 1.5 acres of maintained lawn, but a rise overlooking the lawn is left largely to nature. Take a short hike along the path to the benches for sunset views. No restrooms.

Thunderbird Open Space

5100 block Hollister Avenue to 100 block Walnut Lane

(805) 681-5650

sbparks.org/parks

FREE

From Highway 101, take Patterson Road toward the beach, then turn left onto Hollister Road.

This nearly 1-acre lawn off busy Hollister Avenue offers plenty of room to run on a maintained lawn or rest in the shade of a variety of trees — from palms to pines.

☞ Tierra de Fortuna Park

6692 Fortuna Road

(805) 968-2017

ivparks.org

FREE

From Highway 101, take the Los Carneros exit and head for the ocean. Turn left on El Colegio road, right onto Camino Corto, then right onto Fortuna.

This is a wonderful park with an old-school feel. At publication time, it included timeless playground classics including an increasingly rare merry-go-round and a seesaw for six. Our kids have witnessed the near extinction of this type of priceless play equipment, so they're particularly fond of this park. The quiet, 2.5-acre lot is ideal for families with very small children because it is away from busy streets. Other amenities include a gazebo, swings, a dinosaur-shaped climbing structure, tire swing, grass, shade, picnic table and drinking fountain. There's a basketball standard at the end of the street just outside the park gate. This park is not particularly wheelchair accessible, nor does it have restrooms.

Kids' Trail (p. 106) leads directly from this park, past another play structure and south to the beaches or east to the Camino Corto Open Space & Del Sol Vernal Pool Reserve (p. 98).

Tipi Village

6634 Sueño Road

(805) 968-2017

ivparks.org

FREE

From Highway 101, take the Los Carneros exit and head for the ocean. Turn left on El Colegio road, right onto Camino Del Sur, then right onto Sueño.

As Isla Vista sang its hippy swan song in the 1970s, this site remained home to the tents and tipis of countless squatters. The tipis are long gone, but the half-acre park still serves as a public meeting place. The park includes a play structure, picnic tables, lawn, drinking fountain and shade trees. No restrooms.

Trigo-Pasado Park

6633 Pasado Road

(805) 968-2017

ivparks.org

FREE

From Highway 101, take the Los Carneros exit and head for the ocean. Turn left onto El Colegio road, right onto Camino Del Sur, then left onto Pasado Road.

An 11-foot-tall boulder designed for family climbing is the centerpiece of this tiny midblock park. The boulder includes child-sized routes as well as challenging reaches for full-grown climbers. A paved pathway provides access through the park, which also includes a picnic table, drinking fountain, lawn and shade trees. No restrooms.

☞ Tucker's Grove

Turnpike Road at Cathedral Oaks Road

(805) 967-1112

countyofsb.org/parks

FREE

From Highway 101, take Turnpike road north.

This 120-acre park with ample shade, play structures, lawn, picnic areas and barbecues is particularly popular for large family-friendly gatherings, but dog walkers and lone hikers, bird watchers and artists are just as likely to frequent the space.

At the park's entry off Cathedral Oaks, a large children's play area includes play structures for toddlers and older children. A large lawn offers room to run, or play a pickup game of recreational soccer or toss a Frisbee. Both are conveniently located within long-arm's reach of a group barbecue area. Just across the parking lot are several individual picnic tables under the sycamore trees along bubbling San Antonio Creek. Each of these tables has its own small, raised barbecue.

The parking lot continues through the park until it terminates just below Kiwanis Meadow, another venue popular for large group gatherings. A trail past the meadow follows the gentle curves of the creek for about 2 miles to San Marcos Pass Road. This flat, well-maintained, dirt trail is an ideal introductory hike for toddlers or other beginning hikers, or an easy walk in the shade for adults.

The park also includes restrooms, and dogs are allowed off leash in Kiwanis Meadows Monday through Friday from 8 a.m. to 10 a.m. and 4 p.m. to sunset, except when that group area is reserved.

Twin Lakes Golf Course

6034 Hollister Ave.

(805) 964-1414

twinlakesgolf.com

$-$$

From Highway 101, take Fairview south, then turn right onto Hollister Avenue.

This straightforward, nine-hole golf course adjacent to the freeway is designed for beginning golfers and offers affordable golf, a pro shop, golf instruction, club rentals and juniors program. The facility also includes a driving range with lights for night practice.

University Circle Open Space at San Jose Creek
Merida Drive between Hana and Agana drives
(805) 568-2461
countyofsb.org/parks
FREE

From Highway 101, take Patterson Avenue north; turn left onto Berkeley Drive and either right or left onto Merida Drive.

A trail meandering through some 5 acres of undeveloped land along San Jose Creek leads to a 1.5-acre landscaped park area that includes a ball backstop and play structure. Follow the path up the creek to the footbridge leading to Kellogg Tennis Courts (p. 105), where portable toilets typically are available.

University Village Walkway
7100 block Phelps Road to 7200 block Davenport Road
(805) 968-6848
www.cityofgoleta.org/index.aspx?page=206
FREE

From Highway 101, take Storke Road toward the beach, then turn right onto Phelps Road.

Winding trails on more than 3 acres of landscaped drainage provide car-free space for family bike rides on a "secret" path kids will love. No restrooms.

Walter Capps Memorial Park
6709 Del Playa
(805) 681-5650
countyofsb.org/parks
FREE

From Highway 101, take the Los Carneros exit and head for the ocean. Turn left onto El Colegio road, right onto Camino Del Sur, then right onto Del Playa.

This nearly 3-acre park atop the Isla Vista bluff was going through the planning and approval stage at publication time. Plans call for a natural meadow area, lawn, boardwalk, curving pathways, seating areas and a public restroom. The park was named for a former UCSB professor and member of the U.S. House of Representatives.

Winchester I Open Space

7600 block Calle Real

(805) 968-6848

www.cityofgoleta.org/index.aspx?page=206

FREE

From northbound Highway 101, take Winchester Canyon Road, then turn right onto Bradford Drive, and then right onto Calle Real. From southbound 101, take the Hollister Avenue exit and turn left at the end of the ramp. After crossing over the freeway, turn right onto Calle Real, which turns toward the mountains and becomes Winchester Canyon Road. Turn right onto Bradford Drive, then right onto Calle Real.

A nearly 3.5-acre neighborhood park offers a large, maintained lawn, shade trees and restrooms.

Winchester II Open Space

7700 block Calle Real

(805) 968-6848

www.cityofgoleta.org/index.aspx?page=206

FREE

From northbound Highway 101, take Winchester Canyon Road, then turn right onto Calle Real. From southbound 101, take the Hollister Avenue exit and turn left at the end of the ramp. After crossing over the freeway, turn right onto Calle Real which turns toward the mountains and becomes Winchester Canyon Road, then turn right onto Calle Real.

This 1.5-acre neighborhood park offers swings, a backstop and room to run. No restrooms.

Window to the Sea Park

6691 Del Playa Drive

(805) 968-2017

ivparks.org

FREE

From Highway 101, take the Los Carneros exit and head for the ocean. Turn left onto El Colegio road, right onto Camino Del Sur, then left onto Del Playa.

Sadly, and for reasons that may be obvious, Windows to the Sea Park is commonly known locally as Dog S**t Park. In fact, many local residents know this lovely, 1.3-acre, blufftop park by no name other than the unfortunate alternative, so you may want to cover the ears of anyone who may be offended.

Names official and local aside, this splendid location features unique, wooden sunning decks, as well as volleyball courts, a lawn area and picnic tables. The coastal bluff trail leads west to a safe access point to Isla Vista Beach, then further west to Coal Oil Point Reserve (p. 99).

This park becomes an off-leash dog run Monday through Friday from 8 a.m. to 10 a.m. and from 4 p.m. to sunset. There are no restrooms.

OTHER ADVENTURES

Elings Aquatic Center
Dos Pueblos High School
7266 Alameda Ave.
(805) 968-2541
www.channel-league.org/_swim
$

From Highway 101, take Glen Annie Road toward the mountains. Turn left onto Cathedral Oaks, then left onto Alameda Avenue.

This relatively new Olympic-size pool is available for public use each summer, including recreational swimming, lap swimming and children's lessons. The pool also serves as a training facility for the associated high school and club swim and water polo teams.

☞ Fairview Gardens Farm
598 N. Fairview Ave.
(805) 967-7369
fairviewgardens.org
FREE

From Highway 101, take Fairview Avenue and head for the hills.

At first glance, only the produce stand on the corner appears to differentiate this plot from myriad other agricultural efforts in the area. However, hidden behind the rise, out of sight from the road, is one of the state's oldest organic farms still in operation. The place is so green that even the toilets compost.

Give yourself at least an hour to walk through more than 12 acres of nectarines, peaches, apples, plums, the unique cherimoya, strawberries and root vegetables. More than 20 interpretive panels offer brief explanations of crops, farming methods and environmental issues. (A Spanish-language version is available in booklet form at the produce stand.) Follow the flags, stay on the paths and don't pick the veggies. Lazy goats and pest-pecking chickens also welcome visitors, so dogs are not allowed. The greenhouse also is open for viewing.

In addition to farm walks, the garden offers farm-based education programs for kindergarteners through 12th graders and homeschool groups, cooking classes for all ages, home and school garden consultation, and other services. Open for tours 10 a.m. to sunset, daily. Rain cancels.

Goleta Valley Community Center
5649 Hollister Ave.
(805) 967-1237
www.thegvcc.org
FREE

From Highway 101, take Fairview Avenue south (away from the mountains), then turn left onto Hollister Avenue.

his beautiful, two-story, Spanish-style structure was originally built as an elementary school in 1927. In the mid-1970s, the building found new life as a community center. Today, it is home to daycare centers, food and training programs, church meetings, various classes and clubs, the Goleta School of Ballet, South Coast Karate, Headstart and the Goleta Valley Senior Center.

The community center's park-like setting includes a gazebo, basketball courts, a tennis court, athletic field, restrooms, a picnic area and beautiful courtyards begging for visitors.

Isla Vista Teen Center
889 Camino Del Sur
(805) 685-9170
www.ciymca.org/youth_family/YouthFamilyServices-IslaVistaTeenCenter.html
FREE
From Highway 101, take the Los Carneros exit and head for the ocean. Turn left onto El Colegio road, then right onto Camino Del Sur.

While most things in Isla Vista are dominated by college students, this center offers teens a space of their own. Free membership for area youth enrolled in sixth through 12th grades includes access to recreation programs, pool tables, pingpong tables, computers and a computer center. The center also offers tutoring and homework help most weekday evenings.

The center is open Monday through Friday. Call for current offerings.

Santa Barbara Airport Visitors Center
45 Hartley Place
(805) 964-7622
www.flysba.com/?pageID=51
FREE
From Highway 101, take Fairview Avenue away from the mountains. Turn right onto Hollister Avenue, then left onto Hartley Place.

The only Santa Barbara County airport that offers a visitors center also offers free public tours by reservation. The center hosts special events, periodic classes and hands-on exhibits. The center and tours both are available by reservation.

University of California, Santa Barbara
Mesa Road
(805) 893-8000
www.ucsb.edu
FREE-$$$
From northbound Highway 101, take the Airport/UCSB exit (Highway 217). From southbound 101, take Storke Road/Glen Annie Road away from the mountains, then turn left onto El Colegio Road. Public parking by permit is available in Lot 22. Permit dispensers are in the parking lot.

One of the greatest resources in Santa Barbara County is the University of California, Santa Barbara. Though designed to serve its more than 20,000 full-time students, the university also offers a vast array of programs and facilities to the community at large. These include not only on-campus galleries, recreational facilities, libraries and theaters, but off-campus natural areas from Sedgwick Reserve (p. 229) near Los Olivos and a portion of the Carpinteria Salt Marsh (p. 83). Many of the university's specialized departments feature community outreach programs, exhibits, lectures and performances.

The campus itself is a veritable outdoor playground. Check out the lagoon. Touch wildlife at the Marine Lab by reservation (893- 8765). Take a walk along Devereaux Slough. Catch a wave at Campus Point. Soak up rays on Sands Beach. Stroll along tree-lined pathways or park yourself in any number of great nooks and crannies for quiet meditation. The campus hosts an open house each spring during which students, faculty and staff pull together to show the best of their university.

Though many facilities are limited to students, some provide public access for specialized programs. The Recreation Center, for instance, was designed to meet the needs of students, but its pools are open for community use on weekends and during summer holiday. The center also offers a variety of aquatics programs for area youth, including water polo and swimming lessons. The center also runs a variety of other recreation programs, adventure programs, summer camps and leisure programs. UCSB also offers the Family Vacation Center, an all-inclusive vacation destination for active families (www.familyvacationcenter.com).

☞ Zodo's Bowl & Arcade

5925 Calle Real
(805) 967-0128
www.zodos.com
$

From Highway 101, take Fairview Avenue toward the mountains, and turn right onto Calle Real.

When California banned smoking in public places, bowling centers dropped like cigarette butts as bowlers opted for smokes over pins. But Zodo's figured out how to make it work. The 24-lane, fully automated facility offers open bowling, leagues for youth and adults, bumpers available on every lane, even ball ramps to help the littlest bowlers and others who could use an assist. There's also an arcade and restaurant.

Special events include light shows every Thursday, Friday and Saturday night, glow-in-the-dark bowling Saturday and Sunday afternoons and after 9 p.m. Wednesdays. Youth bowling is typically held Saturday mornings and the facility also is available for party rentals.

Open from 8:30 a.m. to 2 a.m. every day of the year except Thanksgiving and Christmas days.

Chapter 6

Santa Ynez & Solvang

Delineating between neighboring Santa Ynez Valley communities poses a bit of a challenge. Nowhere is drawing the line more difficult than between Solvang, incorporated in 1985, and Santa Ynez, an unincorporated area of Santa Barbara County. Like other communities in this east-west valley, both Santa Ynez and Solvang share the county's warmest, driest climate, which makes for hot summer days and fabulously warm summer evenings. Winter months can be downright frigid in Central Coast terms. But Santa Ynez and Solvang differ in style and purpose.

In 1804, the Catholic Church built Mission Santa Inez, the 19th in a chain of 21 California missions. This location served as a resting place between Mission Santa Barbara (p. 28) and La Purísima Mission (p. 150) while the Church strove to convert to Catholicism the indigenous Chumash people. It wasn't long before the community of Santa Ynez sprung up to help support the endeavor and eventually residents that made this valley home.

More than a century later three Danes, aiming to create an ideal community for Danish-Americans, purchased more than 9,000 acres of Rancho San Carlos de Jonata, once the site of Alajulapu, a Chumash village. They named their new, planned community Solvang, Danish for "Sunny Fields." By the 1950s, word had spread and visitors were flocking to see the community that treasured all aspects of Danish heritage. Solvang had become not only home to families from halfway around the globe, but it also supported Atterdag College, an institution of learning dedicated to preserving Danish culture. Today, it remains one of the state's major tourist destinations while continuing to promote Danish arts and culture.

ARTS

Solvang Theaterfest
420 2nd St., Solvang
(805) 922-8313
www.solvangtheaterfest.org
$-$$$

From Highway 101, turn east onto Highway 246/Mission Drive, then turn right onto 5th Street, left onto Oak Street, then right onto 2nd Street. From Highway 154, turn onto Highway 246/Mission Drive, turn left onto Alisal Road, then right onto 2nd Street.

Warm summer evenings are ideal for outdoor performances. The Santa Maria-based Pacific Conservatory of the Performing Arts (PCPA) theater training company and its patrons take advantage of the wonderful weather with productions in the 700-seat amphitheater from June through October.

When purchasing tickets, pay special attention to the company's strict enforcement of age limits. Children under age 5 are not welcome, even with paid admission, and there are no refunds.

LETTERS

Santa Ynez Branch Library
3598 Sagunto Street, Santa Ynez
(805) 688-4214 (Solvang)
www.sbplibrary.org
FREE
From Highway 101, take Highway 246/Mission Drive east, turn left onto Edison Street, then right onto Sagunto. From Highway 154, turn right onto Highway 246/Mission Drive, right onto Meadowvale, and right onto Sagunto.
This small, neighborhood library is open Saturdays from 2 p.m. to 5 p.m. Though it is compact, it is part of the greater Santa Barbara Public Library System and even more expansive Black Gold Library System from which books, CDs and DVDs may be ordered from many Central Coast libraries.

Solvang Branch Library
1745 Mission Drive, Solvang
(805) 688-4214
www.sbplibrary.org

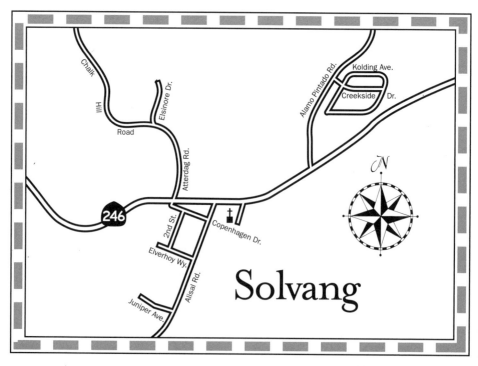

FREE

From Highway 101, turn east onto Highway 246/Mission Drive. From Highway 154, turn onto Highway 246/Mission Drive.

Like most libraries on the Central Coast, this one also is part of the enormous Black Gold Library System. If this small, community library doesn't have what you need, just place a request for it and the title will be delivered to the front desk for pickup.

This branch of the Santa Barbara Public Library system is open Mondays through Saturdays. Call for current hours. It also hosts special events ranging from regularly scheduled story times, including a Spanish-language series, to presentations by guest lecturers and performing artists.

HISTORY

☞ Elverhøj Museum of History & Art

1624 Elverhøj Way, Solvang

(805) 686-1211

www.elverhoj.org

FREE

From Highway 101, turn east onto Highway 246/Mission Drive, then turn right onto Alisal Road and right onto Elverhøj Way. From Highway 154, turn onto Highway 246/Mission Drive, turn left onto Alisal Road, then right onto Elverhøj Way.

This pleasant little museum with a beautiful garden boasts a wealth of information about the history of Solvang and its relationship to Denmark. Friendly docents cater to children as they lead visitors on a walk through room after room of fine art, crafts, historic photos and other artifacts of the community's shared heritage.

The structure itself is fascinating. In 1950, artists Viggo Brandt-Erichsen

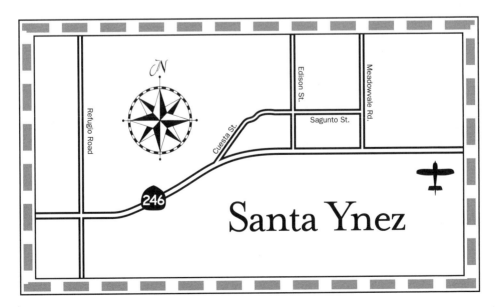

Children particularly are welcomed at the Elverhøj Museum of History & Art, which offers special activities from grade-appropriate treasure hunts to hands-on activities. Docents are fabulous with the children, and tours are available by previous arrangement.

and Martha Mott Brandt-Erichsen began building their dream home in the spirit of the 18th Century Danish country homes. The spacious rooms provide ample accommodations for exhibits, as well as visitors interested in details such as the wooden front door. The carving depicts Viggo Brandt-Erichsen's rendition of a scene from Elverhøj, or Elves' Hill, the Danish opera for which the home was named.

The museum is open Wednesdays and Thursdays from 1 p.m. to 4 p.m. and Fridays through Sundays from noon until 4 p.m. Group tours also can be made by reservation. The museum hosts annual events with hands-on activities. The Living History Festival, held the third weekend in September, provides visitors a firsthand look at crafts in the making including, Viking spinning and weaving, Danish paper cutting and bobbin lace making. Check the Web site or call for the current schedule of special offerings.

Hans Christian Andersen Museum

Upstairs in The Loft Bookstore
1680 Mission Drive, Solvang
(805) 688-2052
www.bookloftsolvang.com/museum.htm
FREE
From Highway 101, turn east onto Highway 246/Mission. From Highway 154, turn onto Highway 246/Mission Drive.

This compact collection dedicated to Danish author Hans Christian Andersen includes books, paper cutouts, silhouettes, sketches and collages related to the stories he told.

Old Mission Santa Inés

1760 Mission Drive, Solvang

(805) 688-4815

www.missionsantaines.org

$

From Highway 101, turn east onto Highway 246/Mission. From Highway 154, turn onto Highway 246/Mission Drive.

After building Mission Santa Barbara and La Purísima Mission, the founders determined a midway point was required for weary travelers. Mission Santa Inés, the 19th of 21 California missions, filled that purpose, while its occupants strove to convert the indigenous Chumash people.

Like many of the missions, Santa Inés fell out of the Church's hands for several years. In 1846, Governor Pio Pico sold it, allegedly without the Church's permission, and in 1862 President Lincoln rescinded the sale, thereby returning the mission to the Church.

But the years had taken their toll. Portions of the mission had completely caved in during the 1812 earthquake, a Chumash uprising in 1824, then again during the Church's absence. Since restoration of ownership, Church leaders, members and supporters have worked diligently to rebuild and improve the facility.

Today, the mission is particularly noted for its gardens, accessible after paying an admission fee. The self-guided property tour includes the Chapel of

the Madonna, church, gardens and the museum, which houses mission relics. Open daily.

Santa Ynez Valley Historical Museum & Parks-Janeway Carriage Museum

3596 Sagunto St., Santa Ynez

(805) 688-7889

www.santaynezmuseum.org

FREE-$

From Highway 101, take Highway 246/Mission Drive east, turn left onto Edison Street, then right onto Sagunto. From Highway 154, turn right onto Highway 246/Mission Drive, right onto Meadowvale, then right onto Sagunto.

Located in the town of Santa Ynez, this pair of museums features art and artifacts related to the Western lifestyle. The historical museum features displays of Chumash, pioneer and early ranching life in Santa Ynez Valley. There also are rotating exhibits that shed more light on particular details. The adjacent Parks-Janeway Carriage Museum offers a spacious venue for its growing collection of horse-drawn vehicles, many donated by prominent Santa Ynez Valley families.

The museums are open Wednesdays through Sundays from noon until 4 p.m. and by appointment Tuesdays through Fridays. They also offer a pair of entertaining annual fundraisers to benefit the museums. Collectors of cowboy artifacts, from antique harnesses to saddles that truly are works of art, gather each autumn for the Vaquero Show & Sale. A summer dinner-auction provides entertainment and fundraising for the museum.

NATURE

Alisal Commons

Juniper Avenue at Alisal Road, Solvang

(805) 688-5575

www.cityofsolvang.com

FREE

From Highway 101, turn east onto Highway 246/Mission Drive, then right onto Alisal Road. From Highway 154, turn left onto Highway 246/Misson Drive, then left onto Alisal Road.

This 2-acre park designed for quiet walks, stroller rides along pathways and picnics under shade trees has room to grow. No restrooms.

Bike Paths

See Santa Barbara County Bike Map

(805) 963-7283

www.trafficsolutions.info/biking.htm

FREE

455532.4534564 33323444433223333433

From Highway 101, turn east onto Highway 246/Mission Drive. From Highway 154, turn left onto Highway 246/Mission Drive.

There are several popular bike routes throughout the Santa Ynez Valley, which hosts numerous competitive cycling events every year. Family friendly, off-street riding also is available on the dedicated bike route off the north side of Mission Drive. The easy, relatively flat, paved, striped, two-lane route begins just east of Alamo Pintado on the north side of Highway 246/Mission Drive and extends 1 ½ miles east to Santa Ynez High School.

Creekside Open Space
Kolding Avenue at Rebild Drive, Solvang
(805) 688-5575
www.cityofsolvang.com
FREE

From Highway 101, turn east onto Highway 246/Mission Drive, left onto Alamo Pintado Road, then right onto Creekside Drive which ends at the park. From Highway 154, turn left onto Highway 246/Mission Drive, right onto Alamo Pintado Road, and right onto Creekside Drive.

This 6-acre undeveloped open space along Alamo Pintado Creek provides room to explore nature, but there are no facilities. A paved sidewalk along the edge of the park provides easy access for wheelchairs and strollers.

☞ Hans Christian Andersen Park
633 Chalk Hill, Solvang
(805) 688-5575
www.cityofsolvang.com
FREE

From Highway 101, turn east onto Highway 246/Mission, then left onto Atterdag Road, which becomes Chalk Hill. From Highway 154, turn onto Highway 246/Mission Drive, then turn right onto Atterdag Road.

This 52-acre park on the west side of town is not a typical stop for tourists. Tucked away on a neighborhood street, it provides ample open space, four tennis courts, a 1.3-mile equestrian/hiking/biking trail, four group barbecue areas, two restrooms and acres of unimproved, natural area to explore.

Solvang Skate Park is housed just inside the main entrance. The concrete-pool-style park is open after school hours and on weekends. Bicycles are not allowed in the skate park, and riders are required to wear knee and elbow pads and helmets. Spectators are required to stay outside the fenced area, but there's a small play structure, benches and other amenities for younger visitors and guardians waiting in the wings.

Head deeper into the park and you'll find a second, more modern play structure protected from summer sun by three towering sycamores. The park also is home to Atterdag Bowl, a natural amphitheater equally useful for performances or family picnics. Future plans include a dog park, basketball courts, sand volleyball pits and a botanical garden.

This park's main entry is off Chalk Hill, but it can also be accessed on horseback, foot or bicycle via the bike path off Mission Drive/Highway 246 east of Skyte Mesa Drive.

Kronborg Open Space
Kronborg Drive at Elsinore Drive, Solvang
(805) 688-5575
www.cityofsolvang.com
FREE

From Highway 101, turn east onto Highway 246/Mission Drive. From Highway 154, turn west onto Highway 246/Mission Drive. From Mission Drive, turn right onto Atterdag Road, which becomes Chalk Hill Drive, then turn right onto Elsinore Drive.

At publication time, this park consisted of nearly 3 acres of undeveloped open space in a residential neighborhood. There is no off-street parking and there are no restrooms.

River Course at the Alisal
150 Alisal Road, Solvang
(805) 688-6042
rivercourse.com
$$$

From Highway 101, turn east onto Highway 246/Mission, then right onto Alisal Road. From Highway 154, turn onto Highway 246/Mission Drive, then left onto Alisal Road.

This public, 18-hole, 6,830-yard, par-72 course offers wonderful views as well as junior golf, private and group instruction, a pro shop and practice areas. Tee times are available by reservation.

Santa Ynez County Park
3400 block Cuesta Street, Santa Ynez
(805) 934-6123
www.sbparks.org
FREE

From Highway 101, take Highway 246/Mission Drive east, then turn left onto Cuesta Street. From Highway 154, turn west onto Highway 246/ Mission Drive, then right onto Cuesta Street.

In summer, temperatures in the valley skyrocket, but trees in this park provide ample shade for picnickers. The park includes play structures, a volleyball court, picnic table, ball fields, horseshoe pits and restrooms. The park also offers, by reservation only, two group picnic areas each with room for 100 hungry visitors, and a kitchen building.

Solvang Park
Parkway at Mission Drive, Solvang
(805) 688-5575

www.cityofsolvang.com
FREE
From Highway 101, take Highway 246/Mission Drive east. From Highway 154, take Highway 246/Mission Drive west.

This triangular park located on less than an acre in the center of Solvang's business district is a popular resting place for visitors and locals alike. A large bust of Hans Christian Andersen is displayed midway between the park's bandstand and picnic tables. Generally clean public restrooms are adjacent to the public parking lot here.

☞ Sunny Fields Park & Rotary Centennial Playground

900 Alamo Pintado Road, Solvang
(805) 688-5575

www.cityofsolvang.com
FREE
From Highway 101, take Highway 246/Mission Drive east, then turn left onto Alamo Pintado Road. From Highway 154, turn west onto Highway 246/Mission Drive, then right onto Alamo Pintado Road.

One of the community's newest parks is the result of a joint private/ public partnership. Local Rotary Clubs banded together to raise funds for and build the fanciful play structure, which includes local touches: a Viking ship, windmill and a playhouse. The structure also includes bench seating and a kid-sized picnic bench.

The rest of the park includes a Little League diamond, horseshoe pits, restrooms and barbecues. Reservations also are available for a group picnic area, as well as the park's kitchen/snack bar.

OTHER ADVENTURES

Alisal Guest Ranch and Resort

1054 Alisal Road, Solvang
(805) 688-6411
www.alisal.com
$$$
From Highway 101, turn east onto Highway 246/Mission, then right onto

Alisal Road. From Highway 154, turn onto Highway 246/Mission Drive, then left onto Alisal Road.

This exclusive resort offers an expansive list of recreational opportunities for adults and children alike, ranging from fishing on its private lake to riding horseback throughout the property. The Ranch Course is a 6,500-yard, par-72 course open to guests and members only. The associated pro shop provides supplies, as well as group and private lessons. Electric carts, handcarts and clubs are all available for rent here, too.

Apple Lane Farm
1200 Alamo Pintado Road, Solvang
(805) 688-5481
www.applelanefarm.com
FREE

From Highway 101, take Highway 246/Mission Drive east, then turn left onto Alamo Pintado Road. From Highway 154, turn west onto Highway 246/Mission Drive, then right onto Alamo Pintado Road.

This family-owned, pesticide-free farm offers old-school, country entertainment – pick-it-yourself fruit gathering. Apple picking generally begins in August with Gala apples, and continues through summer with Golden and Red Delicious apples in September and early October. Fujis and Granny Smiths are available in October with Granny Smiths wrapping up the tail end of the season in November. Group tours also are available by reservation.

Bella Cavalli
959 E. Highway 246, Solvang
(805) 688-7108
www.bellacavallifarms.com
$$$

From Highway 101, turn east onto Highway 246/Mission. From Highway 154, turn onto Highway 246/Mission Drive.

This 50-acre equestrian facility is among the newest in the valley. It lies on property formerly owned by Flag is Up Farm (page 132), and now provides equine boarding facilities, breeding, equine rehabilitation services and training for horse and rider.

☞ Flag is Up Farm
901 E. Highway 246, Solvang
(805) 688-6288
www.montyroberts.com
FREE

Take the Buellton/Solvang exit from Highway 101, turn east and drive through Buellton. Flag is Up Farms is the second large ranch on the left. Pull up to the gate and follow the directions on the electronic entry system.

The valley that separates the Santa Maria Valley from the county's south coast is filled with pastures and paddocks, show rings and stables filled with some of the country's most fantastic horses. While many of the ranches lock out strangers by means of heavy gates, the Roberts family has opened its 59-acre ranch to anyone who cares to drop in for a few minutes or a full day.

The farm provides a peaceful, pastoral setting for easy walks between lush paddocks, along tree-lined paths and amidst the smell of hay and horse. Visitors are welcome to meander through the farm anytime between 8 a.m. and 5 p.m. Monday through Friday. Most areas are wide open, including the Mare Manor, Stallion Barn and various training facilities including a race track. Other facilities on view include the Monty Roberts International Learning Center in the heart of the ranch, and round pens behind the training barn.

A staffed information booth located just outside the training barn provides information about the ranch, the Monty Roberts training method and various paraphernalia is for sale. Visitors must sign a waiver stating they understand the dangers of being on a farm filled with animals, which can at times behave erratically. Visitors are warned not to stick their fingers in stalls (lest those fingers be mistaken for carrots) and not to enter paddocks or pastures. The center aisle of the training barn is off limits to visitors, and there's no animal feeding allowed.

Morrell Nut & Berry Farm
1980 Alamo Pintado Road, Solvang
(805) 688-8969
www.localharvest.org/farms/M23356
FREE-$$$

From Highway 101, take Highway 246/Mission Drive east, then turn left onto Alamo Pintado Road. From Highway 154, turn west onto Edison, then immediately right at the T intersection onto Baseline, then right onto Alamo Pintado Road.

The next best thing to growing your own food is picking your own food grown in a healthy environment. From June through September, head to Morrell's any Thursday through Sunday to pick your own raspberries and blackberries. In late fall, walnut trees are thumped for their nuts, which are dried, then available for sale here and at the Solvang and Santa Barbara farmers markets (p. 235).

Quicksilver Ranch

1555 Alamo Pintado Road, Solvang

(805) 686-4002

www.syv.com/qsminis

FREE

From Highway 101, take Highway 246/Mission Drive east, then turn left onto Alamo Pintado Road. From Highway 154, turn west onto Highway 246/ Mission Drive, then right onto Alamo Pintado Road.

Aleck and Louise Stribling welcome visitors to park, wander, take photos and talk to dozens of their miniature horses, which are clearly visible behind waist-high chain-link fences. They ask visitors not to enter any pens or feed the horses.

This breeding facility opens its doors to visitors every day except Christmas and Thanksgiving. Stop in any time between 10 a.m. and 3 p.m. for a free self-guided tour of the barn and 20 acres of pastures, or call ahead for reservations for a group tour (fee). If you visit in spring, foaling time, you're likely to see darling foals.

Santa Ynez High School pool

2975 E. Highway 246, Santa Ynez

(805) 686-2037

www.ciymca.org/santa_ynez

$

From Highway 101, turn east onto Highway 246/Mission Drive. From Highway 154, turn west onto Highway 246/Mission Drive.

This 25-yard pool is the only publically accessible pool in northern Santa Barbara County offering springboard diving. The pool features two 1-meter boards in the 11-foot deep end, and easy entry in the 4-foot shallower end. While provided chiefly for student use, a cooperative agreement with the Stuart C. Gildred Family YMCA provides public access and lessons for all ages and abilities, as well as lap swim and recreation. Call for current hours and lesson/class scheduling.

☞ Solvang Vintage Motorcycle Museum

320 Alisal Road, Solvang

(805) 686-9522

motosolvang.com

$

From Highway 101, turn east onto Highway 246/Mission, then right onto Alisal Road. From Highway 154, turn onto Highway 246/Mission Drive, then left onto Alisal Road.

This private collection of motorcycles acquired over the past two decades offers an impressive view of motorcycle history. Start with the 1910 FN, complete with starting pedals, and the 1920 ABC Sopwith, a glorified heavy-duty bicycle complete with luggage rack over the back tire. Imagine taking an epic road trip on the brick-red 1946 Indian Chief, or racing the 1955 Moto Guzzi. The clean, shiny motorcycles are packed into a clean, relatively kid-friendly space, but keep little ones in hand. Open weekends 11 a.m. to 5 p.m. and by appointment.

Valley Baby
1984 Old Mission Drive, Santa Ynez
(805) 245-5700
myvalleybaby.com
$-$$$

From Highway 101, turn east onto Highway 246/Mission Drive. From Highway 154, turn west onto Highway 246/Mission Drive.

This gym designed specifically for the 4-and-under set offers a variety of classes, including gymnastics, music and movement, yoga and Pilates. Parents can grab a snack and some time to themselves each Friday during Mom's Coffee Break – kids ages 5 and younger are supervised in groups of eight or fewer while parents are provided nearly an hour to enjoy a free coffee. Programming changes regularly, so call for current offerings and schedule.

Windhaven Glider Rides
Santa Ynez Valley Airport
900 Airport Road, Santa Ynez
(805) 688-2517
www.gliderrides.com
$$$

From Highway 101, take Highway 246/Mission Drive east, then turn right onto Airport Road. From Highway 154, take Highway 246/Mission Drive west, then turn left onto Airport Road.

One of the most unique recreational activities in Santa Barbara County is soaring above Santa Ynez Valley in an aircraft with no engine. Tow vehicles give the gliders their initial lift, but thermals may provide additional lifts throughout the course of any given flight.

The rides in the two-seated gliders aren't inexpensive, but they're exhilarating for fans of flight. Flights range from 15 minutes to half an hour and can accommodate passengers of any age in good health, no taller than 6' 4" and no heavier than 250 pounds.

Chapter 7

Buellton

Buellton is a small community divided by Highway 101. It was established in the heart of Buell Ranch in 1918 when construction of the Santa Ynez River Bridge and associated highway bisected the property. Undaunted by progress, the Buell family opened a roadside tavern that paved the way for a community built to address travelers' needs. In 1924, Anton and Juliette Andersen opened a café that soon became famous primarily for Juliette's split pea soup.

Today, some 4,000 people live in the city that soup built, but the community continues to embrace its agrarian heritage. Cattle still range on the rolling hills and valley floor surrounding the town. Cowboys and horsewomen are as likely to wander into neighborhood restaurants as are world travelers.

ARTS

Parks Plaza Theater
515 McMurray Road
(805) 688-7434
mrmovietimes.com
$

From Highway 101, take the Highway 246/Solvang exit and head east toward Solvang. Turn left onto McMurray Road.

If you are looking for the least expensive indoor movie theater in Santa Barbara County, you might not even miss stadium seating. This five-screen theater offers first-run movies, an old-school setting and affordable ticket prices.

LETTERS

Buellton Library
140 W. Highway 246
 (805) 688-3115
www.cityoflompoc.com/library/info.htm
FREE

From Highway 101, take Highway 246 west.

From the outside, this small library may look a little too small but it actually offers a healthy collection. It also is a member of the Black Gold Library system, so books can be delivered here from as far away as Santa Paula and Templeton. Open daily except Sundays.

Avenue of the Flags, once the main north-south route through Buellton, is evolving into a picturesque promenade integrating art and nature.

HISTORY

Buellton Historical Society History Room

Andersen's Pea Soup
376 Avenue of the Flags
(805) 688-5581·
www.buelltonhistory.org
FREE

From southbound Highway 101, take the Avenue of the Flags exit and proceed straight ahead. From northbound Highway 101, take the Highway 246/Solvang exit, turn west (left) onto Highway 246, then right onto Avenue of the Flags.

If you like to look at old pictures or read about local history, this dedicated space inside the storied restaurant is worth a stop. While Andersen's history is prevalent, the room also includes information about other area businesses and personalities. Open daily.

NATURE

Avenue of the Flags Park

Avenue of the Flags
(805) 688-7474
www.cityofbuellton.com/Parks&Rec
FREE

From southbound Highway 101, take the Avenue of the Flags exit and

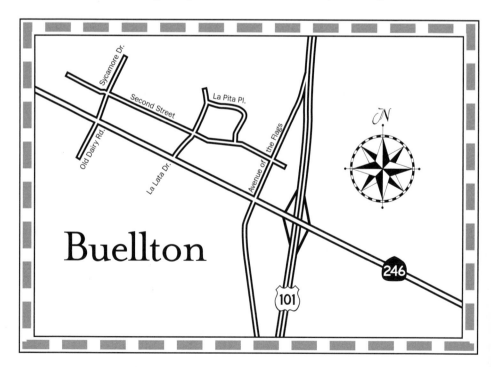

proceed straight ahead. From northbound Highway 101, take the Highway 246/Solvang exit, turn west (left) onto Highway 246, then right onto Avenue of the Flags.

Avenue of the Flags is divided by a wide, landscaped central strip that could loosely be described as a park. If you need a quick and easy spot for stretching your legs, this may be the spot for you. A path winds through the park which also includes lawn, bronze sculptures, benches and flags honoring the country and its military.

☞ Oak Park

401 Sycamore Drive

(805) 688-7474

www.cityofbuellton.com/Parks&Rec

FREE

From Highway 101, take the Highway 246/Solvang exit and proceed west on Highway 246. Turn right onto Old Dairy.

This community park adjacent to Oak Valley School provides play structures, swings, restrooms, picnic tables, shade structures, trees and ample lawn area.

PAWS Off-leash Dog Park

568 Dawn Drive

(805) 688-7474

www.syvpaws.org

FREE

From southbound Highway 101, take the Avenue of the Flags exit; turn right onto Second Street, then right onto Dawn Drive. From northbound 101, take Highway 246/Solvang west. Turn right onto Avenue of the Flags, left onto Second Street, then right onto Dawn Drive.

The Santa Ynez Valley's first off-leash dog park still developing at press time, but its design calls for separate fenced areas for large and small dogs.

River View Park

151 Sycamore Drive

(805) 688-7474

www.cityofbuellton.com/Parks&Rec

FREE

From Highway 101, take the Highway 246/Solvang exit and proceed west on Highway 246. Turn left onto Sycamore Drive.

This new park features play structures, wide open spaces for running or kite flying, baseball diamonds, basketball courts, soccer fields, picnic tables, barbecues and restrooms. Walk across the pedestrian bridge at the west end of the park to explore the neighboring Buellton Botanical Garden (page 139). Five group barbecue areas, each of which can accommodate up to 40 people, and an event pavilion with room for 150 may be reserved in advance for a fee.

Santa Ynez Valley Botanic Garden
151 Sycamore Drive
(805) 688-2115
www.cityofbuellton.com/Parks&Rec
FREE

From Highway 101, take the Highway 246/Solvang exit and proceed west on Highway 246. Turn left onto Old Dairy.

This brand-new botanical garden, still under construction as this book was being published, promises to provide peaceful, manicured walking paths among landscaped gardens featuring California native plants.

OTHER ADVENTURES

Buellton Community Recreation Center
301 Second Street
(805) 688-1086
www.cityofbuellton.com/Parks&Rec
$

From southbound Highway 101, take the Avenue of the Flags exit and then turn right onto Second Street. From northbound 101, take Highway 246/ Solvang west, turn right onto Avenue of the Flags, then left onto Second Street.

This joint-use facility located on the Jonata School campus provides students with space for athletic programs and other special events, and the community with an indoor public play place.

The facility is home to a variety of community recreation classes and camps. It also includes a weight room that is open before school, weekday evenings and on Saturdays. The basketball area is open for free pickup games Monday, Wednesday and Friday evenings. And The Zone, a drop-in meeting place for kids in sixth to 12th grades, is open daily after school until 6 p.m. The Zone includes homework space and recreational activities such as pingpong, billiards, foosball and video games.

Ostrichland
610 E. Highway 246
(805) 686-9696
www.ostrichlandusa.com
$

From Highway 101, take Highway 246 east toward Solvang.

A 33-acre, sparsely vegetated parcel houses this herd of pet ostriches, formerly a breeding herd. A gift shops sells ostrich meat and eggs collected from other farms, feather art and other ostrich-related items. Fee to view, and to feed more sociable emus. Open 365 days a year, 10 a.m. to 5 p.m. during the winter and 9 a.m. to 7 p.m. during summer months.

Chapter 8

Los Olivos

Movie makers were not far from the mark when they chose this tiny inland village for the re-creation of Mayberry R.F.D. At just one square mile and not a single traffic light, the unincorporated community is entirely walkable. The community events calendar boasts an eclectic variety of activities well attended by locals and visitors alike.

Los Olivos is a great place for a low-key, old-town, country kind of day. Park the car on the edge of town, then walk the pedestrian-friendly streets to check out the galleries, park, unique locally owned shops and random acts of public entertainment offered by the Grange Hall. Los Olivos also boasts several restaurants with delicious menus, some with outdoor seating that takes advantage of warm summer days. Once you have had your fill, head out for more active adventures on nearby farms and forestland.

ARTS

Judith Hale Gallery

2890 Grand Ave.
(805) 688-1222
www.judithhalegallery.com
FREE

From Highway 154, turn south onto Grand Avenue.

While an ominous sign posted prominently on the front door notes the gallery welcomes serious buyers, the proprietress has a history of welcoming responsible art enthusiasts of all ages. The gallery supports local and nationally acclaimed artists with a heavy emphasis on Western art. Works on exhibit may vary from Western-themed hat hangers to detailed oil paintings.

Perhaps the best feature for budding artists, however, is the sculpture garden behind the gallery. Open daily 11 a.m. to 5 p.m.

☞ Wilding Art Museum & Goodall Education Center

2928 San Marcos Ave.
(805) 688-1082
wildlingmuseum.org
FREE

From northbound Highway 154, take Alamo Pintado Road west, then turn right onto San Marcos Avenue. From southbound Highway 154, take Grand

Avenue right, turn left onto Jonata Street, then right onto San Marcos Avenue.

This compact gallery features works of local and national artists with emphasis on images placed in natural settings. The museum encourages families to visit, and even provides a full-time room dedicated to painting on a whim. Walk through the museum; if you are inspired, head into the painting room designed to accommodate itinerant artists of all ages and abilities. Open Wednesdays through Sundays from 11 a.m. to 5 p.m.

LETTERS

Los Olivos Branch Library
Santa Ynez Valley Grange Hall
2374 Alamo Pintado Ave.
(805) 688-4214 (Solvang)
www.sbplibrary.org/hourslocations/los-olivos.html
FREE
From Highway 154, turn south onto Grand Avenue, then right onto Alamo Pintado Avenue.
Really intended as a locals' library escape, the small library welcomes all comers most Saturdays from 10 a.m. to 1 p.m., but check the Web site or call ahead for current hours and offerings.

NATURE

Figueroa Mountain Wildflowers & Snow
Figueroa Mountain Road
(805) 925-9538
www.fs.fed.us/r5/lospadres/recreation/trails/slrd
FREE
From Highway 154, turn north onto Figueroa Mountain Road.
This popular Sunday drive leads through spectacular displays of wildflowers in spring, and during particularly cold, wet winters rewards with snow near the summit. For more information, see its full listing on p. 201.

Lavinia Campbell Park
Grand Avenue at Alamo Pintado Road
(805) 693-5090
www.polosyv.org/lcpark.htm
FREE
From Highway 154, turn south onto Grand Avenue.
Named for the donor of this city-center property, this tree-shaded lot packs cooling lawn and picnic tables comfortably into less than a quarter acre. The park is often the central point for community events.

OTHER ADVENTURES

☞ Clairmont Farm Lavender Company

2480 Roblar Ave.

(805) 688-7505

clairmontfarms.com

FREE

From Highway 154, turn south onto Grand Avenue, which becomes Roblar Avenue. From Highway 246, turn north onto Alamo Pintado Road, right onto Santa Barbara Avenue, then right onto Grand Avenue/Roblar Avenue.

Visitors to this family-owned, 5-acre, organic lavendar farm are welcome to stroll through the lavender field, picnic among the rows, set up canvas and paints to enjoy nature's inspiration, or learn how lavender is distilled on site. The friendly staffers are happy to answer questions, and group tours are available by appointment. Open daily 10 a.m. to 6 p.m.

Quacken Farms

2921 Ontiveros Road

quackenfarms.com/ourhours.htm

FREE

From Highway 154, turn west onto Roblar Avenue for less than a quarter mile to a Y, where you continue straight onto Ontiveros Road.

This farm and produce stand promotes family fun with a pumpkin patch, pony rides and tractor rides. Open seasonally.

Santa Ynez Valley Grange No. 644

2374 Alamo Pintado Ave.

www.syvgrange.com

FREE-$$

From Highway 154, turn south onto Grand Avenue, then right onto Alamo Pintado Avenue.

This is Los Olivos' community center, complete with a busy calendar of events ranging from children's art classes to advanced yoga, community service organization meetings to live performances.

Chapter 9

Lompoc & Vandenberg Village

While Santa Barbara County is largely identified by its metropolitan southern shore, it includes an array of communities; pockets of humanity that defy the silver screen's attempt to pigeonhole this region. Lompoc, a locals' town with a rotating door for the military's migratory base employees, is one of those places.

The Lompoc Valley, located on the northwestern edge of the Santa Ynez Fault, has been the epicenter of Chumash life, not one, but two, California mission sites, a temperance-based community and the ornamental floral seed industry. In more recent years, Camp Cooke, now known as Vandenberg Air Force Base, has provided a fairly steady flow of work, and a mighty rotation of citizenry as the base has evolved from World War II training center to 21st Century space base.

The valley is geographically unique. Once submerged in the Pacific Ocean, today it is home to the largest collection of diatomaceous earth in the world. The specialized material used in products varying from water filters to parasiticals is the result of a huge eddy that once covered the southern portion of the valley and provided diatoms a perfect home. The single-cell plants were able to form protective shells from high concentrations of silica — a volcano byproduct that may have saturated the ocean at that time.

A highlight of visiting this laid-back community comes each summer as hundreds of acres of colorful flowers decorate the valley with their banner of colors. According to the Lompoc Valley Chamber of Commerce, Lompoc was the Mustard Seed Capital of the World in the early 20th Century. When sweet peas were introduced, the community changed its title to Flower Capital of the World. The blooms are staggered from late spring through late summer, but generally peak in late June. The fields are easy to spot, but please stay on paved roads and pull completely off the road if you stop to take photos or plan to get out of your vehicle. It is also illegal to hike in the fields, allow children or dogs to run on these private parcels, or to pick any of the flowers without express permission.

To get to Lompoc from the north, take Highway 101 south to the Clark Avenue exit south of Santa Maria. Turn right onto Clark Avenue, left onto Highway 135, merge onto Highway 1 south, then turn left at Vandenberg Air Force Base to continue south on Highway 1, which becomes H Street in Lompoc.

From Buellton and points east, take Highway 246, which becomes East Ocean Avenue.

From the south, take Highway 101 north to Highway 1, which leads directly to East Ocean in Lompoc.

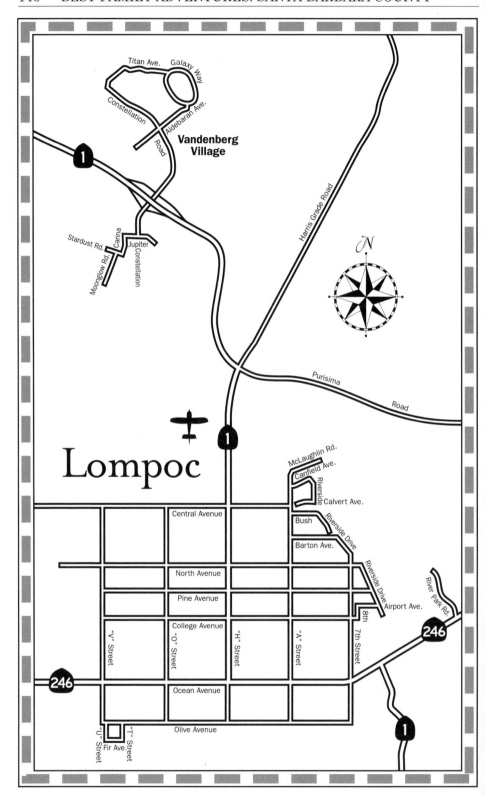

ARTS

Cypress Gallery
119. E. Cypress Ave.
(805) 737-1129
www.lompocvalleyartassociation.com
FREE

From the north, take H Street south, turn left onto Cypress Avenue. From the south and east, take Ocean Avenue into town, turn left on H Street, then right on Cypress Avenue.

This compact gallery, managed by the Lompoc Valley Art Association, features works of local artists, including painters, photographers, jewelry makers, ceramicists and others. This is an ideal spot to begin a tour of Lompoc's downtown murals. Open Tuesdays through Sundays from noon until 5 p.m. during summer months, noon until 4 p.m. in winter months.

The gallery is adjacent to Centennial Square (p. 154) and across the street from the Lompoc Museum (p. 151).

Gemini Twin Theater
1028 North H St.
(805) 736-1306
$

From the north, take H Street into town. From the south and east, take Ocean Avenue west, then turn left onto H Street.

This aging theater includes two screens showing first-run movies, and of course a snack bar and restrooms.

Grossman Gallery
Lompoc Library
501 East North Ave.
(805) 736-3477
www.cityoflompoc.com/library
FREE

From the north, take H Street south, then turn left onto North Avenue. From the south and east, take Ocean Avenue west, turn right onto A Street, then left onto North Avenue.

Located inside the city's library (p. 148), this gallery features new exhibits of local artists monthly. Open during library hours.

☞ Lompoc Mural Walk
Downtown Lompoc
(805) 736-4567
www.lompocmurals.com
FREE

Since 1988, muralists from throughout the country have traveled to Lompoc to adorn city alleyways, parking lots, the visitors center and other available exterior walls with images memorializing the city's historic events and figures. Many emphasize the local flower industry, while some others memorialize Lompoc's first firefighters, and the Chumash people.

Pick up a map of the murals online, at Cypress Gallery (p. 147) or at the Lompoc Chamber of Commerce (p. 234). Wheelchair accessible.

Movies Lompoc
220 West Barton Ave.
(805) 736-1558
$

From the north, take H Street south, turn right onto Barton Avenue. From the east and south, take Ocean Avenue west, turn right on H Street then left onto Barton Avenue.

The city's newest theater includes 4 screens showing first-run movies. Snackbar, restrooms and easily accessible via the city's plentiful bike paths.

LETTERS

Charlotte's Web Children's Library
218 South I St.
(805) 736-3477
www.cityoflompoc.com/library/CharlottesWeb.htm
FREE

From the north, take H Street south, turn right on Cypress, then left onto I Street. From the south and east, take Ocean Avenue west, and turn left onto I Street.

This brand-new children's library, still under construction at publication time, is designed entirely for children ages 14 and younger. It will include books and other materials, a homework center, and serve as a forum for special events. The library sits on property donated by former mayor Charlotte Benton and is designed on principles of sustainable architecture.

Lompoc Public Library
501 E. North Ave.
(805) 736-3477
www.cityoflompoc.com/library
FREE

From the north, take H Street south, then turn left onto North Avenue. From the south and east, take Ocean Avenue west, turn right onto A Street, then left onto North Avenue.

The community's library includes a healthy selection of books, magazines, CDs and DVDs as well as a variety of programs for patrons of all ages, including literacy programs and youth art programs. Story times are held

Tuesdays at 6:30 p.m., Wednesdays at 3:30 p.m. and Thursdays at 1:30 p.m., plus Spanish-language story time Thursdays at 6:30 p.m.

The library is open Mondays through Thursdays from noon to 8 p.m., and Fridays through Sundays from noon until 6 p.m.

Vandenberg Village Branch Library
3755 Constellation Road
www.cityoflompoc.com/library/village.htm
FREE
From Highway 1 north of Lompoc, take the Constellation Road exit and head east.

This community library is a branch of the City of Lompoc library system. Programs include story time (10:30 a.m. Wednesdays), after school homework help, literary groups, teen gaming and other social and cultural events. Check online for current hours and offerings.

HISTORY

Artesia School Museum
Chestnut Street west of H Street
(805) 736-3888
www.lompocmuseum.org/artesia.php
FREE
From the north, take H Street south, then turn left onto Chestnut Street. From the south and east, take Ocean Avenue west, turn right onto H Street, then left onto Chestnut Street.

This schoolhouse was the first of a dozen country schools that served families living throughout Lompoc Valley. Artesia School was built in 1876 and, until 1961, served students in the Artesia Road area west of Lompoc. In 1972, the structure, damaged by fire, was moved to its existing site on the El Camino School grounds. It was renovated in 1995, and then furnished to reflect its earliest days.

Today, visitors are invited for a glimpse of the past during museum open houses the fourth Saturday of each month from 2 p.m. to 4 p.m., during special events and by reservation for group tours.

Fabing-McKay-Spanne House
207 North L St.
(805) 735-4626
lompochistory.org
FREE
From the north, take H Street south, turn right on Chestnut Avenue, then left onto L Street. From the south and east, take Ocean Avenue west, then turn right onto L Street.

In 1875, this new home was the first two-story, wooden residence in Lompoc. Today, it is home to the Lompoc Valley Historical Society, which has renovated it and decorated it in Victorian style. The museum offers a look back in time. The kitchen and pantry reflect the pre-electric era. The teenage girls' room, children's room and nursery demonstrate the simplicity of life before electronics. Other features include the blacksmith shop and carriage house.

The museum is open to visitors each Monday and Thursday from 9 a.m. to 11 a.m. and on the fourth Saturday of each month from 1 p.m. to 4 p.m. Docent-led tours also are available by reservation.

☞ La Purísima Mission State Historic Park

2295 Purísima Road
(805) 733-3713
lapurisimamission.org
$

From the north, take Highway 1 south. At the Lompoc split, continue straight onto Purísima Road. From the east, take Highway 246 west, veer right onto Purísima Road. From the south, take Highway 1 north, turn right onto Ocean Avenue/Highway 246, left onto Mission Gate Road.

Of the 21 Spanish missions built throughout California in the late 18th Century, La Purísima is among the rare few that still offer a rural setting.

While homes and businesses, streets and highways have encroached on city missions like those found in San Luis Obispo, San Francisco and even tiny San Miguel, La Purísima retains much of its natural surroundings.

The Lompoc mission was originally established four miles southwest of its current site. A quarter century later, it was destroyed in the 1812 earthquake, and church fathers opted to move to the present location. When the mission was abandoned by the church, it passed into private hands and served a variety of purposes from private residence to barn.

Today, the park includes the mission, a visitors center, museum, picnic areas, biking and hiking trails, equestrian trails, educational exhibits and programs and guided tours. Special events are held throughout the year, supported in large part by a marvelous group of docents who bring character to the place. Check out Village Days for a Chumash focus and Purísima's People Days that emphasizes the life and times of mission residents. Mission Life Days emphasize mission-era crafts, including functioning displays of the blacksmith shop, weaving, spinning, soap making,

candle making, carpentry, pottery and baking in the hornos — adobe brick ovens. Other special events include candlelight tours, Mountain Men Rendezvous and Founding Day Celebration.

The site has traditionally been open from 9 a.m. to 5 p.m. daily except Christmas, Thanksgiving and New Years' Day, but recent state budget cutbacks may result in a changed schedule. Call ahead.

La Purísima Vieja
South end of F Street
(805) 875-8100
www.lapurisimamission.org
FREE

From the north, take H Street south; turn left onto Locust Avenue, then right onto F Street. From the east and south, take Ocean Avenue west, then turn left onto F Street.

There isn't much left of the original mission; built in 1787, it was destroyed by an earthquake in 1812. Today, two lots on opposite sides of South F Street provide a memorial ground for the mission. The lot on the east side of the street includes a grassy berm, a few decomposing walls, portions of the water system and bits of an aqueduct as well as interpretive signage in an otherwise open lot. To the west of the site marker at the end of the street is another open lot that provides a tree-shaded bench and open space.

Lompoc Museum
200 South H St.
(805) 736-3888
www.lompocmuseum.org
$

From the north, take H Street south. From the south and east, take Ocean Avenue west, then turn left onto H Street.

The 1910 Carnegie Library is preserved today as the home of the city's history museum. Exhibits emphasize the history of Lompoc, but also include information about Santa Barbara County as a whole. The Clarence Ruth Gallery provides a special focus on Chumash artifacts. The annex, built in 1925 for the First Church of Christ Scientist, is used today for museum lectures and performances.

The museum is open from 1 p.m. to 5 p.m. Tuesdays through Fridays and 1 p.m. to 4 p.m. Saturdays and Sundays. Guided tours for groups are also available by appointment.

The structure is Lompoc's Historical Landmark No. 1 and is listed on the National Register of Historic Places.

NATURE

Barton Neighborhood Park

West Barton Ave.

(805) 875-8100

www.cityoflompoc.com/parks_rec/Barton.htm

FREE

From the north, take H Street south, then turn left onto Barton Avenue. From the south and east, take Ocean Avenue west, turn right onto H Street, then left onto Barton Avenue.

This promising 5-acre park was still undergoing improvements at publication time. Play equipment, benches and single-track dirt trails throughout the property were already in place. When completed, plans call for the inclusion of a basketball court, walking path, lawn areas and access to the East-West Channel Bike Path. An area dedicated for dog use, Barkin' Dog Park, also is in the works here.

☞ Beattie Park

Olive Avenue at 5th Street

(805) 875-8100

www.cityoflompoc.com/parks_rec/Beattie.htm

FREE

From the north, take H Street south, turn left onto Olive Avenue. From the south and east, take Ocean Avenue west, turn left onto 7th Street, then right onto Olive Avenue.

This 50-acre park along the southern outskirts of the city is certainly the city's most well-developed park, offering an array of recreational opportunities. Our children particularly enjoy the play structures, swings and the path past a 2-million-year-old whale vertebra and other fossils. The nature trail, extensive stroller-friendly fitness trail, and the gazebo with wonderful views across the Lompoc Valley are among my highlights. Others may find an affinity with the park's other amenities: athletic fields, horseshoe pits, basketball courts, individual picnic areas with barbecues, group barbecue area with not one, but four, large barbecue pits, an urban forest, memorial grove, even a swinging bench memorializing "all pets waiting for us beside the rainbow bridge." The park also includes restrooms and ample parking.

Like many Central Coast parks adjacent to undeveloped wild land, a mountain lion warning has been issued for this park.

Burton Mesa Ecological Reserve
Highway 1 from La Purísima Mission to north of Vandenberg Village
(805) 640-8019
www.dfg.ca.gov/lands/er/region5/burtonmesa.html
FREE

Though there are several popular entrances to this vast reserve, consider taking Highway 1 to Contellation Road turning north into Vandenberg Village. Follow the road to its end at Cabrillo High School where parking is ample after school hours, on weekends and school holidays.

This vast expanse of public land adjacent to La Purísima Mission State Park and surrounding Vandenberg Village includes approximately 5,735 acres of marine chaparral, the last significant natural stand of its kind in Central California. The area is particularly noted for its squat, gnarled oaks, Purísima manzanita, Lompoc ceanothus and other local species. It also is home to a variety of rare fauna, including the threatened vernal pool fairy shrimp, California tiger salamander and California red-legged frog.

While the area includes some 28 miles of designated trails, untold miles of trails crisscross the dry, largely sandy territory. The entire property is limited to hikers and dogs on leashes. No mountain bikes or horses are allowed. Those who bushwhack or take lesser-traveled trails risk contact with poison oak, which thrives here. Mountain lions have been seen here, and deer often are spotted, particularly during early-morning walks.

Informational kiosks are slated to be installed at half a dozen undetermined locations throughout the reserve. Some likely are to be placed at the most heavily used trailheads, including the north end of Constellation Road, Harris Grade Road north of Burton Mesa Boulevard and the Little League Fields at the west and of Albireo. The 100 block of Oak Hills Drive is also a popular approach.

For an easier access to the habitat, visit the Burton Mesa Chaparral Restoration Area at Hancock College's Lompoc Campus. Volunteers from the Lompoc Valley Botanical and Horticultural Society maintain largely stroller-friendly paths through about 7 acres of this 37-acre area. The easy, flat trails wind through the vegetation dotted with benches, including one particularly restful spot overlooking an undeveloped portion of the natural reserve.

Cabrillo Aquarium
Cabrillo High School
4350 Constellation Road
(805) 742-2888

cabrilloaquarium.org

FREE

From Highway 1, take Constellation Drive east.

This extremely nontraditional high school classroom provides the community with the most extensive marine mammal exhibits and educational programs available between Santa Barbara and Monterey. The visually pleasing, curvilinear structure welcomes visitors inside to explore any of three touch tanks, gaze into aquariums dedicated to various coastal species from moon jellies to chain-link eels, view students at work on the monstrous filtration system or enjoy a discussion in the amphitheater.

Students in the school's tourism program are largely responsible for running the place, from caring for the tanks to promoting the center, leading tours and teaching each other. They also display student-built remote operating vehicles. Students are so involved in the program they volunteer throughout school holidays and summer vacations.

"This program is truly amazing. I don't know what I would do without it," said 2009 Curator Amanda Schaller, a senior with three years experience at the aquarium.

The facility is open to the general public during periodic open houses. Private group tours also are available by reservation.

Centennial Square

Cypress Avenue at H Street

(805) 875-8100

www.cityoflompoc.com/parks_rec/Centennial.htm

FREE

From the north, take H Street south. From the south and east, take Ocean Avenue west, then turn left on H Street.

This very small, city-center square at a busy intersection isn't particularly quiet, but it provides a place to rest during the mural walk, or room to wear down little legs before heading to the neighboring Lompoc Valley Arts Association Cypress Gallery (p. 147) or Lompoc Museum (p. 151) across the street. This park includes benches, a gazebo and works of public art, but no public restrooms.

College Park

College Avenue at J Street

(805) 875-8100

www.cityoflompoc.com/parks_rec/College.htm

FREE

From the north, take H Street, then turn right on College Avenue. From the south and east, take Ocean Avenue west; turn right onto H Street, then left onto College Avenue.

The main outdoor feature of this 4.6-acre park is a 10,000-square-foot, concrete collection of ramps, rails and ridges for skateboarders. The skate park's mellow obstacles are ideal for young shredders, but experienced kids are unlikely to be amused for long.

The riding area is surrounded by tree-shaded lawn and is just across the parking lot from the Lompoc Aquatic Center (p. 162) and YMCA, both also located on the park property.

Falcon Open Space

Falcon Drive at Scorpio Road

(805) 934-6123

www.sbparks.org/2007/OpenSpaces/falcon.html

FREE

From Highway 1, take Constellation east, turn right onto Sirius, left on Rigel, right on Falcon Drive.

This small neighborhood park in Vandenberg Village provides a lawn for passive play, picnic tables, play structures and beautiful trees ideal for climbing. The trees, however, are fenced off, and, in true California style, "no tree climbing" signs are posted. No restrooms.

Johns-Manville Park

Chestnut Avenue from A Street to C Street

(805) 875-8100

www.cityoflompoc.com/parks_rec/JM.htm

FREE

From the north, head south on H Street, turn left onto Chestnut Street. From the south and east, take Ocean Avenue west, turn right onto A Street, then left onto Chestnut Avenue.

This 6.5-acre, neighborhood park includes new play structures, as well as lighted Little League fields that double as soccer and football fields. Other amenities include individual barbecues, basketball court and large shade trees, but no restrooms.

☞ Ken Adam Park

2999 Lompoc Casmalia Road/Highway 1

(805) 875-8100

www.cityoflompoc.com/parks_rec/KenAdam.htm

FREE

From the north and south, take Highway 1. From the east, take Highway 246 to Highway 1. Turn left onto Hancock Drive. Once on campus, turn right and follow the driveway around the large parking lot on the left to a smaller parking lot on the right.

Trees. That's all you really need to know about this 118-acre city property. The 42 developed acres of Ken Adam Park include some of the most fantastic, accessible, gnarly oak trees in the county's long list of public parks. The park also includes play structures, a volleyball court, swings, horseshoe pits, several picnic tables, benches and a group barbecue area with a large pit.

Take a short walk southeast of the play structure and you'll find yourself facing a newly established memorial grove, a crescent of young trees that promise to provide shelter from everyday winds and sun as they continue to grow.

Carry on along the service road, bearing left and down the gentle slope into the ravine, then back up the other side for a beautiful half-mile round-trip walk to the three-flagpole war memorial. Except for passing traffic below on Highway 1, this portion of the park is fairly quiet as it seems to be visited rarely.

La Purísima Golf Course

3455 Hwy. 246

(805) 735-8395

www.lapurisimagolf.com

$$-$$$

From the north, take Highway 1 to Purísima Road east, then merge onto Highway 246 east. From the east, take Highway 246 west. From the south, take Highway 1 north; turn right onto Ocean Avenue/Highway 246.

This 18-hole, 6,657-yard championship course comprises 300 oak-studded acres and offers play for golfers from juniors to professionals. The facility also offers a driving range, practice bunkers, chipping and putting greens, club rentals and a restaurant.

Lompoc Valley Multipurpose Trail System

Various locations

(805) 963-SAVE

www.trafficsolutions.info

FREE

Lompoc seems to be doing its best to become a bicycle-friendly community. In recent years, it has forged ahead on a network of Class I bike paths – routes that keep bicycles and motorized vehicles largely separate. Today, it is possible to ride along the west side of town from Pine Avenue to within a block of Ryon Park on dedicated paths. Construction has begun on a parallel route further west along Bailey Avenue with off-street spurs linking to its eastern counterparts.

The brand-new, two-lane, paved Riverbend Multipurpose Trail undulates and meanders 2¼ miles along the western bank of the Santa Ynez River from River Bend Park to College Avenue. A roundabout provides easy access onto a spur leading to Central Avenue. The trail also provides access to a maze of dirt trails for more advanced riders. There are several starting points. Here's a central spot: From the north, take H Street south, then turn left onto Pine Avenue. From the south and east, take Ocean Avenue west, turn right onto 7th, then left onto Pine Avenue.

The V Street route provides a paved, off-street, often tree-shaded ride from Pine Avenue to Olive Street. Follow the path east on Olive Street to O Street to complete the route, then turn left for one block of street riding north on O Street to reach Ryon Park.

A 1-mile segment from H Street to V Street along the East-West Channel is a close third in length, for the time being. This paved path curves along the channel, behind commercial and residential properties.

The other major car-free route stretches along Bailey Avenue from Central Avenue to North Avenue, but plans call for that path to continue south along the length of Bailey, and extend east to tie into the V Street trail near College Avenue.

Mackie Mountain (aka Muffin Hill)
Galaxy Way
(805) 966-4520
www.sblandtrust.org/openspaces.html
FREE
From Highway 1, take Constellation east, turn right onto Aldebaran, left onto Eldorado.

These short uphill hikes offer relatively easy family escapes featuring views over the surrounding Burton Mesa Ecological Reserve (p. 153). Several unmaintained dirt trails meander throughout the 17-acre open space, most leading about a quarter mile to the top of the hill where heavy use has resulted in the complete removal of vegetation. No shade. No water. No facilities.

Marshallia Ranch Golf Course
Vandenberg Air Force Base
734-1333
www.30svs.com/svbg.html
$-$$$
Take Highway 1, turn north onto San Antonio Road West, swing left at the Y onto Lompoc-Casmalia Road, then immediately right onto Marshallia Ranch Road.

This 6,875-yard course is on base property, but the general public is welcome to golf here. Rates vary based on relationship to the base, age and military rank. Junior rates are half that of their sponsor's rate. Discounts also are given for play beginning after noon, and another discount for tee times after 3 p.m.

In addition to the championship course, the serene setting includes a driving range and a fairly new clubhouse that offers a pro shop, snack bar, restaurant and outdoor dining, as well as locker rooms, storage facilities and rentals of clubs and carts.

Miguelito County Park
3051 San Miguelito Road
(805) 934-6123
sbparks.org

FREE

From the north, take H Street, turn right onto Ocean Avenue, then left onto I Street, which becomes San Miguelito Road. From the east and south, take Ocean Avenue west, turn left onto I Street.

This very popular, very quiet park along Miguelito Creek just three miles out of town offers lots of running room and plentiful, fairly dense shade under the canopy of twisted oaks, even redwoods. Children creep, crawl and swing on play structures while their caregivers rest on nearby benches or sprawl on the grass under shade trees.

The park also includes horseshoe pits, barbecue grills, restrooms and a group barbecue area.

Ocean Beach Park & Surf Beach

Ocean Park Road

(805) 934-6123

sbparks.org

FREE

From Lompoc, take Highway 246 west about 13 miles, turn right onto Ocean Park Road.

A 36-acre park and nature reserve adjacent to the Santa Ynez River estuary provides access to Surf Beach (p. 161). The park offers plentiful paved parking, barbecue grills, picnic tables, a playground, wheelchair-accessible restrooms and beach access via the paved trail under the viaduct. The trail can be flooded when the estuary is high. If the underpass is flooded, return to Ocean Avenue and continue west another mile or so to the parking lot at Amtrak's Surf station. Here, you'll have to cross the railroad tracks to reach the beach, so be particularly careful with children and pets.

While this beach can be windy and downright cold, it provides coastal access within a few minutes of town, and for those interested in digging their toes into the sand, wildlife viewing and surf fishing, this may be the beach for you. From March 1 to Sept. 30, Ocean Beach is off limits to human visitors and their canine companions in an effort to protect the endangered western snowy plover.

During periods of heavy runoff, check water quality first at www.sbcphd.org/ehs/oceanmn.htm.

Pioneer Park
Pine Avenue at 4th Street
(805) 875-8100
www.cityoflompoc.com/parks_rec/Pioneer.htm
FREE

From the north, take H Street south, then turn left onto Pine Avenue. From the south and east, take Ocean Avenue west, turn right onto 7th, then left onto Pine Avenue.

This 5-acre community park includes play structures, individual barbecue areas, picnic benches, tree-shaded lawn, a Babe Ruth baseball field, paved paths, a sand pit, restrooms and a preschool building.

Providence Landing Park
Mercury Avenue, Vandenberg Village
(805) 875-8100
www.cityoflompoc.com/parks_rec
FREE

From Highway 1, take Constellation Road west; turn left onto Jupiter Avenue, and then right onto Mercury Avenue.

This brand-new, 12-acre community park is tucked away in one of Vandenberg Village's newest housing developments. The wheelchair-accessible park provides ample parking for everyday use of facilities, which include tennis courts, basketball courts, baseball diamonds, picnic tables, a concessions stand, paved paths, play structures and restrooms.

☞ River Park
Highway 246 at Sweeney Road
(805) 875-8100
www.cityoflompoc.com/parks_rec/River.htm
FREE

From the north, take H Street sout, turn left onto Ocean Avenue/Highway 246. From the east, take Highway 246 west. From the south, take Highway 1 north, then turn right onto Ocean Avenue/Highway 246.

The 35 camping spots in this city park seem to be popular year round, but particularly in winter months, when snowbirds who have discovered the Central Coast come to roost for the season. All sites include full hookups, and there is an on-site camp host. The campground also includes a group area, hike/bike camping area, showers, a public toilet and a dump station.

After wending through the campground, you'll find some 40 additional acres of outdoor recreation opportunities for individuals or very large groups. The central feature of the park may be Kiwanis Kids Lake, a lake developed on the premise that all children need a local fishing hole. The lake is planted with fish quarterly by sponsors, and fishing is free for children.

The 45-acre park also includes a pair of aging playgrounds with structures varying from swings to old-school climbing structures. Other park features include horseshoe pits, fitness trails, sand volleyball courts, Vietnam Veterans Memorial, individual barbecue area, as well as five group barbecue areas, some of which can accommodate up to 150 people. The Shack Paintball Field (p. 164) is also located on park property.

Riverbend Community Park

1600 block North A Street

(805) 875-8100

www.cityoflompoc.com/parks_rec/Riverbend.htm

FREE

From the north, take H Street south, turn left onto Central Avenue, then left onto A Street. From the south and east, take Ocean Avenue west, then turn right onto A Street.

With more than 30 acres, much of it still undeveloped, this park at a bend in the Santa Ynez River is chiefly a Babe Ruth Baseball complex at this printing. Lizzaraga Field features a skinned infield, scoreboard, batting cages and spectator seating. There also is a large barbecue area.

The park is at the northern terminus of the Riverbend Multipurpose Trail (p. 160). Long-term plans include multiuse athletic fields for soccer, youth football, Little League baseball and girls softball.

Ryon Memorial Park

Ocean Ave at O St.

(805) 875-8100

www.cityoflompoc.com/parks_rec/Ryon.htm

FREE

From the north, take H Street south, then turn right onto Ocean Avenue. From the south and east, take Ocean Avenue west.

Since 1916, a Spanish-style arch has announced visitors' arrival at Ryon Park, now more than 22 acres of recreational space. The park is home to many of the city's major events, including cultural festivals, art fairs and an annual dog show.

Everyday facilities include play structures, a lighted softball field and six lighted tennis courts. Other amenities include restrooms, baseball fields, multisport athletic fields, group barbecues and individual barbecue areas, paved pathways and a raised stage.

Sagan Park

Sagan Court, Vandenberg Village

(805) 875-8100

www.cityoflompoc.com/parks_rec

FREE

From Highway 1, take Constellation Road west, turn right onto Jupiter Avenue, left onto Carina Drive, right onto Stardust Road, left onto Moonglow and finally left onto Sagan Court.

At less than a quarter acre, this tiny park is ideal for toddler play sessions. The park includes a play structure, benches and limited running room on a quiet neighborhood street.

Surf Beach
Vandenberg Air Force Base
Ocean Avenue/Highway 246 west of Lompoc
(805) 733-2903
FREE
From Lompoc, take Highway 246 west about 14 miles.
This wild, rugged coastline serves as Lompoc residents' local beach, but it is less than ideal for family visits involving very young children. The current here is dangerous and it is often windy, cold and/or heavily overcast.

Still, this beach, with its own dedicated stop on the Amtrak passenger rail line, offers miles of sand to explore. Facilities also include a parking lot and restrooms. Beach access can be limited or completely blocked during snowy plover nesting season March 1 through Sept. 30.

During periods of heavy runoff, check water quality first at www.sbcphd.org/ehs/oceanmn.htm.

Thompson Park
College Avenue at R Street
(805) 875-8100
www.cityoflompoc.com/parks_rec/Thompson.htm
FREE
From the north, take H Street south, turn right on College. From the south and east, take Ocean Avenue west, turn right onto R Street.
This 5-acre park includes play structures, a softball field, swings, picnic benches with small barbecues and restrooms.

Village Hills Little League Fields
Alibreo Avenue off Constellation Road
(805) 733-1076
sbparks.org
From Highway 1 north of Lompoc, take the Constellation Road exit and head east, then turn left onto Alibreo Avenue.
Village Hills Little League maintains this 7-acre, two-field youth baseball complex located adjacent to the Cabrillo High School campus and Burton Mesa Ecological Reserve (p. 153).

Westvale Park
1300 block West Fir Ave.
(805) 875-8100
www.cityoflompoc.com/parks_rec/Westvale.htm

FREE

From H Street and Ocean Avenue, take H Street south, then turn right onto Olive Street, then left onto T Street and right onto Fir Avenue.

This neighborhood park includes play structures, picnic benches with barbecues and lawn on about 2.5 acres.

OTHER ADVENTURES

Anderson Recreation Center

125 W. Walnut Ave.

(805) 875-8100

www.cityoflompoc.com/parks_rec/anderson.htm

FREE

From the north, take H Street south, then turn left onto Walnut Avenue. From the south and east, take Ocean Avenue west, turn right onto H Street, then left onto Walnut Avenue.

This structure, built in 1942, was one of three United Service Organization facilities serving those stationed at Camp Cooke (now called Vandenberg Air Force Base) during World War II. The building continued to serve local citizens as City Hall from 1947 to 1980. Today, it houses the administrative offices of the Lompoc Parks & Recreation Department.

In addition to offices, the 11,000-square-foot building includes a gymnasium, kitchen, classrooms, and meeting rooms. Many of the rooms are available for rent by reservation.

Civic Auditorium

217 South L Street

(805) 875-8100

www.cityoflompoc.com/parks_rec/civic.htm

FREE

From Ocean Avenue and H Street, take Ocean Avenue west, then turn left onto L Street.

This 430-seat auditorium and related rehearsal spaces are used throughout the year by area performing arts groups for rehearsals and performances. The facility is available for rent.

☞ Lompoc Aquatic Center

207 W. College Ave.

(805) 875-2700

www.cityoflompoc.com/parks_rec

$

From the north, take H Street south and then turn right on College Avenue. From the south and east, take Ocean Avenue west, turn right onto H Street, then left onto College Avenue.

This four-pool, indoor aquatic facility offers lap swimming, play pools, water slides and a therapeutic pool. Hours vary to include recreational swim; family swim in the 90-degree therapy pool; warm water leisure (quiet time in the therapy pool reserved for adults and people with disabilities); water exercise classes such as aqua step, aqua aerobics, arthritis relief, aqua Pilates and deep-water aqua; lap swim early mornings, midday, evenings; parent/tot hours; swim lessons; junior lifeguarding; water safety instruction; parent-tot classes; open water polo for adults ages 18 and up; and pool rentals. There is a classroom and patio area, too.

Lompoc Valley Community Center
1501 E. Ocean Ave.
(805) 875-8100
www.cityoflompoc.com/parks_rec
FREE
From the north, take H Street south, then turn left onto Ocean Avenue. From the east and south, take Ocean Avenue west.
This 9,000-square-foot recreation facility focuses primarily on senior activities, but the property includes several classrooms, meeting rooms, a banquet room and kitchen, all available for rent.

Return to Freedom American Wild Horse Sanctuary
Directions provided upon making reservation
(805) 737-9246
Returntofreedom.org
FREE-$$$
This 310-acre ranch, open to visitors by reservation only, provides sanctuary for more than 200 American Mustangs, some gathered as intact family groups. Most run wild on the slopes, but ambassador horses, including the model for the animated film "Spirit," are maintained for public education. Tours and walks are scheduled regularly and volunteers are welcome to take part in work days and occasional campouts. Other programs include photography tours, horse clinics and kids' days.

Space and Missile Heritage Center

Vandenberg Air Force Base

(805) 606-3595

www.vandenberg.af.mil

FREE

From Highway 101, take Clark Avenue west, turn south onto Highway 135/ Broadway, take the Highway 1 exit toward Lompoc and proceed straight to the base's main gate.

Budding astronauts, rocket scientists and historians may be interested in visiting this interpretive center located at Space Launch Complex 10, a National Historic Landmark. The facility was originally built in 1958 for ballistic missile testing, but it was later retooled for space launch programs, and supported dozens of satellite launches until 1980.

Public tours of the launch facility and heritage center are available to visitors ages 10 and older. Reservations are required, and adult visitors must bring two forms of photo identification. Arrive half an hour before the scheduled 10 a.m. departure on tour days which are the second and fourth Wednesdays of each month. The tour includes a bus ride through the base and a visit to the center that also includes rocket engine displays, missile silo mock-ups and an old missile control station.

The Shack Paintball Field

Ryon Memorial Park (p. 160)

Highway 246 at Sweeney Road

(805) 737-9600

theshackpaintball.com

$-$$

From the north, take H Street south, turn left onto Ocean Avenue/Highway 246. From the east, take Highway 246 west. From the south, take Highway 1 north, and then turn right onto Ocean Avenue/Highway 246.

Paintball didn't sound like fun until I finally caved and tried it. In fact, the related strategy games combined with exercise and tag-like aspects proved the sport exciting, exhausting and highly entertaining.

The Shack's fields are open from 10 a.m. to 4 p.m. Saturdays and Sundays. They include a speedball course with inflatable bunkers and a whizzball field, aka scenario field, with obstacles including trees and wooden structures. Bring your own equipment, or rent it there. Discounts are given for groups larger than 10 players. Call ahead for group reservations.

Several rules apply. Among them: players must be 10 or older to participate and parents must sign a release of liability for children; no pink paint allowed; barrel plugs are prohibited; all players must use barrel bags; face and ear protection required at all times; no walkie-talkies; no alcohol on site.

Bleacher seating and launch countdown announcements are provided at the Corral Road public viewing area. Take Lompoc-Casmalia Road north from Highway 1, then turn right onto Corral Road. For launch schedule, visit www.vandenberg.af.mil.

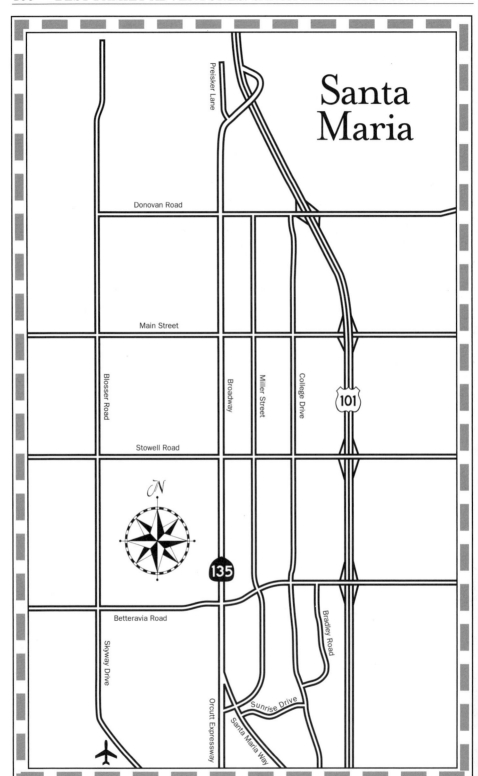

Chapter 10

Santa Maria & Orcutt

Two centuries ago, the flood-prone patch of land separating Rancho Punta de la Laguna and Rancho de Suey was notable only in that California's mission trail passed through it. That changed in the late 19th Century when four landholders donated 4 square miles of land to form Grangeville, later named Central City, and ultimately incorporated in 1805 as Santa Maria.

The community built on the farming industry has grown to include more than 22 square miles, but while it is the single most populous city in Santa Barbara County, it retains its agricultural focus. Surrounding fields abound with broccoli, lettuces, cabbages, grapes and strawberries, among other crops. Cattle graze on historic farmland nearby. Outlying unincorporated communities, not the least of which is Orcutt, also continue to grow. For a closer look at area farms, ranches, and cooling and processing facilities, contact the Santa Maria Valley Visitors Bureau (805-925-2403), which arranges agricultural tours for groups of 30 or more people.

Given its relatively large population, Santa Maria's public recreation offerings have been slow to develop. In recent years, however, growth and political sentiment have allowed for the development of several new parks, expansion of a children's museum, addition of several museums specializing in various aspects of the community's history and construction of a dedicated recreational trail system.

Orcutt comprises the unincorporated area south of Santa Maria city proper. It includes both Old Orcutt, the oil-boom community established at the turn of the 20th Century, and more modern developments that spread east across Highway 101.

ARTS

Betteravia Gallery
Government Center
511 E. Lakeside Parkway
(805) 965-9644
www.sbartscommission.org/exhibitions
FREE
From Highway 101, take Betteravia Road west. Turn left onto Centerpointe Parkway, then left onto Lakeside Parkway.
This gallery, located inside the county government building, aims to provide art to the general public. The gallery features regularly changing exhibits by local artists.

Edwards Santa Maria 10
1521 S. Bradley Road
(805) 347-1164
www.regmovies.com/theatrelocations
$

From the north, take Highway 101 south to Stowell Road exit, then turn left at the end of the ramp. From the south, take Stowell Road exit, turn left at the end of the ramp onto Stowell Road, then left onto Bradley Road.

This 10-screen theater offers major blockbusters, plus ample snacks and drinks at theater prices. During summer months, this theater provides free movies for children, typically running a G-rated movie and a PG-rated movie concurrently to meet the entertainment needs of local families. Stop by in May to pick up the summer schedule.

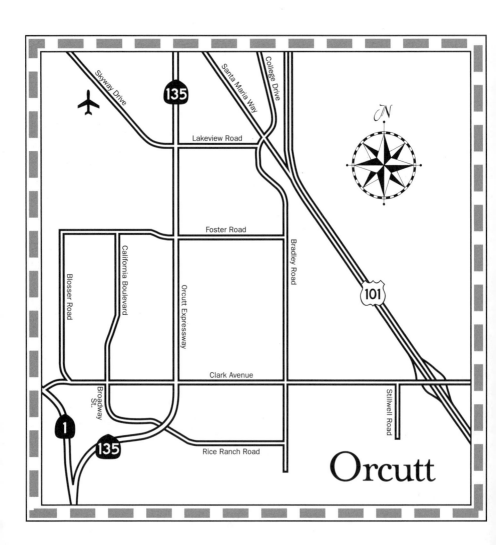

Foxworthy Gallery
Hancock College
800 S. College Drive, building L
(805) 922-6966, ext. 3465
www.hancockcollege.org
FREE

From northbound Highway 101, take the Stowell Road exit and turn right onto Stowell Road, then turn right onto College Drive. From southbound 101, take Main Street exit and proceed straight ahead onto College Drive at the end of the ramp.

This small gallery generally welcomes well-behaved children to experience art by students and faculty, as well as regional and national artists. Open Monday through Thursdays 8 a.m. to 8 p.m. and Fridays 8 a.m. to 3 p.m. Fee for on-campus parking. Restrooms nearby.

☞ Hi-Way Drive-in
3085 Santa Maria Way
(805) 937-3515
www.drive-ins.com/theater/cathigh
$

From the south, take Highway 101 north to Santa Maria Way and turn left at the end of the ramp. From the north on Highway 101, take Betteravia Road west, then turn left onto Santa Maria Way.

For half a century, Santa Marians have enjoyed open-air, big-screen productions at this classic drive-in. At its peak, California was the world's drive-in capital with more than 220 theaters in operation during the late 1960s, but interest declined in the '70s, and theaters continued to close through the turn of the century. By 2009, the Hi-Way was one of two remaining drive-ins on the Central Coast. (The other is San Luis Obispo's Sunset Drive-In.)

This one-screen theater provides affordable access to first-run movies in a family-friendly setting. One of the best ways to enjoy the drive-in involves comfortable camping chairs, blankets and a gaggle of friends and family members piled into one vehicle. Once in the drive-in, pull out the chairs and blankets, line them up and enjoy. Theater sound is provided via traditional window speakers or by local broadcast available on any vehicle's FM radio. The snack bar provides popcorn, nachos, candy and other theater-quality treats, and restrooms also are available.

Mckeon-Phillips Art Gallery & Winery
2115 S. Blosser, Suite 114
(805) 928-3025
Mckeonphillipswinery.com
FREE

From Highway 101, take Betteravia Road west, then turn right onto Blosser Road. A median prevents a left turn into the driveway, so make a U-turn at the first turning lane to return to the gallery.

This winery offers regularly rotated exhibits of works by local artists, including the winery's own winemaker, Ardison Phillips. The second Friday of each month brings an art opening paired with a wine and food reception.

Pacific Conservatory of the Performing Arts (PCPA)
800 S. College Drive
(805) 922-8313
pcpa.org
$ - $$$

From northbound Highway 101, take the Stowell Road exit and turn right onto Stowell Road, then turn right onto College Drive. From southbound 101, take Main Street exit and proceed straight ahead onto College Drive at the end of the ramp.

Since 1974, this conservatory has served up musicals, comedy, classics and contemporary works. PCPA operates out of Hancock College's Marian Theater and Severson Theater from November through May. In June through October, they perform at Solvang's Festival Theater. Fee for on-campus parking.

Santa Maria Civic Theatre
1660 N. McClelland
(805) 922-4442
smct.org
$$

From Highway 101, take Donovan Road west, then turn right onto McClelland.

This 100-seat black box theatre provides a venue for local talent, family fun and performing arts programs for area children.

Town Center Gallery
Town Center West in the breezeway
(805) 349-7303
www.thetowncentergallery.com
FREE

From Highway 101, take Main Street west, turn left onto Broadway and right into Town Center (mall).

This small, community-supported art cooperative provides exposure for area artists. The open spaces and friendly volunteer staff welcome all art lovers. Open 11 a.m. to 5 p.m. Tuesdays through Sundays. Restrooms nearby.

LETTERS

Orcutt Library
1157 East Clark Ave., Unit K
(805) 937-6483
www.ci.santa-maria.ca.us/3092.shtml
FREE

From Highway 101, take Clark Avenue west.

This small branch library, located in a shopping center, loans books for children and adults, as well as videos, local publications and a bank of internet-accessible computers. Library supporters do what they can with the limited space, but the key here is to make full use of the Black Gold Library System. It provides patrons access to collections from Santa Paula to San Miguel. For a small fee, materials from any of these libraries are delivered to any other library in the system, including Orcutt.

This branch is open from 10 a.m. to 6 p.m. Saturdays and Mondays through Thursdays; closed Fridays and Sundays. No restrooms.

Santa Maria Public Library
421 S. McClelland Street
(805) 925-0994
www.ci.santa-maria.ca.us/210.html
FREE

From Highway 101, take Main Street west. Turn left onto Miller, right onto Cook, then left onto McClelland.

There may be no better place to enjoy a good book than under the

Santa Maria's new library includes a large section dedicated to children's literature as well as a gift shop, cafe and comfortable seating throughout.

sprawling branches of a tree. In Santa Maria, children can enjoy this pleasure, even during the toughest winter storms, thanks to the library's Enchanted Forest — a contemplative place surrounded by books all under the branches of an artfully rendered artificial tree. In 2008 the city celebrated the grand opening of its brand new, creatively designed library.

State-of-the-art library services include traditional book loans, as well as a lending library of music, videos, magazines and more. The library also provides venues for local artists to display their work and for clubs and organizations to gather. Shepherd Hall Gallery is located off the main lobby and may be used for meeting space or as exhibit space. Permanent displays throughout the library include the Shepard Family Miniatures, Ainley Family Egyptian Antiquities and Bob Hoffman's scale model of Columbus's "Santa Maria."

The library offers a variety of special events, including performances. Preschool story time, available by reservation only, includes stories, songs, finger plays and a book on DVD. It is strictly limited to children ages 3 to 5 years old; even parents are not allowed.

Open Mondays through Thursdays 10 a.m. to 9 p.m. and on Fridays and Saturdays from 10 a.m. to 6 p.m. Closed Sundays.

HISTORY

☞ Natural History Museum of Santa Maria
Reuben Hart Home
412 S. McClelland
(805) 614-0806
naturalhistorysantamaria.com
FREE

From Highway 101, take Main Street west. Turn left onto Miller, right onto Cook, then left onto McClelland.

I'd lived in Santa Maria for more than a decade before I stepped through the doors of this museum located in an historic home. The tiny building was too small, I thought, to be of much interest. That was my first mistake.

In fact, this volunteer-driven museum packs a lot of information in its constantly evolving collection that represents the area's natural history. See rock and fossil exhibits, native bird displays, the bat room and a room dedicated to the oak woodland. Tectonic plates and the ancient sea are featured in the back room, where a short film about the geology of Santa Maria Valley also is presented. The touch table is a hit with most visitors, and

docents lead group tours by reservation. An outdoor picnic table and sand pit also are available.

Want to give your children an appreciation for the modern conveniences of home? Give them a tour of the tiny Hart Home, then point out it grew to this size after more than one addition!

This home, originally built in 1877 at the corner of Broadway and Church Street, was moved later to its current location. Docents can provide information about the house, or ask for the audio tour for a family-friendly lesson in times past.

Check the calendar for regular programs, including story time and, on the first Saturday of each month, visits with live animals. The museum is located in the historic Reuben Hart Home (page 172), and audio tours are available during museum hours. Open Wednesday through Saturday 11 a.m. to 4 p.m. and Sundays from 1 p.m. to 4 p.m. Public restrooms.

Santa Maria Valley Historical Society Museum

616 S. Broadway

(805) 922-3130

www.santamariahistory.org

FREE

From Highway 101, take Main Street west, then turn left onto Broadway.

This small, free museum in the heart of Santa Maria offers pictures and various other memorabilia commemorating the valley's history. Although small, the value in this museum is in its library and institutional knowledge. Museum docents are happy to answer questions, and the library includes just about everything ever written about Santa Maria, its ranches, businesses, homes and characters. The museum also houses thousands of photographs taken throughout the city's more than 100-year history. Open Tuesdays through Saturdays from noon until 5 p.m.

The historical society also organizes and sponsors The Valley Speaks, a series of talks featuring local residents of interest. The talks are given at 11 a.m. on the second Saturday of each month at the Santa Maria Public Library (p. 171).

☞ Santa Maria Museum of Flight

3015 Airpark Drive

(805) 922-8758

smmof.org

$

From Highway 101, take Santa Maria Way north, turn left onto Bradley Road, then immediately turn right onto Lakeview Road, which becomes Skyway Drive west of Broadway/Highway 135. Turn left onto Hangar Street, then right onto Airpark Drive.

Flight has been an important element in the modern history of Santa Maria since the establishment of the Allan Hancock Air Field in 1927 and Allan Hancock School of Aeronautics the following year on the midtown

property that now serves as Allan Hancock College. Hancock's field, school and pilots ultimately trained military pilots until the Army Air Field (now the Santa Maria Municipal Airport) was built across town. There, pilots trained on P-38s, and, later, Santa Maria's Army Air Field was home to the first U.S. Army Air Force jet fighter squadron.

Today, the airport features regular fly-ins by aircraft of historic or military interest, private aircraft and commercial flights. It is also home to the Santa Maria Museum of Flight, appropriately housed in a hangar. Fans of flight may enjoy listening to the regular take-offs and landings on the nearby runway while perusing World War II and modern aircraft and artifacts in the museum.

The museum is open Fridays through Sundays from 10 a.m. to 4 p.m. with group tours available by reservation.

NATURE

☞ Abel Maldonado Community Youth Center

600 S. McClelland St.

(805) 925-0951, ext. 252

www.ci.santa-maria.ca.us/3090.html

FREE

From Highway 101, take Main Street west, turn left onto Miller, right onto Cook, then left onto McClelland.

This midsize recreation center is designed to serve the youth of Santa Maria. Students in seventh through 12th grades are welcome to play indoor sports, arcade-style games, use a computer lab, fitness equipment, billiard tables and homework center after school hours. There also is a snack bar, and meeting rooms are available to organizations serving youth.

The center, free to area youth, is open from 2:30 p.m. to 8:30 p.m. Mondays through Thursdays, 2:30 to 10 p.m. Fridays and Saturdays, and 3:30 to 7 p.m. Sundays.

Adam Park

600 W. Enos St.

(805) 925-0951, ext. 260

www.ci.santa-maria.ca.us/3083.html

FREE

From Highway 101, take Stowell Road west; turn left onto South Depot and left onto Enos Street.

This large, city park straddling Enos Street includes a basketball court, play structures, a sand volleyball court, baseball diamonds, restrooms, lighted tennis courts and 10 acres of soccer fields. The Minami Community Center, home to several city recreation programs, also is located here.

Alice Trefts Park

510 E. Park Ave.

(805) 925-0951, ext. 260

www.ci.santa-maria.ca.us/3083.html

FREE

From southbound Highway 101, take Main Street west; turn left onto College Avenue, right onto Park Avenue then left onto Oakwood Drive. From northbound 101, take Stowell Road west, turn right onto College Avenue, left onto Park Avenue, then left onto Oakwood Drive. The park is accessed via the parking lot to the right of Elwin Mussell Center.

This 5-acre park is dedicated to providing residents their own gardening plots. Plots are available by reservation for $27 per year on a first-come, first-served basis. Portable toilets are on site, or head into the neighboring Elwin Mussell Senior Center for the flush variety during open hours.

Armstrong Community Park

1000 E. Chapel St.

(805) 925-0951, ext. 260

www.ci.santa-maria.ca.us/3083.html

FREE

From Highway 101, take Main Street west; turn right onto Concepcion Avenue, then right onto Chapel.

This 2-acre park next door to Fesler Junior High School includes shade trees, lots of lawn, play structures, swings, picnic areas and restrooms.

Atkinson Community Center & Park

1000 N. Railroad Ave.

(805) 925-0951, ext. 260

www.ci.santa-maria.ca.us/3083.html

FREE

From northbound Highway 101, take Main Street west, then turn right onto

Railroad Avenue. From southbound 101, take Donovan Road west, then turn left onto Railroad.

This very popular, 6.5-acre park includes a community hall, play structures, basketball courts, multipurpose fields, shade trees and a restroom. Four tennis courts also are available on a first-come, first-served basis.

Bike Paths & Multipurpose Trails

Throughout Santa Maria

(805) 925.0951, ext. 260

www.ci.santa-maria.ca.us

FREE

In 2009, the city completed its Bikeway Master Plan, a comprehensive study of existing bike paths in the valley and $62 million proposal for 139 additional miles of bike paths. Nearly 60 miles of the proposed paths would provide cyclists routes entirely separate from vehicle traffic.

At publication time, several paths were already in place. The Santa Maria River Levee Multipurpose Trail is a wide, largely unpaved segment that runs more than 4 miles from the 2000 block of east end of Main Street to the west end of Atlantic Place. The trail is easily accessed via paved entryways at: Bull Canyon Road; Seaward Drive and Magellan Drive; Seaward Drive at Carlotti Drive; Seaward Drive at Mariah Drive; North Broadway east of Highway 101; the north end of Preisker Lane; and along Atlantic Place at North Railroad Avenue, Bicknell Avenue and Blosser Road. A somewhat parallel path runs below the levee intermittently, with long segments completed along Atlantic Place, Poplar Place and Seaward Drive. This paved portion includes landscaping, benches and some shaded areas.

Another popular off-street segment begins at Foster Road west of Broadway. The paved path undulates slightly, but is largely flat. It crosses Skyway Drive at Airpark Drive, then curves along the west side of Waller Park (p. 187) along the abandoned railroad bed. Eventually, this path is slated to extend some 4 miles north to the levee trail.

And on the southwestern edge of town, a newly developed network of off-street paths connect Maramonte Park (p. 180) and Fletcher Park (p. 177).

In nearby Orcutt, new housing developments were sparking new parks and paths. The Orcutt Creek Multipurpose Trail stretched from Bradley Road to Olive Hill Road, but will eventually link to paths off Stillwell Road near Cobblestone Creek Open Space (p. 177). Another planned segment in Old Orcutt would link California Avenue with Foxenwood Lane. For more information on Orcutt paths, contact County Parks (805-934-6123) or Traffic Solutions (trafficsolutions.info or (805) 963-SAVE).

Buena Vista Park

800 S. Pine St.

(805) 925-0951, ext. 260

www.ci.santa-maria.ca.us/3083.html

FREE

From southbound Highway 101, take Main Street west; turn left onto Broadway then right onto Park Avenue. From northbound 101, take Stowell Road west; turn right onto Broadway, then left onto Park Avenue.

This heavily used, 4-acre neighborhood park includes play structures, a barbecue pit and group picnic area, picnic tables, basketball courts, horseshoe pits and lots of lawn. The park is particularly busy during the neighboring high school's lunch periods, after school and on weekends.

Cobblestone Open Space

Stillwell Road, Orcutt

(805) 934-6123

countyofsb.org/parks

FREE

From Highway 101, take Clark Avenue west, then turn left onto Stillwell Road.

This 2-acre park offers lots of room to run, on grass or on a trail system that could someday tie in with the Orcutt Multipurpose Trail. The park also includes a play structure for the smaller set, swings, benches and a paved path. No restrooms.

Domino Open Space

Domino Avenue at Via Fedora, Orcutt

(805) 934-6123

countyofsb.org/parks

FREE

From Highway 101, take Clark Avenue west; turn left onto Bradley Road, right onto Rice Ranch Road, then right onto Domino Avenue.

This secret park is a neighborhood gem offering expansive lawn, landscaped beds, concrete paths, play structures and swings. No restrooms.

Edwards Community Center & Sierra Vista Park

809 Panther Drive

(805) 925-0951, ext. 260

www.ci.santa-maria.ca.us/3083.html

FREE

From Highway 101, turn east onto Donovan Road/Panther Drive.

Among the city's newer public facilities, this center includes a multipurpose room, kitchen, gymnasium with volleyball and basketball courts, and bleacher seating. The center, located in Sierra Vista Park (p. 185), is used extensively by the city's recreation programs.

Fletcher Park

2200 S. College Drive

(805) 925-0951, ext. 260

www.ci.santa-maria.ca.us/3083.html

FREE

From Highway 101, take Betteravia Road west, then left onto College Drive.

At nearly 3 acres, this newer park surrounded by some of the city's busiest streets includes a nice playground, covered picnic area and raised barbecue pit. A skate park has been added just north of the drainage ditch, and a relatively flat, paved path curves along four residential blocks before crossing busy Bradley Drive to continue toward the freeway and south into Orcutt.

Parking here is a challenge unless the parking lot for the soccer fields across the street is open. Consider parking at the massive asphalt lot in the shopping center off Bradley Road, then walking, running or cycling the path from Bradley Road at Crossroad Lane. No restrooms.

Grogan Park

1155 W. Rancho Verde

(805) 925-0951, ext. 260

www.ci.santa-maria.ca.us/3083.html

FREE

From Highway 101, take the North Broadway exit; turn left onto Taylor Avenue, right onto Blosser Road, then right onto Rancho Verde.

This quiet park on the western edge of town includes 6 acres of recreational opportunities, including play structures, picnic areas, open lawn area, public restrooms and a community hall that is available for rent.

Hagerman Sports Complex

3300 Skyway Drive

(805) 925-0951, ext. 260

www.ci.santa-maria.ca.us/3083.html

FREE

From Highway 101, take Santa Maria Way north, turn left onto Bradley Road, then immediately turn right onto Lakeview Road, which becomes Skyway Drive.

The city's largest competitive sports complex includes four multipurpose fields for soccer, softball or baseball. The facility also includes bleachers, snack bar and playground. It is home to the city's major softball tournaments but not generally available for pickup games. Restrooms available.

Jim May Park

809 Stanford Drive

(805) 925-0951, ext. 260

www.ci.santa-maria.ca.us/3083.html

FREE

From Highway 101, take Donovan Road east, turn left onto Carlotti Drive, then left onto Stanford Drive.

Though this 22-acre park is adjacent to the freeway, it is remarkably welcoming with its 11-acre lake surrounded by a paved walking path. Along the south end of the lake is lawn for passive play, play structures, a covered picnic area and restrooms.

Joe White Park
500 S. Palisade Drive
(805) 925-0951, ext. 260
www.ci.santa-maria.ca.us/3083.html
FREE

From Highway 101, take Main Street east, turn right onto South Palisade and follow the loop around to the park.

This quiet, 2-acre neighborhood park includes two basketball keys with nets, a play structure, picnic tables, shade trees, paved paths and plenty of lawn for passive play. No restrooms.

☞ Las Flores Ranch Park
Dominion Road
(805) 928-7816
www.ci.santa-maria.ca.us/3083.html
$

From Highway 101, take Clark Avenue east, then turn right onto Dominion Road.

This brand spankin' new outdoor recreation area still was under development at publication time. The 1,774-acre park is the first of its kind in the Santa Maria area, a byproduct of the community's need for a new landfill, which will eventually be located nearby. The park includes about 8 miles of aging ranch roads now dedicated to horseback riding, mountain biking and hiking. None were particularly challenging and all were wide enough to accommodate group walks or rides. New trails were in the planning stage and may include single-track options for more rugged individualists.

Most of the routes are out-and-back adventures, but there are loop potentials. Consider this easy loop: Beginning at the Dominion Road entrance, follow the main trail south, veer left at the T intersection, then veer right onto East La Cuesta Trail. Loop through the oaks on the Acorn Trail, check out the Big Oak Trail spur and amphitheater, then head north on the Valley View Trail. Cut back to the parking lot on the Manzanita Trail to complete the 2-mile loop or continue to Lower Trail which also leads back to the entrance road for a total of 2.4 miles.

Check the current calendar for opening hours and restrictions. At publication time the park was only open to the general public Fridays through Sundays. On Thursdays access was limited to equestrian users.

The park can also be accessed from Highway 101 at exit 161 where horse corrals are provided for equestrian visitors.

All visitors are required to register at the visitors center upon entry and exit. The first visit entails viewing a short video about potential dangers on the property while filling out liability waivers and other simple forms in exchange for a park permit. On subsequent visits, just drop the permit at the desk on the way in, and pick it up on the way out.

Lee West Open Space

700 block Glen Cairon Drive, Orcutt

(805) 934-6123

countyofsb.org/parks

FREE

From Highway 101, take Clark Avenue west; turn right onto Cherry Avenue, then right onto Glen Cairon Drive.

This hidden park bounded by residences provides a large lawn area for pickup games of soccer or tag. There's a playground and backstop, too. No restrooms, and parking is limited.

☞ Maramonte Park

620 E. Sunrise Drive

(805) 925-0951, ext. 260

www.ci.santa-maria.ca.us/3083.html

FREE

From Highway 101, take Betteravia Road west; turn left onto College Drive, then right onto Sunrise Drive.

This 9-acre park, known to many locals as Sunrise Park, includes two tennis courts, a basketball half-court, play structure, baseball fields, horseshoe pits, covered picnic area, open lawns and restrooms. The park also is home to Maramonte Community Center, a small, clean, brightly lit room available for rent.

North Preisker Ranch Park

801 W. Boxcar Place

(805) 925-0951, ext. 260

www.ci.santa-maria.ca.us/3083.html

FREE

From Highway 101, take the Broadway exit; turn right onto Preisker Lane, left onto Hidden Pines, left onto Railroad Avenue, then right onto Boxcar Place.

Santa Maria added several new parks at the turn of the 21st Century, including this one adjacent to Tommy Kunst Junior High School. Tennis courts and basketball courts are available to the public whenever the school isn't using them. The remainder of the park includes a paved path that meanders around the lawn area, picnic tables, restrooms and a railroad-themed play structure that is placed unfortunately close to the street.

Oakley Park
1200 N. Western Ave.
(805) 925-0951, ext. 260
www.ci.santa-maria.ca.us/3083.html
FREE
From Highway 101, take Donovan Road west, then turn left onto Western Avenue.
This palm-tree-lined park adjacent to Oakley School includes a Little League baseball field, play structure, picnic areas and a lot of open lawn. Parking is all on street. No restrooms.

Orcutt Aquacenter
Hummel Drive off Union Valley Parkway, Orcutt
(805) 714-9292
www.orcuttaquacentersmv.org
$
From Highway 101, take Santa Maria Way west, turn left onto Bradley Road, then right onto Union Valley Parkway.
For decades, community organizers have dreamed of a pool for Orcutt. In 1998, the donation of 14.5 acres to the cause brought that dream closer into focus, and groundbreaking was slated for 2009.

When completed, the plan calls for an indoor recreation pool, outdoor Olympic-sized competition pool, physical therapy pool, water slides, bleachers, picnic and barbecue areas, and a 16,500-square-foot community building. Call ahead or watch the website for the latest developments, hours and programs.

☞ Orcutt Community Park
Sage Crest Drive, Orcutt
(805) 934-6123
countyofsb.org/parks
FREE
From Highway 101, take Clark Avenue west. Turn left onto Bradley Road, right onto Rice Ranch Road, then left onto Sage Crest Drive.
This 27-acre park with a view to the Orcutt Hills features plenty of room to run, soccer fields, baseball diamonds, play structures, covered barbecue and picnic areas, a dedicated dog park, hiking trails and restrooms.

A bridge crosses a seasonal waterway that divides the play structure and restrooms from the sports facilities, so parents with children of divergent interests may have a challenge keeping an eye on both camps. Overcoming the challenge is as simple as traveling in packs, with parents dividing the duties as kids scatter.

Paul Nelson Aquatics Center

516 S. McClelland St.

(805) 925-0951 ext. 252

cityofsantamaria.com

$

From Highway 101, take Main Street west, turn left onto Miller, right onto Cook, then left onto McClelland.

This year-round facility includes two pools. The Olympic-size pool offers lap swimming throughout the year, and recreational swimming during school holidays and other special days. (See the recreation schedule for the latest.) A second, warmer pool includes four 25-yard-long lanes with a side entry that resembles beach access. Children easily can walk the gentle slope into this pool's dedicated play area, which features a turtle slide, frog slide and a water mushroom.

The pool is home to the city's own swimming lesson program, as well as the Santa Maria Swim Club, which offers year-round, coached swimming for all abilities and ages.

The pool is located immediately adjacent to the Abel Maldonado Community Youth Center (p. 174), which provides showers, locker rooms and restrooms, among other facilities.

Perlman Park

100 N. Broadway

(805) 925-0951, ext. 260

www.ci.santa-maria.ca.us/3083.html

FREE

From Highway 101, take Main Street west; turn right onto McClelland, then left at the end of the building into the park's parking lot.

Were it not for the heavy traffic on Broadway and Main Street which border the park, this 3.5-acre botanical pleasure would be a sanctuary. The park includes a gazebo and waterfall, a rose garden and a native plant garden, as well as play structures and a restroom.

Pioneer Park

1000 W. Foster Road

(805) 925-0951, ext. 260

www.ci.santa-maria.ca.us/3083.html

FREE

From Highway 101, take Santa Maria Way north; turn left onto Bradley Road, then right onto Foster Road.

This quiet park commemorating the city's founding families is a popular place for large group barbecues and family picnics alike. The 15-acre park, lined with eucalyptus trees, includes baseball diamonds, horseshoe pits, play structures, restrooms, unimproved areas for nature exploration and a group barbecue area for up to 900 guests.

Pioneer Valley High School Pool
675 Panther Drive
(805) 925-0951
$

From Highway 101, turn east onto Donovan Road, which becomes Panther Drive.

After this heated, outdoor, lap pool was opened for student use in 2008, it was made available to the public through a cooperative agreement with the city. Hours are limited and vary by season. Call the city for current offerings.

Preisker Park
2301 Preisker Lane & 330 Hidden Pines Way
(805) 925-0951, ext. 260
www.ci.santa-maria.ca.us/3083.html
FREE

From Highway 101, take the Broadway exit, then turn right onto Preisker Lane.

We've spent a lot of time pretending, daydreaming and making up our own fairytales on the decks of the concrete ship at anchor in the duck pond. But this 40-acre park with ample parking also includes loads of room to run, play pickup games of baseball, soccer, volleyball or horseshoes, picnic, roam or stretch out for a nap. There also are barbecue areas, paved walkways, a gazebo, shade trees and restrooms. The city holds special events here throughout the year, including various festivals, summer musical performances, cook-offs, car shows and more.

Rice Park
700 E. Sunset Ave.
(805) 925-0951, ext. 260
www.ci.santa-maria.ca.us/3083.html
FREE

From Highway 101, take Donovan Road west; turn left onto College Drive, then right onto Sunset Avenue.

This 3-acre park adjacent to Rice School is unique among Santa Maria's parks because it offers picnic space in a grove of redwood trees. The park offers lots of room to run, a baseball field, picnic areas and play structures. Restrooms available.

Rice Ranch Open Space
5400 block Orcutt Road, Orcutt
(805) 934-6123
countyofsb.org/parks
FREE

From Highway 101, take Clark Avenue west, then turn south onto Orcutt Road.

This neighborhood park is basically a large, open lawn area that spans the depth of one city block. A few trees provide shade around the outskirts, and a paved ramp provides access up the short hill from Orcutt Road. Portable restrooms available.

Rod Rodenberger Park
2700 Santa Barbara St.
(805) 925-0951, ext. 260
www.ci.santa-maria.ca.us/3083.html
FREE

From southbound Highway 101, take Betteravia Road west; turn left onto College Avenue, right onto Sunrise, then right onto Santa Barbara Street. From the south, take Highway 101 north to Santa Maria Way, turn left at the end of the ramp, turn right onto College Avenue, left onto Sunrise, then right onto Santa Barbara Street.

This 5-acre park is one of a complex of adjacent parks that provide expansive recreational opportunities at the southern edge of town. Rodenberger Park offers play structures, softball fields, a fitness trail, paved walkways and a covered picnic area. For restrooms, walk south across Sunrise Drive to Maramonte Park (p. 180).

Rotary Centennial Park
2625 S. College Drive
(805) 925-0951, ext. 260
www.ci.santa-maria.ca.us/3083.html
FREE

From Highway 101, take Betteravia Road west, then turn left onto College Avenue.

When area Rotary Clubs joined forces to commemorate the city's 100th birthday, the result was this medium-sized park, which includes a basketball court, play structures, lawns for free play, a gazebo, a fitness trail, picnic tables, play structures and restrooms. The park also houses Robin Ventura Field and a Little League field.

Russell Park
1000 W. Church St.
(805) 925-0951, ext. 260
www.ci.santa-maria.ca.us/3083.html
FREE

From Highway 101, take Main Street west, turn left onto Western, then turn right onto Church Street.

This tree-shaded neighborhood park offers a play structure, picnic benches and barbecue pits on 1.5 acres of lawns. Mature trees provide ample shade. Portable restrooms are available.

Santa Maria Valley Sustainable Garden
624 W. Foster Road
(805) 568-3546
www.ci.santa-maria.ca.us/3115-Landscaping.html
FREE
From Highway 101, take Santa Maria Way north; turn left onto Bradley Road, then right onto Foster Road.

This landscaped park is designed to teach locals how to garden with natives and other plants that tolerate Santa Maria Valley's dry conditions. Take a self-guided tour of paved walkways and unpaved paths. Check out paving options; analyze the plants, which are labeled for identification. The garden also offers some alternatives to lawn, information about composting and is occasionally home to sustainable gardening education programs.

Sierra Vista Park
809 Panther Drive
(805) 925-0951, ext. 260
www.ci.santa-maria.ca.us/3083.html
FREE
From Highway 101, turn east onto Donovan Road, which becomes Panther Drive.

This park adjacent to Edwards Community Center (p. 177) offers 5 acres of running room, including a Babe Ruth baseball field complete with bleachers. Restrooms are available in the community center.

Simas Park
516 S. McClelland St.
(805) 925-0951, ext. 260
www.ci.santa-maria.ca.us/3083.html
FREE
From Highway 101, take Main Street west, turn left onto Miller Avenue, right onto Cook Street, then left onto McClelland Street.

Though primarily identified with Elks Field, the baseball park that served as the long-time home of the Santa Maria Indians semi-professional baseball team, this park also includes the South Side Little League Field, Abel Maldonado Community Youth Center (p. 174), and Paul Nelson Aquatic Center.

The park is also home to Joslyn Bowling Green, home turf for the Santa Maria Lawn Bowling Club (349-9838). While typically depicted as a sport for the elderly, bowls is actually an international competitive sport that dates back more than seven centuries. The local club welcomes players of all ages and abilities. Club members provide free lessons and tips for beginners interested in trying out the sport. Call ahead for an appointment. The green is open from 9 a.m. to noon Tuesdays through Saturdays, but members can play any daylight hour. Wear flat-soled shoes, and bring a sense of humor.

This park is ideally located for a car-free day out. It is across the street from the city's new library, half a block south of the city's central bus terminal and adjacent to the Natural History Museum of Santa Maria (p. 172). The Santa Maria Valley Discovery Museum (p. 192) is one block south.

Stanley Park
2600 La Costa Drive
(805) 925-0951, ext. 260
www.ci.santa-maria.ca.us/3083.html
FREE

From northbound Highway 101, take the Santa Maria Way exit, turn left at the end of the ramp onto Santa Maria Way, turn right onto Broadway, left onto McCoy Lane, then left onto La Costa Drive. From southbound 101, take Betteravia Road west, turn left onto Broadway, right onto McCoy Lane, then left onto La Costa Drive.

This quiet, 2-acre, neighborhood park offers a play structure, short dirt path, trees and a large, open lawn area. No restrooms.

Stonebrook Open Space
4400 block Stonebrook Road, Orcutt
(805) 934-6123
countyofsb.org/parks
FREE

From Highway 101, take Clark Avenue west, turn right onto California Boulevard, right onto Old Mill Lane, then left onto Stonebrook Road. The park also is accessible from California Boulevard.

There is plenty of room to run on this large patch of lawn with shade trees. The neighborhood park also includes a baseball backstop and a grass volleyball court (bring your own net). There are no restrooms.

Tunnell Park
1100 N. Palisade Drive
(805) 925-0951, ext. 260
www.ci.santa-maria.ca.us/3083.html
FREE

From Highway 101, take Donovan Road east; turn right onto Bay Avenue, left onto Dena Way, then right onto North Palisade Drive.

More than 5 acres of lawn adjacent to Tunnell School are available for public recreational use. The ample lawn and redwood trees house picnic areas and a play structure.

Veterans' Memorial Park
313 W. Tunnell St.
(805) 925-0951, ext. 260
www.ci.santa-maria.ca.us/3083.html
FREE

From the north, take Highway 101 south to Broadway. Continue south on Broadway, then turn left onto Tunnell Street. From the south, take 101 north to Main Street west, then turn right onto Pine Street.

Ample shade below a variety of mature trees is a highlight in this 2-acre park across the street from Veterans' Memorial Community Center. The park includes a play structure, and restrooms are across the street at the community center.

Veteran's Memorial Community Center
313 W. Tunnell Street
(805) 925-0951, ext. 260
www.ci.santa-maria.ca.us/3083.html
FREE

From the north, take Highway 101 south to Broadway. Continue south on Broadway, then turn left onto Tunnell Street. From the south, take 101 north to Main Street west, then turn right onto Pine Street.

While this community center is typically rented for special events, recreation programs and a variety of classes, it remains a worthwhile stop in your tour of Santa Maria. The Spanish-style structure built in 1934 features a peaceful courtyard with a fountain that small children are bound to enjoy. It also provides the closest public restroom to Veterans' Memorial Park (p. 187) across the street.

☞ Waller Park
3070 Orcutt Road
(805) 934-6211
sbparks.com
FREE

Waller Park's ducks are particularly responsive to feeding on cold winter days when fewer visitors venture here.

From Highway 101, take Betteravia Road west. Turn left onto Broadway, right onto Waller Lane and immediately left onto the Frontage Road.

For generations, this 153-acre park has hosted sporting events and wedding receptions, group barbecues and romantic picnics. Thousands of children have taken their first pony ride here, fed the ducks, even raced bikes on a track long since replaced by soccer fields and group barbecue areas.

Kids still enjoy pony rides during summer months, as well as duck and goose feeding year round. The park also boasts four playgrounds of varying difficulty, barbecue and picnic areas, disc golf course, soccer fields, a gazebo and three manmade ponds, two of which are connected by a manmade stream. Meander to the back of the park for the Winners of Off-leash Freedom-Political Action Committee (WOOF-PAC) Dog Park, complete with coin-operated, self-service dog bath.

The park is open daily from 8 a.m. to sunset, and includes several restrooms.

Westgate Ranch Park

1800 S. Westgate Road
(805) 925-0951, ext. 260
www.ci.santa-maria.ca.us/3083.html
FREE

From Highway 101, take Betteravia Road west, then turn right onto Westgate Road.

This quiet, 7-acre park adjacent to Liberty School includes nice play structures, barbecue pits and plenty of room to run on manicured lawns. A paved pathway provides a nice, relatively flat loop for the littlest cyclists. Portable restrooms are available.

OTHER ADVENTURES

Boomers!

2250 North Preisker Lane

(805) 928-4942

boomersparks.com

$

From Highway 101, take North Broadway south, then turn right onto Preisker Lane.

This commercial recreation center offers two miniature golf courses, two go-cart tracks, 10 batting cages, a bumper boat pool, a climbing wall and countless arcade games. The batting cages can be reserved Mondays through Fridays.

Central Coast Sports Arena

Santa Maria Fairpark

937 S. Thornburg, Gate 7

(805) 739-0920

www.centralcoastsportsarena.com

$

From Highway 101, take Stowell Road west, turn right onto Thornburg.

The Central Coast's only indoor roller skating rink offers league roller hockey play, as well as public open skate hours complete with skate rentals (sizes youth-10 and larger). Open skate includes adult-supervised teen night each Friday, public skate Saturday nights, family night Sunday evenings, and pickup hockey Sunday nights. Call or check the Web site for current hours, game schedules and hockey sign-up information.

Motionz
218 Town Center East
(805) 922-6922
Motionz.net
$$

From Highway 101, take Main Street west.

It feels a little strange to play a game of tag without running, but such is the rule at safety-conscious Motionz laser tag center. The 7,000-square-foot play area includes ramps, platforms, catwalks, walls and other obstacles in a darkened room, where music booms. An observation deck provides the peanut gallery with a bird's-eye view. The arena can accommodate up to 30 players per game and is available for walk-in play as well as group reservation.

The Pitchout
2305 A St.
(805) 739-9090
$

From Highway 101, take Betteravia Road west, then turn left onto A Street.

This indoor batting range provides baseball and softball players of all abilities the opportunity to practice hitting year round. Cages include three pitching speeds. Though The Pitchout is open Tuesdays through Sundays, the facility is also available to groups by reservation Mondays.

☞ Rancho Bowl
128 E. Donovan Road
(805) 925-2405
$

From Highway 101, take Donovan Road west.

Rancho Bowl hasn't survived merely because it's the only bowling alley in town. The business carries on because it continues to incorporate new and interesting attractions, programs and special events for all ages. In addition to the old standby league bowling, Rancho Bowl offers the incredibly popular all-you-can-bowl night, particularly popular with families and teens. Arrive early if you want to get a lane. Call for the current schedule of programs and events.

The facility includes 32 bowling lanes, with bumpers available on all lanes for no additional fee. There also is a video arcade, coffee shop, bar, pool tables and bowling accessory shop.

Rancho Maria Golf Course
1950 State Highway 1
(805) 937-2019
www.ranchomariagolf.com

$$-$$$

From the north, take Highway 101 south, turn west on Stowell Road, then left onto Highway 1. From the south, take Clark Avenue west, then turn right onto Highway 1.

The public is welcome to golf just nine holes or go all-in for an 18-hole round at this course west of town. The par 72 course offers tree-lined fairways and the additional challenge of the valley's afternoon winds. The facility also includes a practice bunker, chipping and pitching greens, a driving range, golf instruction and social clubs.

Range Master of Santa Maria

2004 Preisker Lane, Unit I

(805) 346-2501

www.rangemasterofsantamaria.com

$$

From Highway 101, take Broadway, then turn left onto Preisker Lane.

This indoor pistol range offers target practice, competitions and firearm training courses. Open Tuesdays through Sundays.

Santa Maria BMX

Elks-Unocal Events Center

4040 Highway 101

(805) 868-4762

www.santamariabmx.com

$

From southbound Highway 101, take the Santa Maria Way exit; turn right at the end of the ramp, then left and immediately right onto the frontage road. From northbound 101, take Santa Maria Way, turn right, then right again onto the frontage road.

After a two-decade absence, bicycle motocross found its way back to Santa Maria in 2008 with the creation of this track. Enthusiastic supporters offer local races almost every Saturday, and public practices are held on Tuesday and Thursday evenings from 5 p.m. to 7 p.m.

Riders of all abilities are welcome. To hit the track, they must wear helmets with chin straps, long-sleeved shirts, long pants or shorts with knee and shin protection, and clipless shoes. They should also consider injury prevention measures, including pads on the bicycle's top tube, handlebar and handlebar stem. Just about any bike in good condition is welcome on practice nights, but kickstands, reflectors and chain guards must be removed prior to riding on the track.

Santa Maria Gun Club

3150 Telephone Road

(805) 925-6673

www.santamariagunclub.org

$

From the south, take Highway 101 north to Clark Avenue east, then turn north again onto Telephone Road. From the north, take 101 south, Betteravia Avenue east, then turn south onto Telephone Road.

This 42-acre facility associated with the Amateur Trapshooting Association offers a dedicated setting for target and trap shooting, as well as an indoor pistol range. The club offers nine traps, including three lighted traps and two wobble traps that provide a greater challenge through more erratic flight of the clay targets. There also is an archery course.

The club maintains a busy calendar, including public shooting hours, competitions and firearm safety courses. Check the Web site or call for current hours and special events.

☞ Santa Maria Valley Discovery Museum

705 S. McClelland Ave.

(805) 928-8414

www.smvdiscoverymuseum.org

$$

From Highway 101, take Main Street west, turn left onto Miller, right onto Cook, then left onto McClelland

My children were pretty disappointed when Santa Barbara County's only children's museum pulled up stakes to move across town. But since establishing itself in its new home, the museum has done nothing but grow better with age. Exhibit offerings continue to evolve, and the museum's activity calendar continues to expand.

The museum is one of only a few locations in the Santa Maria Valley that provides space for active play on rainy days. On any given day, visitors can learn about agriculture, check out creepy crawly insects and cool aquariums, make crafting messes in someone else's crafting space and literally climb the walls. The museum is open Mondays through Saturdays from 10 a.m. to 5 p.m. and Thursdays until 7 p.m.

Sunset Ridge Golf Center

1424 Fairway Drive

(805) 347-1070

$

From Highway 101, take Betteravia Road west; turn left onto Skyway Drive, then right onto Fairway Avenue.

This easygoing, nine-hole golf course is a local favorite, open to the general public seven days a week. While other courses in the region may specialize in championship challenges, this course is a hidden gem for beginning golfers, as well as experienced golfers out for an easy swing around the course. The course offers First Tee, a youth golf development program for players 16 and younger. Call for the latest information.

Chapter 11

Guadalupe

At first glance, Guadalupe looks like something out of an Old West movie — a border town where you might find rowdy cowboys and outlaws eyeing each other tensely over a card table. But get out of the car and give it some time. The community offers great food, friendly people and a comfortable atmosphere: kids playing outside, teens walking from pizza joint to park to home again, adults strolling with toddlers to and from the grocery store, seniors taking an evening jaunt amidst it all.

In addition to being a true California farm town, Guadalupe also is the entrance to the Guadalupe-Nipomo Dunes Preserve and Guadalupe-Nipomo Dunes National Wildlife Refuge. The community is rallying behind efforts to develop museums and cultural centers, and annual events bring out the local crowd as well as visitors interested in enjoying the atmosphere only a small town can provide.

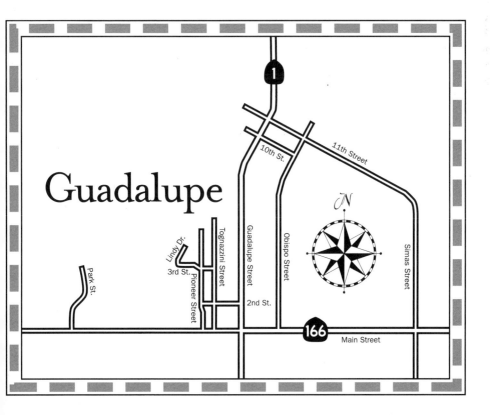

ARTS

Guadalupe Cultural Arts & Education Center

1065 Guadalupe St.

(805) 34302939

www.guadalupecultural-arts.com

FREE

From Highway 101, take Santa Maria's Main Street exit and drive west 9 miles, then turn right onto Guadalupe Street.

This home, originally built in 1909, was entirely revamped by Margie and Joe Talaugon to house a community center focused on cultural history and art. Today, their daughter, Karen, runs the place, which includes cultural relics, regularly changed works of artists of local interest, and the Guadalupe Sports Hall of Fame. The center is open Tuesdays through Saturdays from 10 a.m. to 4 p.m., and by appointment for group tours and special events.

LETTERS

Guadalupe Library

4719 W. Main St., Suite D

(805) 343-1405

www.ci.santa-maria.ca.us/3092.shtml

FREE

From Highway 101, take Santa Maria's Main Street exit and head west.

This branch of the Santa Maria Library system is open Mondays through Thursdays and Saturday afternoons. Story time has been offered occasionally, but call ahead or stop in to check on latest offerings.

HISTORY

Rancho Guadalupe Historical Museum

Veteran's Memorial Building

1005 Guadalupe St./Highway 1

(805) 343-5901

www.guadalupemuseum.org

FREE

From Highway 101, take Santa Maria's Main Street west, then turn right onto Highway 1.

This small venue hosts artifacts representing Guadalupe area history. It is also home to the Guadalupe Historical Society (p. 194).

NATURE

Central Park

9th Street at Pacheco

(805) 343-1340

ci.guadalupe.ca.us

FREE

From Highway 101, take Santa Maria's Main Street exit, head west, and turn right onto Highway 1/Guadalupe Street, then right onto 9th Street.

A paved path gently curves through more than an acre, which includes a large lawn area and the city's towering water tank. No restrooms.

Dunes Center

1055 Guadalupe St.

(805) 343-2455

www.dunescenter.org

FREE

From Highway 1, take Santa Maria's Main Street exit and head west. Turn right onto Highway 1/Guadalupe Street.

A Craftsman-style home built in 1910 now serves as the information hub for the Guadalupe-Nipomo Dunes complex that includes the Guadalupe-Nipomo Dunes Preserve and National Wildlife Refuge (p. 195), and Oso Flaco Lake (p. 224).

The center offers various hands-on activities, interactive displays and a short film featuring a history of the Dunite community that made its home in the beach's farther reaches during the 1920s and '30s. There are also classes, lectures and regularly scheduled docent-led walks. The center is open from 10 a.m. to 4 p.m. Thursdays through Sundays.

☞ Guadalupe-Nipomo Dunes Preserve & National Wildlife Refuge

West Main St.

(805) 343-2455

www.dunescenter.org/dunes.htm

FREE

From Highway 101, take Santa Maria's Main Street exit, cross Highway 1 and continue to the road's end at the beach.

From time immemorial, visitors have explored this coastline and dunes habitat on foot, on horseback, in carriages and buggies and, until 1982, in a variety of motorized vehicles from the earliest automobiles to all-terrain vehicles of the late 20th Century.

Today, motorized vehicles are banned from some 22,000 acres of preserved sprawling mountains of sand and 8 miles of lonesome, white-sand beach. Instead, the dunes complex, which envelopes the preserve and 2,553-acre Guadalupe-Nipomo Dunes National Wildlife Refuge, is accessible only on foot. Wheelchair access is limited to the parking lot, which also includes a restroom, picnic tables and an information kiosk.

The beach here is often windy and the surf is heavy and very dangerous for swimmers and surfers. During periods of heavy runoff, check water quality first at www.sbcphd.org/ehs/oceanmn.htm. No camping, off-highway vehicles,

The long stretch of uninterrupted sand at Guadalupe Beach beckons visitors interested in long walks along the crashing surf. Dangerous currents here, however, are deadly reminders of nature's power. Even wading is not advised, particularly for children.

fires, horses or sand surfing — think snowboarding on sand — are allowed. Between March 1 and September 1 each year, dogs are banned from the beach in an effort to protect nests of the endangered California least tern and Western snowy plover — among the 200 species of migrant and resident birds in the preserve.

Even with so many limitations, there still is plenty to do at the Guadalupe Dunes. Hiking along the beach and through the dunes is allowed throughout the year, though some areas are fenced off during nesting seasons. Surf fishing and sandcastle building are certainly high on the list here, and hard-core surfers traveling in protective packs brave the waters.

For the rugged sand walkers, head south along the beach and walk for about an hour to Devil's Landslide, a giant sand dune next to Mussell Rock at the end of the beach. Shimmy up the face of the dune for a fabulous view up and down the coast. Kayakers enjoy paddling Oso Flaco Lake (access from Oso Flaco Road off Highway 1 north of Guadalupe). Botanists tend toward Coreopsis Hill, while those seeking solitude and a very long hike continue south along Paradise Beach to Point Sal (p. 225).

The wind often comes up in the early afternoon, so plan ahead and bring plenty of water. Take a snack with you, but leave the big meals to the cooks at any number of scrumptious restaurants in Guadalupe.

The area also may be accessed via Oso Flaco Lake (p. 224).

Jack O'Connell Park
Calle Cesar Chavez at West Main Street
(805) 343-1340
ci.guadalupe.ca.us

FREE

From Highway 1, take Santa Maria's Main Street exit and head west.
A long line of trees on the western edge of this 14½-acre park is intended to protect its expansive lawn areas from frequent coastal winds. The park includes the community's football field, a soccer field, baseball diamond, horseshoe pits, a playground, barbecues and restrooms.

LeRoy Park
11th St. west of Highway 1
(805) 343-1340
ci.guadalupe.ca.us
FREE

From Highway 101, take Santa Maria's Main Street exit, head west, turn right onto Highway 1/Guadalupe Street, then right onto 11th Street.
Though only 4 acres of this park are developed at this point, the entire property includes 25 acres, much of which remains in its natural state. The existing developments include play equipment, lawn, handball courts and a group barbecue area. Though there are restrooms, we've never found them open, so plan accordingly. The Boys & Girls Club also shares the property.

Paco Pereyra Park
3rd Street at Lindy Drive
(805) 343-1340
ci.guadalupe.ca.us
FREE

From Highway 101, take Santa Maria's Main Street exit, head west, turn right onto Highway 1/Guadalupe Street, left onto 3rd Street.
This grassy park on less than an acre provides picnic tables and room for a pickup game of soccer or Frisbee. No restroom.

Pioneer Street Park
Pioneer Street at 2nd Street
(805) 343-1340
ci.guadalupe.ca.us
FREE

From Highway 101, take Santa Maria's Main Street exit, head west, turn right onto Highway 1/Guadalupe Street, left onto 2nd Street.
This triangular park behind a sheltered bus stop includes shade trees and a third of an acre of lawn. No restrooms.

Tognazzini Avenue Park
400 block Tognazzini Avenue
(805) 343-1340
ci.guadalupe.ca.us

FREE

From Highway 101, take Santa Maria's Main Street exit, head west, turn right onto Highway 1/Guadalupe Street, left onto 3rd Street, then right onto Tognazzini Avenue.

This neighborhood park on less than a quarter acre provides some open space, a playground and horseshoe pits. No restrooms.

OTHER ADVENTURES

Royal Theater

437 Guadalupe Ave./Highway 1

www.goldcoastsoundstudio.com/royal.html

From Highway 101, take Santa Maria's Main Street exit, head west, turn right onto Highway 1/Guadalupe Street.

This movie theater featured first-run movies, classics, Spanish-language films and live performances from 1939 until the mid 1980s. Since then, the venue has changed hands several times. Today it is home to random public events – film, live theater, public meetings, festivals, and other presentations. Watch the community's calendar of events for public events.

Chapter 12

Los Padres National Forest

This national forest comprises 1.75 million acres of coastal mountain ranges, meadows and coastline stretching 220 miles from Monterey to Ventura counties and inland to Kern County. The area includes single-track trails, fire roads, campgrounds, recreation areas, rivers, waterfalls and swimming holes, designated wilderness areas, an off-limits California condor sanctuary, as well as restrooms in high-use areas.

Two ranger districts help manage forestlands and wilderness areas in Santa Barbara County. The Santa Lucia Ranger District (1616 N. Carlotti Dr., Santa Maria, (805) 925-9538) also features a bookstore and demonstration center featuring the forest's predominant reptiles. Call ahead to arrange group tours during feeding time, or stop in during regular business hours for a simpler visit. The Santa Barbara Ranger District (3505 Paradise Road, off Highway 154, (805) 967-3481) offers a small, comfortable visitors center with knowledgeable staff and exhibits related to the forest.

These offices also sell the Adventure Pass, which is required in high-impact recreation areas, including Upper Santa Ynez River, Figueroa Mountain (p. 201) and the maintained campsites east of Santa Maria. To

Zaca Peak in the Figueroa Mountain Recreation Area is just one of several scenic lookouts in the Los Padres National Forestrecreation area.

be on the safe side, carry a day pass in your vehicle every time you venture into the forest, or pick up the annual pass to cover your bases. The passes only are required for visitors traveling by motorized vehicle. Hikers and cyclists are exempt. Depending on the site, there may be additional fees required for camping. Check the Forest Service Web site (www.fs.fed.us/r5/lospadres) for detailed information about the program.

The Los Padres forest maps beckon with names like Happy Hunting Ground and Hot Spring Canyon, but most of this public land is accessible only on foot, horseback or, if not a wilderness area, mountain bike, which limits access for families with very small children or adventurers who depend upon wheelchairs and related assistive devices. Many of the old roads are slowly degrading behind locked gates. Gates to the maintained roads are often locked when the weather turns wet, so check the rangers' offices for closures before heading out.

In addition to those listed here, consider these additional treks for big kids and grownups: Lizard's Mouth, Jameson Lake/Alder Creek and Sluice, Devil's Canyon from East Camino Cielo to Gibraltar Reservoir, Manzanita Schoolhouse, Indian Creek for swimming holes in the late spring, Tequepis Trail, Cold Springs East Fork Trails, Cottonwood Canyon and miles of trails and camping opportunities in the Dick Smith Wilderness. Details of these outings already have been published in some wonderful guides (see Resources, p. 234).

Rather than re-create the wheel, I've focused on some family-friendly favorites. Trailheads located away from established communities are listed here. Trailheads in proximity to cities and towns are listed in those chapters.

Ballinger Canyon Off-Highway Vehicle Area
Ballinger Canyon Road
East of Cuyama
(661) 245-3731
www.fs.fed.us/r5/lospadres/recreation/ohv/mprd
$

From Highway 101, take Highway 166 for 60 miles, turn right onto Highway 33 for four miles, then turn left onto Ballinger Canyon Road.

This 8,000-acre, designated off-highway vehicle use area in the Los Padres National Forest includes nearly 70 miles of trails and roads for motorists to explore. The park also has been used for equestrian endurance events. The rugged area includes everything from sandy washes to scenic ridgelines and tough weather to boot; temperatures here can drop below freezing on winter nights and summer highs are typically well into the 90s.

Ballinger offers one designated campground with picnic tables, fire rings, vault toilets and 20 camp sites. While there's nothing frilly about this campground, the surrounding area offers fantastic wildflower shows when early spring conditions are right, and room to roam year round.

Figueroa Mountain
Near Santa Ynez Valley

From Highway 154, turn north onto Figueroa Mountain Road.
This area is particularly popular for spring wildflowers and the
occasional winter snow. The white stuff doesn't last long when it does
land in Santa Barbara County, but this mountain can capture enough for
snowmen and simple snow play. The area also is available for camping
and miles of hiking and mountain biking trails. Primitive toilets are
offered at the campground and at Figueroa Mountain Lookout, which also
features expansive views across the Santa Ynez Mountains and beyond.

Though it is also a popular road bike ride, Figueroa Mountain Road is
fairly busy and too narrow to comfortably accommodate motorists and
inexperienced cyclists. Hard-core teen and older cyclists may want to
tackle this climb, but children should stick with the safer ascent by car.

This road is the gateway to several day use and campgrounds, as well
as a network of trails in the Los Padres National Forest (p. 199). Avid
hikers may want to consider taking the 3.7-mile round trip from Figueroa
Camp to Figueroa Peak Lookout (741-foot elevation gain). Take a rest at
Pino Alto day use area, where interpretive signs provide some local
education.

By car, you can continue along Figueroa Mountain Road as it passes
through Sunset Valley, past Davy Brown Campground and ultimately to
Nira Campground, a popular jumping-off point for hikers headed into
Dick Smith Wilderness. (No bicycles allowed in wilderness area.) Davey
Brown Campground, gateway to the Dick Smith Wilderness, is accessible

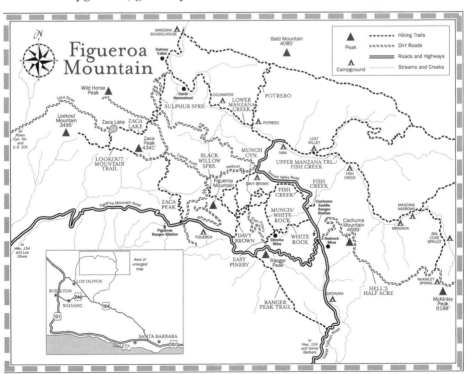

either via 4x4 down the Catway trail from Figueroa Mountain or via Sunset Valley Road from Santa Ynez Valley. By mountain bike, the Catway offers a splendid downhill ride to Davy Brown for those who can finagle a lift back up the road. Otherwise, plan for a long uphill return

Continue on to Zaca Peak for amazing wildflower shows, expansive views, fewer crowds and views to the only natural lake in Santa Barbara County – privately owned Zaca Lake.

As with all Los Padres Forest access, the Adventure Pass (p. 7) is required here. And when hiking in this area, keep in mind that it can be very hot and dry, and there are no services in many areas. Pack sufficient water and snacks for all explorers in your group, carry a first-aid kit, and consider bringing along the cell phone for emergency use, though cell reception is spotty in some areas here.

Gaviota Peak
Off Highway 101 north of Gaviota

From Highway 101, take the Highway 1/Lompoc exit just north of Gaviota, turn east toward the mountain, turn right at the T intersection onto the frontage road which dead-ends in the parking lot.

The hike to Gaviota Peak is a steep, hateful trek for anyone who doesn't run daily or hike very regularly. The steady uphill journey does, however, reward hikers with an absolutely spectacular 360-degree view.

Though your hike will take you into national parks land, this lot is part of Gaviota State Park and thereby subject to state parking fees. A parking fee drop box is clearly marked near the trailhead.

Head up the dirt road that rises just behind the mountain lion warning signs. If you need a flatland warm-up before climbing (or want to avoid the parking fee), park alongside the road about 200 yards from the lot and take the easy, flat walk in.

A well-marked intersection about half a mile up the hill guides hikers either straight up the well-maintained gravel single-track trail a third of a mile to the hot springs, or to the left 3 miles farther to the peak. If the lower portion of the hill has you beat, make it easy on yourself: Take to the hot springs and leave the peak to another day.

In spring months, the hike offers some spectacular pockets and fields of wildflowers, while winter hikers are greeted by a bitterly cold wind by coastal standards. During summer months, the marine layer can obscure the view, but make the trek on any other clear day and the view includes all the Channel Islands, the hills and dales of the Lompoc and Santa Ynez valleys, and points north.

Beware of poison oak, and if you stop by Gaviota Hot Springs (p. 218) on your way back, be aware that many regular visitors treat it as a clothing-optional retreat.

There are portable toilets in the parking lot. No additional facilities.

☞ Knapp's Castle/Snyder Trail
Paradise Road off Highway 154

From Highway 101, take Highway 154 toward Lake Cachuma, then turn onto Paradise Road. About ¼-mile west of the Los Prietos Ranger Station is a wide pullout on the south side of the road featuring an old oak tree with a giant burl. The trailhead sign is just beyond the fence.

This well-traveled, maintained, multiuse trail is a 4-mile hike up the mountain through oak forests, a tunnel of bay trees and along grassy hillsides to the ridge-top East Camino Cielo Road. There are no services, no water, no restrooms anywhere along the route, including the trailheads, so plan accordingly. The route is popular for hiking, mountain biking and equestrian use as well as with the local bear population, though the furry travelers seldom are seen by boisterous humans.

While accessible via a very short walk from East Camino Cielo, this climb to Knapp's Castle is well worth the time and effort. After following the well-worn path, climbers are rewarded with the view from Knapp's Castle, the burned-out shell of a hunting lodge built by George Owen Knapp. The Chicago industrialist built the stone lodge in the 1920s while living in the Santa Barbara area. The house burned in the 1940s, leaving behind only stone remnants. The great room's arched stone doorways and windows with fantastic views over Lake Cachuma and Santa Ynez Valley still stand as testament to the once—spectacular home.

Knapp's Castle is on private land, but there is no fence around the property and the sign at the upper gate reads, "Right to pass revocable." It provides a special spot for scenic picnics at the end of the uphill hike.

The trail offers no flatland warm-up. The upward slope begins just past the information and trailhead signs, where a service road provides the pathway. Beyond the water tanks, the road narrows to a single-track trail. Thanks to trimming and heavy trail use, brush, grass and trees give hikers wide berth.

During our midweek hikes, we seldom cross paths with more than half a dozen walkers and encounter even fewer mountain bikers, but we see horse, deer and dog tracks that tell another story.

Whether you take the long route from the bottom or the short route from the top, the end result is the same: a window to the past at Knapp's Castle.

Mountain bikers racing down the route typically slow — some even wave — as they pass. Others stop to share trail information or chat. A hefty water supply and body armor on many riders tells the tale of the trail. Riders should carry their own water, repair kits, first-aid kits and know their limits. The steep hill can be treacherous for riders, whether they take the speedy downhill ride or the strenuous pump uphill.

Miranda Pine/Sierra Madre Road/Colson Canyon
East of Santa Maria

From Highway 101, take Highway 166 east to Sierra Madre Road.

While the central county's snow spot is Figueroa Mountain, the north county also has its secret snow playground a short drive from the beach. When winter weather patterns are just right, Sierra Madre Road offers easy

access to snow. For the other 363 days of the year, the route offers fantastic views up and down the coast, and over inland valleys.

The main route, Sierra Madre Road, is a graded dirt road passable by most passenger cars with standard road clearance. High-end cars and others with very little clearance should stick to the pavement. The road is maintained to provide access to a variety of towers along the ridge, but remains open for public access except in cases of heavy rain. After a

Miranda Pine campground on Sierra Madre Ridge offers northern Santa Barbara County residents snow on occasion, and camping all year round.

short, winding climb, the road continues 7.5 miles to Miranda Pine Campground which includes picnic tables, barbecue pits, shade trees and pit toilets with spectacular views.

From the campground, continue another 12.5 miles to Bates Canyon where an optional route leads 4.7 miles down to Bates Canyon campground (picnic tables and pit toilets) and the abandoned White Oaks ranger station, then provides a paved route back to Highway 166. Four-wheel drive is a plus on this leg, and the route should not be attempted by any vehicle during inclement weather due to off-camber sections, narrow road, steep drop offs and other hazards.

Those interested in exploring further may continue another 4 miles to McPherson Peak, then backtrack. At Miranda Pine, rather than return via Sierra Madre Ridge, high-clearance vehicles may turn down Miranda Pine Canyon Road for a 17.5 mile descent through Smith Canyon, La Brea Canyon, and finally Colson Canyon. Forest Service campgrounds line the route, and spurs, including Colson Canyon, Wagon Flat, Horseshoe Springs and Brookshire. Other campgrounds are available along the area's designated hiking and motorcycle routes.

Nineteen Oaks
Upper Santa Ynez River

From Highway 154, take Paradise Road across the first river crossing, then turn left following the Upper Oso Campground signs, then park at the end of the road.

This first leg of the Santa Cruz Trail, which eventually leads 10.5 miles up a steep climb to Little Pine Mountain, is among one of the nicest springtime hikes in the Cachuma Lake area. It isn't particularly tough, but you'll want to be sure to bring plenty of water and avoid the area during the heat of summer and autumn months. Watch for snakes, which can be plentiful here, and be aware that, as with all hiking areas on the Central Coast, mountain lions may be present.

From the trailhead, where restrooms are available, follow the clearly marked, dusty service road, which is open to mountain bikers and motorcyclists but no other vehicles.

A cool, clear creek bubbles through the canyon down a steep embankment from the road. Watch closely for swimming holes and well-traveled trails to the creek's edge. Trail blazing here is both unwelcome and dangerous as there are drop-offs and poison oak. The junction with the footpath is clearly marked. A registration book is provided for hikers interested in leaving their marks and their trek plans.

For the most part, this single-track trail appears to be fairly well-traveled. It is relatively clear of brush and the only poison oak we spotted was well clear of our calves and dangling arms. Watch for the occasional large rock, loose gravel and steep drops off the trailside.

The route gently climbs 525 feet to the 19 Oak Campground. There are several creek crossings that provide ample opportunity to dip a hat or shirt in the creek before continuing on. We also found wide spots in the trail where we sought shelter under sycamore trees while resting alongside the creek.

One mile up the trail, watch for a clearly marked 'Y' in the trail. Turn right, away from the creek, and continue a quarter mile up a fairly steep final climb to the campground. Amenities here include picnic benches and fire pits sheltered by ancient oak trees in the middle of a meadow. It's a dusty spot, but there are good flat areas for tents, a nice view down the valley, plenty of fallen deadwood to fuel a campfire and undoubtedly spectacular shows of wildflowers each spring.

☞ Red Rocks & Gibraltar Reservoir Loop
Upper Santa Ynez River

From Highway 154, take Paradise Road to its end.

Locals best know the area along the Upper Santa Ynez River for its deep swimming holes lined with spectacular red boulders. Hikers enjoy the cool water here on their way up the hot canyon to Gibraltar Reservoir, or make the riverside beaches their destination. There are no lifeguards and no

Hikers who continue up the Santa Ynez River beyond the popular Red Rocks swimming hole are rewarded with tranquility and spectacular wildflowers and a bit of scrambling.

services. Make your last pit stop in the restrooms at the paved parking lot. Bring your own food, water and towels. Use your best judgment; jumpers often are injured here.

The 10-minute hike to Red Rock swimming hole is an easy one, regularly traversed by children and ice-chest-toting adults. The greatest challenge is balancing on the rounded river rock with which the trail is cobbled. Expect to get your feet wet in the river crossings during spring months and beware of slippery moss-covered rocks. The water level tends to run very low by late August.

If the swimming hole isn't enough for you, continue up the riverbed trail another 2 miles to Gibraltar Reservoir. Swimming is not allowed here, but fishing is if you plan ahead and pick up a fishing permit from the City of Santa Barbara. Return via the trail or the easier graded-dirt service road.

Rockfront & Buckhorn Ridge Off-Highway Vehicle areas
Near Santa Maria

From Highway 101, take Highway 166 east 25 miles to Rockfront Ranch, or continue east half a mile and turn right onto Sierra Madre Ridge to access the Buckhorn area.

These designed off-highway vehicle use areas span more than 20,000 acres and include more than 50 miles of designated trails for motorized vehicles and countless miles to explore on foot, horseback or mountain bike. The inland area is very warm to downright stifling hot in late summer and early fall, and rains can close these roads in winter, so aim for a spring visit when wildflowers are blooming, temperatures are ideal and the trails are relatively clear.

Sierra Madre Road offers one incredibly long ride along a well-maintained, graded, dirt road with spurs to several campgrounds and potential loops, including a ride down Colson Canyon to Tepusquet Road, a swoop down Bates Canyon past the abandoned White Oaks ranger station, then on to Cuyama Valley. There are several designated campgrounds in the area, including often-blustery Miranda Pine, heavily used Colson Canyon, and more remote Wagon Flats and Horseshoe Springs campgrounds. Campgrounds in this area are primitive, so plan to pack in everything you'll need from food and stove fuel to toilet paper. Vault toilets are available in some of the designated campgrounds; carry a Forest Service map of the area for ease of finding them. The area was heavily damaged in the 2009 La Brea fire.

☞ The Playground
West Camino Cielo near Santa Barbara

From Highway 154, turn west onto Kinevan Road, which becomes West Camino Cielo. Continue about 2 miles and look for a telephone pole immediately adjacent to the road with a short pullout.

Finding this place is only one of the tricks to this rock-lover's paradise. Note to those with small children (particularly if they are not avid hikers): DO NOT TAKE THEM! This hike is great for older kids, say avid 11- to 12-year-olds, energetic teens and adults who have little or no fear of scratches, scrapes, spiders, bats or heights.

Once you've parked, follow the oversized rabbit hole into the hedge on the ocean side of the road. Yep, walk right in there and continue downhill. As the trail opens, you'll find yourself on an abundance of oversized sandstone boulders. Search high and low and you may find the entrance to the Narrows, an aptly named route that made me feel like an ant creeping through the spaces between sand particles. While I hike, mountain bike and camp regularly, I don't recall the last time I spent so much time creeping, crawling and sometimes even dropping my way into big, dark holes that drop straight down, crawling under monstrous fallen boulders, door jamming (feet on a boulder on one side of an opening, back on the other) and such.

Bring water, snacks, a compass or GPS receiver, maps, camera, a 20-foot or longer rope and at least one friend. A first-aid kit isn't a bad idea, either, due to low overhangs and other tight squeezes that tend to surprise visitors.

Chapter 13

Outlying Areas & Day Trips

Santa Barbara County comprises 2,737 square miles, much of it preserved in one fashion or another inside the boundaries of the Los Padres National Forest (p. 199), seven California State Parks, and various reserves, refuges and city and county parks. The geography varies from coastal wetlands, rocky shores and sandy beaches to rolling hills and jagged mountains. There are eight incorporated cities in the county, most of which are featured in their own designated chapters of this book. They account for just over 100 square miles of the massive county, so it stands to reason the outlying areas also would have plenty of recreational opportunities to offer.

For waterfall adventures and unparalleled views, you'll want to focus your travels in southern Santa Barbara County's "front country." Northern Santa Barbara County features a greater focus on agriculture and massive stretches of open space, more solitary trails and campgrounds that are less often visited. And the Santa Ynez Valley, which divides the two, offers storybook rolling hills dotted with ancient oaks and acres upon acres of vineyards.

One potential day trip surveying the county's diversity is the Lake Casitas loop. (Lake Casitas is, technically, outside Santa Barbara County, but the drive swings around the county's lesser visited southern and eastern edges.) Take Highway 101 south to Highway 150, then drive east on the two-lane highway to Lake Casitas. At South La Luna, turn left, then left again onto Highway 33, which winds through the backcountry to Highway 166, where you turn left and continue through Cuyama Valley and along the gently winding road through the mountains to Highway 101, north of Santa Maria.

ARTS

Circle Bar B Dinner Theatre
1800 Refugio Road
Near Refugio State Park (p. 226)
(805) 967-1962
www.circlebarbtheatre.com
$$$
From Highway 101, take Refugio Road for about 3.5 miles up the canyon.
Four miles from the pounding surf of the Pacific Coast in a wooded canyon far from city lights and freeway noise, an old barn that once sheltered horses and cattle now serves as a performing arts venue. Hay has given way to

Gaviota State Park is just one of Santa Barbara County's many jewels outside its cities' boundaries. Some of the tiniest communities have the most wonderful attractions.

Santa Maria-style tri-tip dinners. The shuffle of hooves has made way for tears and laughter, applause and cheers.

The theater offers four shows each year from April to early November. Each performance ticket also includes dinner.

LETTERS

Cuyama Library
60 Newsome St.
New Cuyama
(661) 766-2490
www.ci.santa-maria.ca.us/3092.shtml
FREE

From Highway 101, take Highway 166 east through New Cuyama, then turn right onto Newsome Street.

This branch of the Santa Maria City Public Library also ties in with the larger Black Gold Library System, which provides access to books, magazines and various recordings. This library is generally open Monday, Wednesday and Friday evenings after school, although it's never a bad idea to call ahead to make sure.

HISTORY

Chapel San Ramon
6600 Foxen Canyon Road
Sisquoc
(805) 937-4555
www.sanramonchapel.org
FREE

From Santa Maria, take Highway 101 south to Clark Avenue east; turn left onto Dominion Road, right onto Orcutt-Garey Road, then right onto Foxen Canyon Road. From the south, take 101 north to Highway 154, then turn left onto Zaca Station Road, which becomes Foxen Canyon Road.

In the dry winter of 1875, Frederick Wickenden drove his herd of 5,000 hungry sheep north in hope of finding grass. He found salvation in the plenty of Salinas Valley. Then, he drove the herd on to Redwood City, where its sale provided funding for the redwood boards that would form this family chapel.

The chapel was the county's first official landmark, and is recognized as California State Historical Landmark No. 877. Today, the chapel is open for public service every Sunday at 10:15 a.m. and the grounds, including a historic cemetery, are open weekends for self-guided tours.

Chumash Painted Cave State Historic Park
Painted Cave Road
Near Santa Barbara
(805) 733-3713

www.parks.ca.gov/?page_id=602
FREE
From Highway 154, turn uphill onto Painted Cave Road.
After a slow, white-knuckle drive up a very windy, narrow road (no trailers or RVs), you'll come around a curve to a relatively wide spot in the road, where there is room for, perhaps, three vehicles to park. Walk up the uneven stone steps just beyond the sign to some of the coast's most accessible cave paintings. (Be sure to bring your flashlight so you can see them!) Enjoy the cool shade and the gentle sound of the creek across the road (and down a considerable gully) while considering the history here. No facilities.

NATURE

Arroyo Hondo Preserve
Gaviota Coast
(805) 966-4520 (reservations: 567-1115)
www.sblandtrust.org/arroyohondo.html
FREE
From northbound Highway 101 about 7 miles north of Refugio Road, turn right into the driveway immediately east of Caltrans Call Box No. 101-412. From southbound 101, make a U-turn at the designated turning lane about 7 miles south of Gaviota State Park, then proceed to the driveway at the call box.
This 782-acre preserve has been owned by only two families in the nearly 200 years since Chumash people dominated this land. The preserve was part of the 26,530-acre Rancho Nuestra Señora del Refugio Mexican land grant awarded to Santa Barbara Presidio Commandant Jose Francisco Ortega in 1827. It remained in the Ortega family until 1908 when the Jennie B. Hollister family bought it. The Land Trust for Santa Barbara County purchased it in 2001.
Today, the property, complete with the original 1842 adobe, is open to the general public on the first and third Saturdays of each month. Docent-led hikes begin at 10 a.m. by reservation. Tours tailored for schools and other larger groups are available Mondays and Wednesdays by reservation.
Due to the nature of the area, wheelchair access is limited. Dogs, mountain bikes, horses, hunting, fishing and campfires are not allowed. Restrooms are available.

Cachuma Lake County Park
2200 San Marcos Pass Road/Highway 154
Between Santa Barbara and Santa Ynez
(805) 686-5054
www.sbparks.org
$
From the north, take Highway 101 south to Highway 154/San Marcos Pass

Cachuma Lake offers boating and fishing, camping and hiking, but no swimming, skiing or other body contact with this drinking water reservoir.

east. From the south, take Highway 101 north to Highway 154/San Marcos Pass west.

This, the largest recreation area in the Santa Barbara County Parks system, offers more than 400 campsites on a peninsula that juts into Lake Cachuma. The lake, which serves as Santa Barbara's drinking water supply, is off limits for swimming, but year-round boating, fishing and hiking are allowed. During summer months, the Family Fun Center offers park guests access to a swimming pool, miniature golf course, arcade and snack bar. A busy calendar includes fishing derbies, astronomy nights and ranger lectures.

The park is home to Cachuma Lake Nature Center (805-693-0691). The free facility focuses on Chumash traditions, local history, geology, flora and fauna and includes hands-on displays. Stop in to see the giant bear skin or pet a skunk skin. The Junior Ranger Program (805-688-4515) rewards kids who learn about wildlife and environmental stewardship. Nature walks are offered year round (805-688-4515).

One of our favorite programs here is the year-round Wildlife Cruise (805-686-5050). Visitors strap on life vests and climb aboard large tour boats driven by naturalists who share their extensive knowledge of the lake's flora, fauna, geology and culture. Reservations are strongly recommended, and group tours also are available.

☞ Channel Islands National Park
Santa Barbara Channel
(805) 658-5730
nps.gov/chis
$$$

One of the nation's most unique parks is just off the Santa Barbara County coastline. Channel Islands National Park includes five islands all accessible for public exploration and camping. San Miguel, Santa Rosa, Anacapa and Santa Barbara islands are maintained by the National Parks Service and include camping, hiking, kayaking, tidepooling, snorkeling and scuba diving opportunities. While Santa Cruz Island is the largest in the park, The Nature Conservancy controls most of it and bars camping there. Docent-led tours of the ecological preserve are available by reservation.

Some of the islands are home to North America's smallest wild dogs – the Channel Islands fox. Sly and shy and only 6 pounds on the heavy side, the foxes are unlikely to visit trails and camps when people are evident. During late-winter months, visitors traveling the islands' trail systems may observe native plants, and superb tidepooling is available during low-tides year round.

The park's Robert J. Lagomarsino Visitor Center is located at 1901 Spinnaker Drive in Ventura. The center is open daily (except Thanksgiving and Christmas) from 8:30 a.m. until 5 p.m. In addition to exhibits about each of the islands, the center includes a theater featuring a 25-minute movie about the park. Park rangers host free public programs at 11 a.m. and 3 p.m. on weekends and holidays.

While there is no fee to enter the park or visitors center, there is a camping reservation fee, and unless you have a seaworthy boat of your own, you'll have to pony up for one of the park's two designated commercial boating companies – Truth Aquatics (963-3564) out of Santa Barbara Harbor, or Island Packers (642-1393) out of Ventura and Oxnard harbors.

Chaotic Exotics Orchid Ranch
5375 Campbell Road
Near Lompoc
(805) 736-0040
www.chaoticexotics.biz
FREE
Take Highway 246 to Campbell Road.
This private orchid enterprise includes a large greenhouse surrounded by 9 acres of oak woodland. The greenhouse is home to more than a thousand varieties of orchids, bromeliads, ferns and other unusual greenery. The business is open to the general public Fridays and Saturdays or by reservation any other day of the week.

Circle Bar B Stables
1800 Refugio Road
Near Refugio State Park
(805) 968-3901
www.circlebarbstables.com
$$$
From Highway 101, take Refugio Road 3.5 miles up canyon.

This private guest ranch provides guided trail rides for riders ages 7 and older. The trail-ready horses know the routes that vary in length from 90 minutes to half a day. Private group rides also are available.

Classic Organic Farm & Market

2323 Old Coast Highway, near Buellton
(805) 714-4420
localharvest.org/farms/M18470
FREE

From Highway 101, turn east onto the Old Coast Highway/La Lata Place about 5 miles south of Buellton, then turn left onto Santa Rosa Road/Alisal Road.

Helmut Klauer gazed on with a smile as the organic craze rose to mainstream at the turn of the 21st Century. He's been growing fruits, vegetables and animals the organic way since 1971. The popularity of the farm's roadside produce stand and a desire to make fresh food available come rain or shine led to the development of a full-fledge market in the shelter of the Peace Barn.

The market is open daily from 10 a.m. to 7 p.m., and the farm welcomes visitors every day from 10 a.m. until sunset. Group tours are available by reservation and special events are held on occasion. Educational tours include information about the methods used in growing and harvesting crops here, and, if timing is right, opportunities to participate in hand-pollinatation, harvesting or egg collecting. U-pick crops include pumpkins, strawberries and other seasonal produce.

El Capitan State Park

Gaviota Coast
(805) 968-1033
www.parks.ca.gov/?page_id=601
$

From Highway 101, take the El Capitan State Park exit (No. 117).

This popular state park offers a seemingly endless beach at low tide. The 3-mile-long stretch of sand offers swimming, fishing, surfing and tidepooling. Beach access is via stairs from the blufftop campgrounds or via a long path to a rocky stretch of beach. Neither approach is particularly easy on strollers nor wheelchair friendly.

The park also features a campground we found highly overrated. The freeway noise overshadows any ocean sounds that may climb the steep bluff to the campground. High-walled fire pits allow heat generated by fires to warm faces but block the rest of the campers' chilled bodies from the neck down.

A 3-mile-long paved bicycle path along the bluff links El Capitan State Park to Refugio State Beach (p. 214). The path is decomposing, but passable, and provides access to fairly secluded coves along the shore. For restrooms, return to either park.

Ferrini Park
Bell Street at Centennial Street
Los Alamos
(805) 344-3805
www.sbparks.org
FREE

From Highway 101, take Bell Street west.
This grassy, open space near the city's central flagpole offers room to picnic under the trees or run in the sun. No restrooms.

☞ Gaviota Coast Beach Access
Various spots along Southbound Highway 101
Gaviota to El Capitan
www.gaviotacoastconservancy.org
FREE

All are available from southbound Highway 101. See further directions at each of the following access point listings.
Friends of the Gaviota Coast Conservancy someday hope to see this area become a designated national seashore. Until then, much of the area remains under state ownership and, thereby, accessible to the public.
Beaches and coves along this section of the Gaviota Coast often offer the

When visiting El Capitan's beaches, be prepared to take the stairs or hike the trails.

peace and solitude not available at more easily accessible beaches on the south coast. At high tide, the ocean beats against the bluffs, leading to sloughing, so steer well clear of blufftop edges. Time your visit well and you'll be treated to a beach that may be your own for the day, some great tidepools and some prime surfing spots. Time it poorly and you could be in a wet world of hurt. These beaches also offer no services: no lifeguards, no restrooms and no garbage cans. Pack it in, pack it out, and plan ahead for potty needs. During periods of heavy runoff, check water quality first at www.sbcphd.org/ehs/oceanmn.htm.

San Onofre Creek: 1¼ mile south of Mariposa Reina overpass. Park in the dirt pullout well off the highway and clear of the railroad tracks. Carefully cross the tracks, then follow any of several single-track trails to a series of secluded coves. Beach access is steep and not advised for very small children.

Molino Creek: 2.2 miles south of the Mariposa Reina overpass. A small parking area under a large tree offers very limited access to a single-track trail to the bluff descent.

Tajiguas: 6.4 miles south of the Mariposa Reina overpass, and just south of Tajiguas Creek. This gem of a beach is often overlooked, in large part due to the parking (a dirt pullout on the side of the highway), railroad crossing (beware; very busy), or the rugged trail. The trail is not maintained; it is rutted and often overgrown, but preschoolers should be able to handle it with a little help from their steadier friends and family. A fantastic old eucalyptus tree provides rare shade on this sandy stretch most often visited by local surfers. Unlike most of the Gaviota Coast beaches, this one offers sand even at high tide.

Venadito Cove: 1 mile south of Refugio State Beach overpass. Park well off the highway in the dirt pullout, carefully cross the tracks, then follow the unmaintained, single-track foot trails down the embankment, across the paved bike path and on to a relatively secluded sandy cove. No wheelchair access except along the rough 3-mile bike path that joins El Capitan and Refugio State beaches.

El Capitan Cove: 1.3 miles south of Refugio State Beach overpass. Park off the highway in the dirt pullout, cross the busy rail tracks, climb down the moderately steep embankment to the 3-mile bike path, then follow the easy, posted trail about 1/10 mile to the sandy shore. At low tide, it is possible to walk from this cove clear out to the point at El Capitan State Beach.

Gaviota State Park
Gaviota Beach Road
(805) 968-1033 general information
(800) 444-7275 camping reservations
www.parks.ca.gov/?page_id=606
$

From the south, take Highway 101 to the Gaviota Park exit about 33 miles north of Santa Barbara. From the north, take 101 south to the exit, which is about 13 miles south of Buellton.

The first thing visitors need to know about this park is that it is incredibly

windy most of the time. Rangers
warn visitors who feel inclined to
pitch a tent here that tents should be
both staked down and loaded with
the heaviest camping gear on hand.
Then, expect it to be blown flat.
Better yet, bring an RV or hard-
sided trailer. Make sure you have
reservations; last-minute camping is
not allowed.

The park has enough to offer,
however, to make a visit worthwhile
on all but the windiest days: more
than 18 miles of dirt trails and fire
roads through some 2,000 acres of
oak woodland and chaparral
backcountry; hot sulfur springs;
miles of tidepools; a public fishing
pier with electric boat launch hoist; a
sandy beach; wildlife; and a variety of bridges. In 2009, the park added 43
acres across the freeway, an area formerly known as Gaviota Village. During
our visits, we've spotted countless ravens, lizards, red-tailed hawks and mule
deer. There are signs of coyote and gray fox, tracks of bobcats and slithery
paths of rattlesnakes and king snakes alike. Listen for woodpeckers and
beware of mountain lions.

While enjoying the scenery, consider the area's past. Soldiers of the Gaspar
de Portolà Expedition of 1769 named this area "Gaviota" — Spanish for the
seagulls that make the area their home. Juan Cabrillo also noted the area in
his journals as did Father Juan Crespi. This windy pass served as the main
route for stagecoaches until 1871 when a safer, faster route was established
at San Marcos Pass.

While the stage had abandoned the area and the wind continued to pose its
challenges, settlers would not give up on Gaviota. In 1875, Col. William
Welles Hollister built a wharf here to ship wool, lumber, cattle and grain to
the Atlantic. A quarter century later, the railroad completed its link to points
north with the construction of the 811-foot trestle that is still in use today.

Perhaps the easiest hike in the park is the 3-mile Overlook Fire Road out-
and-back, which offers views of the Channel Islands. From the parking lot,
return toward the freeway, then turn left up the paved road about ¼ mile to
a clearly marked parking area and proceed on foot through the gate. This is
the trailhead for a variety of routes, many of which are posted on the park's
map. For an added challenge, watch for a single-track trail to your left about
half a mile in. Follow the trail about another half mile as it meanders up a
ridge, then up a steeper incline to eroded sandstone called "Wind Caves."

The toughest hike we've done in the park is the climb to Gaviota Peak, a
strenuous 6-mile round-trip trek from a parking lot located 2.5 miles north of
the park's main entrance. While the peak is outside park boundaries (and
inside the Los Padres National Forest), the trail begins inside Gaviota State

Park. From Highway 101 north of Gaviota Tunnel, take the Lompoc/Highway 1 exit, turn east, then immediately right onto the frontage road, which ends at the parking lot. Though brutal at points, particularly for less-practiced hikers, this climb offers splendid views and the added benefit of a side trip to Gaviota Hot Springs.

There are, in fact, several trails that take off from this parking lot. They include the 3.2-mile Gaviota Peak Road (open only to pedestrians and official park vehicles), 2.5-mile Trespass/Tunnel loop trail, 2-mile Beach-to-Backcountry trail, 2.9-mile Hollister Fire Road trail and the .7-mile Hot Springs hike.

There are innumerable natural springs throughout the Central Coast, but Gaviota Hot Springs may be the most easily accessible, hot water spring on nearby public land. The directions are easy, the roads are paved and the trails are well maintained. Friends of the spring have dammed the waters to create three pools for wading and soaking, but don't expect to find time alone there. These same people visit the site daily, most often in the buff, keeping watch on their beloved place of refuge. The hike to the falls is a fairly steep, uphill climb from start to finish. As the route curves left toward Gaviota Peak, water seekers continue straight up the hill along a steep, wide, manicured, all-weather path, lined with gravel.

The foliage grows increasingly green and dense as hikers approach the falls. Around a bend, the soaking pools suddenly come into view. The water smells of rotten eggs, an effect of the sulfur springs. The upper pool collects the clear water immediately as is springs from the black walls of the canyon. Rocks have been strategically placed in the pool to help soakers relax in bath-like water without sitting in the mushy mud.

The water flows down the sides of the upper basin's dam to a second, larger pool. A second spring under that pool also contributes to the more tepid water, which is murky white. The silty soil on the bottom of the pond squishes through waders' toes as they seek the source of the bubbles rising in the middle of the pool.

A third pool nearby has been cut right into the nearly-black soil from whence flows a third spring. Its water is clear until the first swimmer takes the plunge. Within minutes, the soil and water mix to give those outside the pool the feeling they are talking to someone sinking in quicksand rather than enjoying a relaxing soak.

While the park and its beach-side restrooms are open for day use year round, camping is available Oct. 1 to March 31 on Fridays and Saturdays only. Camping is limited to the 41 spaces in the beach parking lot. Trailers up to 25 feet long and RVs up to 27-feet long are allowed. Dogs must be on a leash no more than 6-feet long and are not permitted on the beach or the trails. There are lots of extra rules, like no volleyball, badminton, horseshoes or similar games allowed.

There are additional access points. Vista del Mar, ½ mile south of the Mariposa Reina overpass, comes up quickly on southbound travelers' right. Limited access, no services and relatively remote placement makes this among the loneliest public beaches in Santa Barbara County. After parking clear of the highway, follow the single-track, unmaintained trail through wildflowers (in early spring), across the oil company access road and very carefully over the busy railroad tracks. The old fence that once protected cattle from the danger of crumbling bluffs is long gone, so you're on your own. Keep yourselves, your children and your pets away from the edges, which always are in danger of collapse. Follow the clearly beaten path to the left along the bluff and down a modestly steep ravine to the beach of sand interspersed with uplifted rocks. Bring binoculars for great views of otters and pelicans visiting the kelp beds. (See Gaviota Coast Beach Access, p. 215.)

The park's northern access is the Las Cruces Adobe area, off San Julian Road. Take Highway 101 north to Highway 1 north, turn left onto San Julian Road and continue to the parking lot past Vista de Las Cruces School. There once were restrooms here, but they've been boarded up, and there is no wheelchair access to the park here. This entrance offers access via trails that are, in a word, steep. But the routes are popular with mountain bikers out for a tough climb and the equestrian crowd less concerned about elevation changes.

During periods of heavy runoff, check water quality first at www.sbcphd.org/ehs/oceanmn.htm.

☞ Jalama Beach

Jalama Beach Road
South of Lompoc
www.sbparks.org
(805) 736-6316
$

From Lompoc, take Highway 1 south 4 miles, then turn right onto Jalama Road and proceed 14 miles.

The 23.5-acre parcel of land just north of Point Conception was donated to Santa Barbara County in 1943 by the Atlantic Richfield Oil Company. It has since become a hit with campers from throughout the United States, but somehow remains unknown to many Central Coast residents.

According to County Parks, the area near Jalama Creek was a Chumash settlement until the native people were removed from their homes and shipped to La Purísima Mission by Spanish rule. With fresh water, easy ocean access and plentiful wildlife, the village was no doubt near Utopia.

Even today, visitors are likely to spot deer, foxes and bobcats in the area. Whale watching from shore, or just up the hill, is a popular Jalama pastime in February and March, then again in September through November.

The park provides the public some of the most remote beach access in Santa Barbara County. The long, sandy beach beckons sandcastle builders, joggers and tidepoolers. Bring binoculars and keep a lookout for migrating whales that can often be spotted passing through during the February through April and September through November migrations. The typically windy beach is also popular for kite flying and particularly attractive to kite surfers. Though there are lifeguards here during summer months, swimming is not recommended due to heavy surf. The park is surrounded by private property, so there is no legal hiking off the beach.

The park also is popular for its fishing. According to County Parks, regular catches include halibut, cabazon, kelp bass and four species of perch.

During one of our visits the ebb tide left behind a great big puddle ideal for our small child to wade through, sit in, shovel from and throw rocks into for a big splash. The current and tide combine to bring ashore driftwood that is great for building lean-tos, teepees or tiny houses for toddlers' toys. There are all sorts of rocks — big and small, heavy and strangely light — to collect, sort and stack, then leave behind for others' enjoyment. We found various shells that intrigued our little girl, including crab legs and turban snail shells.

Then there are the tidepools with relatively smooth, slippery rocks that welcome young explorers. In the shallower pools, there were no large animals, but hermit crabs and sea anemones were abundant.

If the kids tire of the beach (not likely), they'll probably have to stop at the play structure before climbing into the car. Or, they may be interested in a treat from the Jalama Beach Store, where ice cream, burgers, hot dogs and grilled cheese sandwiches are popular fare.

The store is, in fact, quite remarkable.

Planned to fish but forgot your license? Pick up one at Jalama Beach Store. Left your rod at home? Check the store. Break an awning strap on your RV? Store. Need mustard? Swimsuit? Frisbee? Store, store, store.

For those interested in a longer stay, the campground offers 117 sites, all available on a first-come, first-served basis. The first-come, first-served reservation rule is strictly enforced, so don't plan to hold a site for

friends arriving later, even if you are willing to pay for it. Campsites are limited to two vehicles each, maximum 8 people per campsite. Each site includes a fire pit and picnic table. Amenities include flush toilets, sinks and pay showers. Other park facilities include a dump station, store and grill.

Imagine the possibilities: Surf by morning; nap on beach; eat hot, juicy, scrumptious burger from Jalama Beach Store; nap on sand some more; surf fish; cook your catch over the campfire for a hot evening meal by the sea; long sunset walk; nestle in tent; fall asleep to sound of waves; start again at sunrise.

During periods of heavy runoff, check water quality first at www.sbcphd.org/ehs/oceanmn.htm.

Live Oak Camp
Live Oak Road
Near Lake Cachuma
(805) 686-5076
www.sbparks.org
$$$

From points north, take Highway 101 south, turn south onto Highway 154 for 19.8 miles, then turn left onto Live Oak Road. From Santa Barbara, take Highway 154 north 12 miles, then turn right onto Live Oak Road.

This county campground is available by reservation for up to 1,500 campers at a time. The property includes 40 undeveloped acres with barbecue grills, group fire rings, picnicking areas, hiking trails, restrooms with hot running water and showers.

The site hosts several public events throughout the year, including the Live Oak Music Festival each Father's Day weekend, Native American powwows hosted by the Santa Ynez band of Chumash people and Sage Hill Competitive Trail Ride.

☞ Los Alamos Park

500 Drum Canyon Road
Los Alamos
(805) 344-3805
www.sbparks.org
FREE

From Highway 101, take the Highway 135/Bell Street exit and turn west into Los Alamos, then turn left onto Centennial Street, which becomes Drum Canyon Road.

This park has become one of our favorite rural stops in Santa Barbara County because we've never found it busy, and always found it relatively well maintained. Ancient oaks provide ample shade for group picnic areas, individual barbecue pits and picnic benches. The park also includes a baseball diamond, volleyball net, play structure, lots of open lawn, restrooms and a 1-mile loop trail that connects the lower portion of the park to an upper meadow. A park ranger in residence keeps tabs on the place.

Los Padres National Forest

This federal landholding covers about one-third of the county and includes numerous trails, campgrounds and other recreational venues. It is, in fact, so large it has been given its own chapter, which begins on page 199.

New Cuyama Aquatic Center

Richardson Park
Hubbard Avenue at Escuela
New Cuyama
(661)766-2270
$

From Highway 166, turn south onto Hubbard Avenue, then immediately left onto Escuela.

This brand-new community pool is located conveniently adjacent to Richardson Park playground (p. 227). The four-lane, 25-yard lap pool offers varying depths up to 6½ feet in at its deepest. Just across the deck is a wading pool for the smaller set. The facility also includes a bathhouse with restrooms and changing areas.

New Cuyama Tiny Tot Park

4800 block Cebrian Ave.
New Cuyama
(661) 766-2270
FREE

From Highway 101, take Highway 166 east, turn right onto Pato Avenue, then left onto Cebrian Avenue.

This small neighborhood park in desperate need of renovation offers a tiny tot play structure, swings, benches, lawn and shade trees. A large dirt rectangle appears once to have been a pool, and a building that once may have been a restroom was boarded up at publication time.

☞ Nojoqui Park & Nojoqui Falls

3100 Alisal Road
Near Buellton
(805) 934-6123
www.sbparks.org
FREE

From Highway 101, turn east onto the Old Coast Highway/La Lata Place about 5 miles south of Buellton, then turn left onto Santa Rosa Road/Alisal Road.

The greatest challenge about Nojoqui Falls Park is not the hike or finding a private spot under a sprawling oak tree, but pronouncing its name. Ask locals and responses include "no-JOKE-ee," "no-HO-kee," and "NAH-wee." According to a parks department employee, however, the proper pronunciation is "NAH-ho-wee."

Nojoqui was a rancho in the Mission La Purísima territory. Local experts say the word "nojoqui" seems to stem from the language of the local Chumash tribe, but its meaning is now unknown.

Any way you pronounce it, Nojoqui Falls and its surrounding park are beautiful. Three-tenths of a mile into the park, the paved road loops around a dirt parking area under a canopy of trees. Large signs mark the trailhead and facilities here include restrooms and a picnic table.

The quarter-mile trail up to the falls is very wide and fairly well groomed. Keep your eyes open for large rocks, ruts and roots that pose tripping hazards farther up the trail. They could frustrate anyone challenged by walking and make the trail impassable to most wheelchairs.

Though quite short by most hikers' standards, the trek along gurgling Nojoqui Creek is a pleasant one and well worth a quick stop, or a lengthy picnic. Benches along the trail invite walkers to relax.

In the farthest corner of the box canyon, a 160-foot-tall white ribbon of cold water cascades down a dark-green, moss-covered rock wall to a small pond. Visitors stretch out on the stone seating area to relax in the dappled shade of sycamore and oak trees and listen to the rush of water on rock. Interpretive signs at the base explain that, while most falls cut a rut into mountainsides, Nojoqui Falls is growing away from the wall as water deposits minerals.

During summer months, the waterfall can become little more than a trickle bubbling through the Venus maidenhair fern and other ferns and mosses that have taken root in the growing mineral deposit. After heavy rains, however, visitors may want to take an umbrella to keep off some of the overspray as the trickle turns to a torrent.

There's more to this park than a lovely hike. According to birders, wildlife in the park includes the yellow-billed magpie, Pacific slope flycatcher, yellow warbler, oak titmouse and California towhee. There are open lawn, barbecue and picnic areas, playground equipment, horseshoe pits and restrooms.

☞ Oso Flaco Lake Natural Area
West end of Oso Flaco Lake Road off Highway 1
San Luis Obispo County
(805) 473-7230

www.dunescenter.org/ottoso.htm

$

Take Highway 1 to Oso Flaco Road. Turn west on Oso Flaco Road which ends at the parking lot.

This natural area offers easy foot access to the dunes (even with stroller). An entrance fee collected by State Parks qualifies visitors to walk the boardwalk over Oso Flaco Lake, through the dunes and out to a vast expanse of sand. Keep an eye out for cormorants drying their wings, ruddy ducks and white pelicans.

Although Oso Flaco Lake is under the general umbrella of Oceano State Vehicular Recreation Area, fees paid to enter the beach by car in Oceano do not translate to pedestrian passage here, or vice versa. Plan to pay separate fees at each gate. Rules here are entirely different, too. No dogs, no horses and no camping are allowed at Oso Flaco, nor are campfires, vehicles, shooting, hunting, bicycling or collecting. Surf fishing, however, is a hit at the beach as are bird watching, kite flying and picnicking.

The non-profit Guadalupe Dunes Center (p. 195) offers educational exhibits, docent-led walks, bird bingo, plant rubbings, scavenger hunts and more throughout the area.

☞ Point Sal State Beach
Point Sal Road
Near Guadalupe
(805) 733-3713
www.parks.ca.gov/?page_id=605
From Highway 101, take Main Street exit in Santa Maria and head west. Turn left onto Ray Road, then right onto Brown Road. Continue west on Brown Road across Highway 1, then follow the road as it curves toward the locked gate at the bottom of Point Sal Road.

While the Bureau of Land Management does not provide public access to its 77-acre Point Sal promontory, State Parks does allow hikers to access Point Sal Beach south of the point. The 9-mile out-and-back trek isn't for the faint of heart, whether traveled on foot or on pedals.

The road that once provided public access to this beautiful stretch of white sand was wiped out by winter storms, and the powers that were opted not to restore it. While many portions of the road remain in decent repair, complete sections have been wiped out. There, only single-track trails remain.

A complete round trip involves a long, unrelenting climb/descent. But the graded dirt road, sections of pavement, and even the single-track that leads down toward the beach are clearly well traveled. The joy in this journey doesn't require reaching the beach. Adventurers who reach the ridge are rewarded with expansive views often accompanied by the sounds of waves and sea lions from the beach below.

If you're planning to hit the water after your hike, check water quality first at www.sbcphd.org/ehs/oceanmn.htm.

Rancho Oso Guest Ranch & Stable
3750 Paradise Road
Between Santa Barbara and Santa Ynez
(805) 683-5110
rancho-oso.com
$-$$$
From Highway 101, take Highway 154 toward Lake Cachuma, then turn onto Paradise Road.

The Rancho Oso Guest Ranch welcomes day visitors for trail rides, horse boarding, children's activities and ranch demonstrations from bucking bulls to stock dogs. Guided trail rides offer riders of all experience levels a chance to hit the trail in Los Padres National Forest. Riders may not exceed 225 pounds and should be at least 8 years old, though age exceptions are made for younger riders with considerable horse experience. The farm also features a variety of friendly animals, including pigs, goats, cattle, chickens and, at press time, one very loud turkey.

The guest ranch provides accommodations in covered wagons and unique cabins set in a Western village motif, as well as camping facilities for equestrian visitors. Guests are welcome to use the heated pool and hot tub. Other facilities include horse boarding, miniature golf, a tennis court, horseshoe pits, volleyball and basketball courts, RV storage and laundry facilities. Chuckwagon meals are available on weekends, but call ahead for details and schedule.

Rancho San Marcos

4600 Highway 154
Between Gaviota and Buellton
(805) 683-6334
www.rsm1804.com
$$$

From points north, take Highway 101 south, turn south onto Highway 154 for 19.8 miles, then turn left onto Live Oak Road. From Santa Barbara, take Highway 154 north 12 miles, then turn right onto Live Oak Road.

This 18-hole golf course offers lessons for all ages with both private and group instruction available. Other amenities include a pro shop, meeting area, practice areas, driving range and bar.

The course does impose a dress code, including soft spikes and no denim. Men are asked to wear collared shirts with sleeves, and shorts that are mid-thigh length. Women are asked to wear either collared shirts, with or without sleeves, or other shirts that cover the shoulders. Shirts without collars must have sleeves. Shorts or skirts should be mid-thigh length.

Refugio Beach State Park

10 Refugio Beach Road
Gaviota Coast
(805) 968-1033

www.parks.ca.gov/?page_id=603
$
From Highway 101, take the Refugio Road exit.
This very popular, 2,700-acre park features beachfront camping and day use. Amenities include picnic areas, designated campgrounds, educational exhibits and programs. Rangers and docents lead guided walks. Swimmers, surfers and kayakers take to the sea. A 3-mile, paved bike path connects this park with El Capitan State Park (p. 214) to the west. Bushes and other plants have begun to encroach on the path, which is in disrepair, but is otherwise passable for cyclists of average skill and physical fitness.
During periods of heavy runoff, check water quality first at www.sbcphd.org/ehs/oceanmn.htm.

Restoration Oaks Ranch/Santa Barbara Blueberries
1980 Highway 101
Gaviota
805-686-5718
www.restorationoaksranch.com
$$

From the south, take Highway 101 to the ranch about 5 miles north of the Gaviota Tunnel. From the north, take 101 south about 5 miles past the Highway 246/Mission Road overpass.
There's nothing like fresh fruit and vegetables, and picking your own can be a great family adventure, particularly for the littlest kids. Those who visit are handed a bucket, then sent into acres of blueberries to pick to their hearts' content before returning to the stand to pay for their harvest. Berry picking is available from 9 a.m. to roughly sunset during harvest season, which is generally May to August.

Richardson Park
Hubbard Avenue at Escuela
New Cuyama
(805) 934-6123
www.sbparks.org
FREE

From Highway 166, turn south onto Hubbard Avenue, then immediately turn left onto Escuela.

This county park has long been a popular pit stop for Highway 166 travelers. A new playground replaced the great old swings and teeter totter here, but the restrooms are always open, there's room for kids of all ages to run wild and there are plenty of picnic benches — even barbecue pits if you'd like to stay a bit longer.

In the 1970s, Radio Emergency Associated Communications Teams (REACT) staffed a trailer to encourage travelers to take a break here. Volunteers offered coffee and hot chocolate free to anyone who would take a breather at the pullout under the trees. Today, the trees still offer shade and rest, but the free coffee is long gone.

☞ Rincon Beach County Park

Bates Road
South of Carpinteria
(805) 568-2461
www.sbparks.org
FREE

From Highway 101, take Bates Road west, then turn right into the parking lot.

Surfers know Rincon Point for its epic winter breaks, but families also enjoy the nearby blufftop park for its views, play structure, picnic tables and beach access for summer swimming sessions. The park also includes restrooms and cold-water showers, plus beach access via a paved pathway. No horses are allowed on this stretch of sand from May 1 to Nov. 1.

Rincon Point can be rounded on foot at low tide, or drive or walk across Bates Road and through the parking lot. Follow the short, relatively flat trail squeezed between the highway and ritzy Rincon Point homes. This nice locals' spot offers a long break along a rocky beach. When the ocean is flat, the water can be quite clear, and dolphins often frequent the area. The beach is very small and freeway noise may bother some, but if you want surf, this is the place to be.

During periods of heavy runoff, check water quality first at www.sbcphd.org/ehs/oceanmn.htm.

San Julian Bridges

San Julian Road near Vista del Mar School
Near Gaviota
FREE

From Highway 101 south of Buellton, take Highway 1 north, turn left onto San Julian Road, then turn left again after the state park lot.

While this is primarily an access for the school and the back door to the state park, it's also a great little stop for bridge fanatics. After turning left at the state park, an old steel span crosses the narrow creek. Just up the dirt road, you'll pass under three modern concrete pillar bridges that hold up passing traffic on Highway 101. Turn around before the cattle guard on this dead-end private driveway, then return to Highway 101 south, exit at Gaviota State Park (p. 216) to see the century-old, 811-foot steel train trestle that made the coastal rail route possible.

Santa Rosa Park

Santa Rosa Road, between Buellton and Lompoc

(805) 934-6211 (reservations)

sbparks.org

FREE

From Highway 101, take the Santa Rosa Road exit about 1 miles south of Buellton, then head west for about eight miles.

This often deserted 21-acre park is an ideal gathering spot for those interested in a more natural setting. Native plants abound here, and the late-spring wildflower show can be superb. The multi-level park also offers picnic areas, barbecues, benches, horseshoe pits, a playground, volleyball court and restrooms.

Sedgwick Reserve

3566 Brinkerhoff Ave.

Near Los Olivos

(805) 686-1941

sedgwick.ucnrs.org/Welcome to Sedgwick

FREE - $

From Highway 154 near Los Olivos, turn east onto Roblar Avenue, then left onto Brinkerhoff Avenue.

When the Sedgwick family bequeathed their 9-square-mile ranch to the University of California system, they opened up a slice of Central Coast

Volunteers at Sedgwick Reserve leader visitors on guided hikes each Saturday, and special tours for all ages by previous arrangement.

heaven held private for more than a century. Through additional acquisitions by the Land Trust of Santa Barbara County, the reserve now spans some 6,000 acres of oak-studded rolling hills, meadows splashed with wildflowers and rugged mountain terrain.

Even after winding along bucolic Roblar and Brinkerhoff avenues, the first glimpse of the reserve from atop a nearby ridge is breathtaking, particularly when wildflowers are in full spring bloom.

Schools may schedule tours during the spring and fall, but the public is welcome to visit for docent-led hikes on the second Saturday morning of each month. Three interpretive hikes, ranging from easy to moderately strenuous, are offered each Saturday for visitors of all ages. Wear long pants, sunscreen, a hat, good hiking footwear, water, snacks, a camera and binoculars. Hikes begin at 8:30 a.m. and reservations are required. Restrooms are available, and camping is available under certain conditions. Call for details.

The reserve also is home to the Sedgwick telescope, part of the Internet-connected Las Cumbres Telescope Global Telescope Network (lcogt.net). With its proximity to Central Coast universities, as well as some of the darkest skies available in the county, the telescope promises to provide a wealth of opportunity for stargazers. The network will allow scientists to track objects in space around the clock without interruption.

Vista Point
Highway 101 south of Gaviota State Beach
Gaviota Coast
FREE

From Highway 101, 3.7 miles south of Mariposa Reina overpass off southbound Highway 101.

For bridge and train buffs, this view point off the southbound route offers a nice picnic spot with wonderful views. We like to picnic in the middle of the Arroyo Hondo highway bridge, built in 1918 but long since closed to vehicle traffic, and watch trains pass on the neighboring steel trestle. No facilities.

OTHER ADVENTURES

Cold Springs Tavern
5995 Stagecoach Road
San Marcos Pass
(805) 967-0066
www.coldspringtavern.com
$-$$$

From Highway 101, take Highway 154, then turn west onto Stagecoach Road.

There are several reasons Best Family Adventures has not focused on dining establishments, the easiest of which to explain is turnover. While some restaurants hang in there, too many others come and go in less time than it has taken to research these books.

Cold Springs Tavern is an exception worth noting, not simply as a restaurant but also as a historic place of note and a fun family setting for a meal or a weekend afternoon. The main structure dates back to the 1860s when it served as a rest stop for travelers on the dusty San Marcos Pass toll route. While coachmen changed horses, travelers enjoyed a meal in the relative wilderness between Santa Barbara and the Santa Ynez Valley. The Road Gang House, built for the Chinese immigrants who did most of the grunt work in Western road and rail construction, and Ojai Jail are popular sights for today's travelers, who stop in for everything from family meals to romantic evenings, or to take in musical performances in the shade of sycamore and bay trees or inside the rustic restaurant. Open daily.

New Cuyama Recreation Hall
4885 Primero St.

New Cuyama

(661) 766-2270

FREE

From Highway 101, take Highway 166 east, take the first right in town (Perkins Road), then immediately turn left onto Primero Street.

If you're looking for recreational opportunities in the Cuyama Valley, this is the place to begin. The old hall, due for renovation, is home to the Cuyama Valley Recreation District offices. At publication time, it included a multiuse room with a stage, kitchen, conference rooms, a recreation room with pool table, as well as district offices.

Quail Springs is an environmentally conscious community where residents share the lessons they've learned while striving to live in harmony with nature.

Quail Springs Learning Oasis and Permaculture Training Center

Highway 33 east of Cuyama
Ventura County
(805) 886-7239
www.quailsprings.org
$$$

From Highway 101, travel east on Highway 166, then south on Highway 33. Call for remaining instructions.

This 450-acre ranch provides public education in sustainable living solutions. Features include straw bale homes, cob homes, natural water systems and sustainable gardens.

The organization offers a variety of educational programs, including Sustainable Vocations, a permaculture training program designed to train students ages 15 to 24 for environmentally conscious careers. Students learn sustainable design, shelter design, natural building basics, home and community food system design, water harvesting and compost systems, while developing leadership skills.

Other offerings have included public tours and family camping weekends. Call for the current schedule.

Santa Maria Speedway

1900 Hutton Road
North of Santa Maria
(805) 922-2232
santamariaspeedway.com
$$

From Highway 101, take the Highway 166 exit, turn west, then turn right onto Hutton Road.

On any given Saturday night from April to October every year since 1964, local drivers and their crews have gathered at this 1/3-mile oval dirt track to prove themselves. The natural amphitheater provides the crowd and track with shelter from coastal sundowner winds and clear views of the track.

Several championship series are held each season, including late-model stock cars, non-winged sprint cars, street stock cars, mini stocks, factory stocks and modified cars. All these vehicles are built for speed, not spectator comfort, so it's not a bad idea to bring ear plugs, particularly for younger race fans.

The track has become increasingly family friendly, most recently with the addition of a designated family section, where no smoking or drinking is allowed. Other amenities include restrooms, snack bar, free parking, and transportation from the parking lot to the seating area for people with disabilities and seniors. Kids ages 5 and younger get in free with a paying adult.

Winchester Canyon Gun Club
6622 W. Camino Cielo
Santa Ynez Mountains
(805) 964-5606
www.wcgc.org
FREE-$$$
From Highway 154, take West Camino Cielo about 3 miles to the end of the pavement.
This non-profit, public, outdoor facility provides year-round shooting opportunities from open use to organized events. The club maintains seven separate shooting areas including short and long ranges for pistols and rifles as wells as trap and skeet ranges. Muzzle loading, sporting clays and other specialties are also encouraged.

Winchester Canyon Gun Club also facilitates firearms instruction including basic and advanced firearm use and hunter safety. The club also regularly holds shooting opportunities for youth with adult supervision and guardian permission.

The rifle and pistol ranges are open to the public from 10 a.m. to 4 p.m. Saturdays and Sundays, while trap and skeet fields are open 10 a.m. to 4 p.m. Wednesdays and weekends. Members may shoot here any day between sunrise and sunset. The club is closed on solstice and equinox.

Zaca Station Motocross
Zaca Station Road off Highway 154
Between Buellton and Los Olivos
(805) 693-1209
www.zacastationmx.com
$$
From Highway 101 north of Gaviota, take Highway 154, then turn left onto Zaca Station Road. Nearly 1 mile down the road, just past the power substation, turn left onto a dirt road and proceed slowly for 3 miles.
This well-maintained trio of dirt tracks on private property is open to the public Saturdays, Sundays and Wednesdays from 9 a.m. to 2 p.m. A 1.3-mile track provides hills, jumps and cambered turns. Two additional shorter tracks provide easier obstacles for less-practiced riders.

Children ages 6 and younger and anyone riding 50cc or smaller motorcycles get in for half price. Memberships are available and provide reduced gate fees, camping privileges and other services.

Resources

BOOKS

Some things are better left alone. This book, always focused on lower-impact, family friendly venues and opportunities, was never intended to replace the great hiking and biking books about Santa Barbara County already available. For a complete rundown of the great outdoors, check out these books, most of which are available at local bookstores and libraries.

Day Hikes Around Santa Barbara, by Robert Stone (2003)

Mountain Biking California's Central Coast Best 100 Trails, by Delaine Fragnoli (1999)

Mountain Biking the Central Coast, Volume 1, by Carol Berlund (1990)

Santa Barbara Trail Guide, by Santa Barbara Group, Los Padres Chapter, Sierra Club (1995)

Santa Barbara County Recreational Map Series, by Ray Ford (1986)

Santa Barbara Day Hikes, by Ray Ford (2000)

CHAMBERS OF COMMERCE

These business associations promote their communities with an emphasis on their member businesses. While these are great places to start your search for local information, keep in mind most omit non-member businesses.

Buellton Visitors Bureau   (805) 688-7829
& Chamber of Commerce
     597 Avenue of Flags, Unit 101
     P.O. Box 231, Buellton, CA 93427
     Buellton.org

Carpinteria Valley Chamber of Commerce   (805) 684-5479
     1056-B Eugenia Place, Carpinteria, CA 93013
     carpchamber.org

Goleta Valley Chamber of Commerce   (805) 967-2500
     P.O. Box 781, Goleta CA 93116
     goletavalley.com

Lompoc Valley Chamber & Visitors' Bureau   (805) 736-4567
     111 S. I St., Lompoc, CA 93436
     Lompoc.com

Los Olivos Business Organization   (805) 315-1292
     www.losolivosca.com

Santa Barbara Conference & Visitors Bureau   (805) 966-9222
and Film Commission
     1601 Anacapa Street, Santa Barbara, CA 93101
     santabarbaraCA.com

Santa Barbara Region Chamber of Commerce   (805) 965-3023
     924 Anacapa St. Suite 1, Santa Barbara, CA 93101
     sbchamber.org

Santa Maria Valley Chamber of Commerce   (805) 925-2403
and Visitor & Convention Bureau
  614 South Broadway, Santa Maria, CA 93454
  santamaria.com
Santa Ynez Valley Visitors Association   (805) 686-0053
  P.O. Box 1918, Santa Ynez, CA 93460
  syvva.com
Solvang Chamber of Commerce   (805) 688-0701
  P.O. Box 465, Solvang, CA 93464
  solvangcc.com
Solvang Conference & Visitors Bureau   (805) 688-6144
  1639 Copenhagen Drive, Solvang, CA 93464
  solvangusa.com

RECREATION AND PARKS DEPARTMENTS

These governmental departments provide activities and amenities for all ages.

Buellton Parks & Recreation	(805) 688-1086
Carpinteria Parks & Recreation	(805) 684-5405 ext. 4
Cuyama Valley Recreation & Parks	(661) 766-2270
Goleta Parks & Open Space	(805) 968-6848
Guadalupe Recreation	(805) 343-1340, ext. 8
Isla Vista Recreation & Parks	(805) 968-2017
Lompoc Parks, Recreation	(805) 875-8100
& Urban Forestry	
Santa Barbara City Parks & Rec.	(805) 564-5418
Santa Barbara County Parks	(805) 568-2461
Santa Maria Recreation & Parks	(805) 925-0951, ext. 260
Solvang Parks & Recreation	(805) 688-7529

FARMERS' MARKETS

It's easier than ever to eat locally grown produce, particularly on the Central Coast where the growing season continues throughout the year. On any given day you can find some sort of farmers' market in Santa Barbara County. They are organized by a variety of associations, and all include produce from local (and sometimes not-so-local) farms. Some also include crafts, games and live entertainment.

The following list of locations and times is subject to change. Check the newspaper listings or chambers of commerce for the latest information or check in with organizers.

Carpinteria
  www.sbfarmersmarket.org   (805) 962-5354
  Thursday, 4 p.m. - 7 p.m. (summer), 3 p.m. - 6 p.m. (winter), 800 block Linden Ave.
Goleta
  www.sbfarmersmarket.org   (805) 962-5354

Thursday, 3 p.m. - 6 p.m., 5700 block Calle Real
Lompoc
www.countyofsb.org/agcomm   (805) 709-6740
Friday, 2 p.m. - 6 p.m., Ocean Ave. @ I Street.
Los Olivos
www.losolivosca.com   (805) 315-1292
Saturday, 8 a.m. - Noon, San Marcos Ave. @ Alamo Pintado Ave.
Montecito
www.sbfarmersmarket.org   (805) 962-5354
Friday, 8 a.m. - 11:15 a.m., 1100-1200 block Coast Village Road
Orcutt
www.countyofsb.org/agcomm   (805) 709-6740
Tuesday, 10 a.m. - 1 p.m., Bradley Road & Clark Ave.
Santa Barbara
www.sbfarmersmarket.org   (805) 962-5354
Tuesday, 4 p.m. - 7:30 p.m. (summer), 3 p.m. - 6:30 p.m. (winter),
500-600 block State St.
Wednesday, 3 p.m. - 6:30 p.m., Harding School, 1625 Robbins St.
Saturday, 8:30 a.m. - 12:30 p.m., Santa Barbara St. & Cota St.
Santa Maria
www.countyofsb.org/agcomm   (805) 709-6740
Wednesday, 12:30 p.m. - 4:30 p.m., 100 block South Broadway
Solvang
www.sbfarmersmarket.org   (805) 962-5354
Wednesday, 4 p.m. - 7 p.m. (summer), 3 p.m. - 6 p.m. (winter),
Copenhagen Drive & First Street

ARTS ASSOCIATIONS

Artists Guild of the Santa Ynez Valley
P.O. Box 1008, Santa Ynez   (805) 686-0090
www.agsyv.org
Carpinteria Valley Arts Council
P.O. Box 597, Carpinteria   (805) 684-7789
www.artscarp.org
Central Coast Woodturners
Santa Maria   (805) 489-5309
www.centralcoastwoodturners.com
Goleta Valley Art Association
P. O. Box 435, Goleta   (805) 967-6601
www.tgvaa.org
Lompoc Valley Art Association
P. O. Box 723, Lompoc   (805) 737-1129
www.lompocvalleyartassociation.com
Lompoc Valley Mural Society
P. O. Box 2813, Lompoc   (805) 736-4567
www.lompocmurals.com

Los Padres Artists Guild
   P.O. Box 2415, Orcutt   (805) 937-4427
   www.lospadresartistguild.com
Los Padres Watercolor Society
   12 Camino Verde, Santa Barbara   (805) 564-7019
Santa Barbara Art Association
   1114 State Street #8, Santa Barbara   (805) 963-1026
   sbartassoc.org
Santa Barbara Contemporary Arts Forum
   653 Paseo Nuevo, Santa Barbara   (805) 966-5373
   www.sbcaf.org
Santa Barbara Fiber Arts Guild
   P.O. Box 30944, Santa Barbara
   sbfiberarts.com
Santa Barbara Printmakers
   Santa Barbara
   www.sbprintmakers.com
Santa Barbara Sculptors Guild
   P. O. Box 2273, Santa Barbara   (805) 705-1499
   www.sbsculptors.org
Santa Barbara Visual Arts Alliance
   3905 State Street, Suite # 7-293, Santa Barbara
   sbva.org
Santa Maria Mural Society
   2429 Professional Parkway, Suite 103, Santa Maria
Santa Ynez Woodworkers Guild
   Santa Ynez Valley   (805) 466-8142
   www.woodwest.com/woodorg.html
Southern California Artists Painting for the Environment (S.C.A.P.E.)
   P.O. Box 30932 Santa Barbara
   s-c-a-p-e.org

MUSIC ASSOCIATIONS
Accordion International Music Society
   (805) 642-7940
   P.O. Box 4511, Santa Barbara
   www.santabarbaraaccordions.com
   Want to learn what an accordion can really do? Perform with others, or just learn to take proper care of your squeeze box.
Camerata Pacifica
   (805) 884-8410
   P.O. Box 30116, Santa Barbara
   www.cameratapacifica.org
   Chamber music with a modern bent.
Central City Chordsmen Barbershop Chorus
   (805) 925-9263
   Orcutt
   www.centralcitychordsmen.org

Teen boys and men alike are invited to sing in four-part a cappella harmony throughout the Santa Maria Valley. Rehearsals weekly; performances regularly.

Coastal Voices
(805) 937-3416
4011 Shellie Court, Santa Maria
coastalvoiceschoir.org

Community Arts Music Association
(805) 966-4324
111 East Yananoli Street, Santa Barbara
www.camasb.org
For nearly a century, CAMA has focused on bringing classical musicians to Santa Barbara's various performance venues.

Channel City Barbershop Chorus
(805) 682-5005
Santa Barbara
Men of all ages are invited to sing in four-part a cappella harmony.

Gents-In-A-Chord Barbershop Chorus
(805) 733-4615
Lompoc
Men of all ages are invited to sing in four-part a cappella harmony serving the Lompoc Valley.

Hancock College Concert Band
(805) 922-6966 ext. 3252
800 S. College Dr. Santa Maria
www.hancockcollege.edu/Default.asp?page=329
Welcomes experienced musicians from throughout the community to join the band which offers public performances throughout the year.

Joyful Sound of Unity
(805) 937-6437
1165 Stubblefield Road, Santa Maria
www.unitysantamaria.org/services.htm
This vocal ensemble performs gospel, Broadway, traditional, and songs of various faiths and backgrounds with a focus on uplifting messages.

Lompoc Concert Association
(805) 735-1408
P.O. Box 1557, Lompoc
lompocconcert.org
Since 1948, bringing professional musicians of various genres to perform in Lompoc Valley.

Lompoc Music Association
(805) 736-8702
P.O. Box 734, Lompoc
lompocconcert.org/lompocmusicassociation.aspx
Since 1964, this volunteer organization has focused on providing four concerts per year typically featuring Central Coast artists with eclectic styles of music.

Lompoc Pops Orchestra
(805) 735-6463
Lompoc
www.lompocpopsorchestra.org
Performs classical and pops concerts and provides music education
and outreach throughout the year.

Lompoc Valley Master Chorale
P.O. Box 24, Lompoc
www.lvmasterchorale.org
Providing public performances varying from classical to Broadway.

Music Academy of the West
(805) 969-4726
1070 Fairway Road, Santa Barbara
www.musicacademy.org
Features public performances of classical works by hand-selected
academy fellows mid-June to mid-August.

Opera Santa Barbara
(805) 898-3890
1330 State St., Suite 209, Santa Barbara
operasb.com
Also offers free student dress rehearsals, learning guides at website
and special family performances.

Prime Time Band
(805) 962-6983
P.O. Box 92055, Santa Barbara
www.ptband.org
An informal community concert band open to instrumentalists ages
50 and older interested in performing for people of all ages.

St. Andrew Academy of Music
(805) 937-0690
3945 S. Bradley Road, Orcutt
Saintandrewumc.com
Non-profit organization providing group and private music
instruction for a variety of instruments.

Santa Barbara Chamber Orchestra
(805) 966-2441
P.O. Box 90903, Santa Barbara
www.sbco.org
Performs classical works. Free ticket for children ages 10 to 18 and
their parents/guardians for certain concerts.

Santa Barbara Choral Society
(805) 965-6577
P.O. Box 3324, Santa Barbara
www.sbchoral.org
A semi-professional community chorus open, by audition, to qualified
singers of all ages and backgrounds.

Santa Barbara City College Music Department
(805) 965-0581, ext. 2379

721 Cliff Drive, Santa Barbara
www.sbcc.edu/music
Offers a variety of performing vocal and instrumental groups
including Concert Choir, Chamber Singers, Quire of Voyces,
Symphony Orchestra, Jazz Ensemble and various recitals.

Santa Barbara Master Chorale
(805) 967-8287
P.O. Box 30803, Santa Barbara
www.sbmasterchorale.org
Offers public performances of major works varying from classical to
Jazz and pops.

Santa Barbara Music Club
(805) 683-0811
P.O. Box 3974, Santa Barbara
www.sbmusicclub.org
Performing club members who pass the audition present an annual
series of free concerts featuring classical and American works.

Santa Barbara Symphony Association
(805) 898-9626
1330 State St., Suite 102, Santa Barbara
www.thesymphony.org
Classical music performances in Santa Barbara for more than half a
century.

Santa Barbara Youth Symphony
(805) 967-0781
www.sbys.org
Provides training and performance opportunities for area youth with
an interest in symphonic music.

Santa Maria Philharmonic Orchestra
(805) 925-0412
120 E. Jones St., Suite 120, Santa Maria
santamariaphilharmonic.org
Bringing classical music performance to the Santa Maria Valley.

Santa Ynez Valley Master Chorale, Youth Chorale and Orchestra
(805) 350-4241
P.O. Box 1902, Santa Ynez
www.syvchorale.org
Musicians of all abilities and experience levels are invited to
audition for this Classical performance group.

Santa Ynez Valley Wind Ensemble
(805) 688-8728
Community concert band provides half a dozen public performances
per year. If you can read music and play a concert instrument, this
may be the place for you. Rehearsals begin at 7 p.m. Thursdays in
the music room at Santa Ynez Valley High School.

Tri City Sound Chorus, Sweet Adelines
(805) 736-7572
Rehearses in Orcutt

Tricitysound.org
Santa Barbara County's only Sweet Adelines chapter. Women with
an interest in learning and performing four-part, a cappella
harmony in true barbershop style are invited to join and take part in
annual performances.

UCSB Department of Music
(805) 893-3261
University of California, Santa Barbara, Goleta
www.music.ucsb.edu
Features more than a dozen instrumental ensembles and more than
half a dozen vocal ensembles and workshops with public
performances and other events throughout the year. Genres vary
from opera to jazz, Middle Eastern to chamber music.

West Coast Chamber Orchestra
1812 La Coronilla Drive, Santa Barbara
www.wccosb.org
Chamber orchestra performances of classical works.

Young Singers Club
(805) 681-7078
Santa Barbara
www.youngsingersclub.com
Offers a variety of vocal performance groups for children 4 to 18.

THEATRICAL AND DANCE ORGANIZATIONS

There are dozens of performing arts schools and programs throughout the
county. This list includes many of those that offer public performances
regularly.

Arlington Theatre
1317 State St., Santa Barbara   (805) 963-4408
www.thearlingtontheatre.com
Historic venue for all performing arts. For more details, see p. 13.

Arts for Humanity! (AH!)
P.O. Box 91522, Santa Barbara   (805) 687-6615
www.artsforhumanity.com
Performing and visual arts outreach programs and education.

Ballet Santa Barbara
2536 Foothill Road, Santa Barbara   (805) 450-7535
balletsantabarbara.org
Contemporary ballet company offering both performances and
training for dancers of all ages.

BOXTALES Theatre Company
P.O. Box 91521, Santa Barbara   (805) 962-1142
www.boxtales.org
Specializes in sharing myths and folktales from around the world
using masks, movement, music, and storytelling.

Center Stage Theater
751 State Street, Santa Barbara   (805) 963-0408

www.centerstagetheater.org

Circle Bar B Dinner Theatre
1800 Refugio Road, Goleta   (805) 967-1962
www.circlebarbtheatre.com
Dinner theater in a cozy ranch setting. (See p. 213 for details.)

Daughter of Zion Aerial Dance Co.
P.O. Box 1586, Santa Ynez   (805) 698-9188
daughterofzion.net
Melds modern dance, theater and low-flying aerial work.

Drama Dogs
P.O. Box 2335, Santa Barbara
www.dramadogs.org
Combines theater, dance and literature for public performances and educational programs.

Ensemble Theatre Company
914 Santa Barbara St., Santa Barbara (805) 965-5400
www.ensembletheatre.com
Santa Barbara's oldest professional theater company.

Hancock College Fine Arts
800 S. College Dr., Santa Maria   (805) 922-6966, ext. 3252
www.hancockcollege.edu/Default.asp?Page=452
Dance, drama and music performed by students and other community members.

Lobero Theatre
33 East Canon Perdido Street, Santa Barbara   (805) 966-4946
www.lobero.com
Performance venue with an active calendar of performing arts from dance and theater to lectures and readings.

Lompoc Civic Theater
P.O. Box 69, Lompoc   (805) 735-2281
lbee.com/LCT
Since 1973, offering local actors a performance outlet including full-length plays, musicals, one acts, dinner theaters, murder mystery parties, and variety shows. Also offers summer workshops.

Marjorie Luke Theatre
Santa Barbara Junior High School
721 E. Cota St., Santa Barbara   (805) 884-4087
www.luketheatre.com
This historic theater with a very active performance schedule is home to dozens of organizations. The theater has served as symphony hall, film venue, dance and theater stage, speakers' podium and more.

Pacific Conservatory of the Performing Arts (PCPA)
800 South College Drive, Santa Maria   (805) 922-8313
www.pcpa.org
Professional conservatory theater with regular performances in Santa Maria at Marian and Seversen theaters and in Solvang at Festival Theater.

Santa Barbara City College Theatre Group
721 Cliff Drive, Santa Barbara   (805) 965-5935
sbcctg.sbcc.edu
Combines professional, community and student talent for
performances in both Garvin Theatre and black box Jurkowitz
Theatre, both on campus.

Santa Barbara Dance Arts
1 N. Calle Cesar Chavez, Suite 100, Santa Barbara (805) 966-5299
Jazz, hip hop, ballet, Broadway, tap and lyrical performances,
classes and camps.

Santa Barbara Dance Alliance
924 Anacapa Street #15, Santa Barbara   (805) 966-6950
www.sbdancealliance.org
Non-profit organization striving to bring the dance community
together. Coordinates dance events, but this is also the place to go
for information about dance studios, schools, companies and private
instruction throughout southern Santa Barbara County.

Santa Barbara Improv Group
Santa Barbara   (805)680-0455
www.sbimprov.com
Improvisational comedy for all with occasional public performances.
Mature teens welcome. Bring a friend.

Santa Barbara Performing Arts League
P.O. Box 20284, Santa Barbara   (805) 563-8068
sbperformingartsleague.org
This concerted effort to coordinate the performing arts in southern
Santa Barbara County maintains a calendar of events by a variety of
troupes.

Santa Barbara Silver Follies Entertainment Group
1600 Garden Street, #9, Santa Barbara   (805) 845-8689
www.sbsilverfollies.org
A precision dance troupe and Follies Singers for performers ages 50
and older, some with a history in the entertainment industry, others
introduced later in life.

Santa Barbara Theatre
P.O. Box 23211, Santa Barbara   (805) 963-7282
www.sbtheatre.org
Professional theater company housed at Lobero Theatre.

Santa Maria Civic Theater
1660 N. McClelland St., Santa Maria   (805) 922-4442
www.smct.org
Community theater in a black box venue.

ShowStoppers
3579 Modoc Road, Santa Barbara   (805) 682-6043
www.showstopperstheatreproductions.com
Musical theater training program for youth with after-school,
summer and ensemble opportunities.

Speaking of Stories

    P.O. Box 21143, Santa Barbara   (805) 966-3875

    www.speakingofstories.org

    Reader's theater brings literature to the stage.

State Street Ballet

    2285 Las Positas Road, Santa Barbara, CA 93105 (805) 563-3262

    www.statestreetballet.com

    Professional dance company.

The Granada

    1214 State St., Santa Barbara   (805) 899-2222

    www.granadasb.org

    Performing arts venue with a very active calendar including both local and traveling dance, theater, music and more.

University of California, Santa Barbara Arts & Lectures

    UCSB, Goleta   (805) 893-3535

    www.artsandlectures.ucsb.edu

    A diverse calendar of performances by artists from around the globe, including dance, music, theater, film, lectures and a variety of other special events.

UCSB Department of Theater & Dance

    UCSB, Goleta   (805) 893-3241

    www.theaterdance.ucsb.edu

    Live performing arts productions by students.

Valley Community Theatre

    Los Olivos   (805) 688-3343

    Community theatre offers performance outlet for local artists, and entertainment for local audience.

Westmont College Theatre Arts

    955 La Paz Road, Santa Barbara   (805) 565-7040

    www.westmont.edu

    Student theater and dance live on stage.

GETTING AROUND
CAR-FREE TRANSPORTATION OPTIONS

The county is full of public transportation options, though some are more convenient than others. Many of the area's buses include bike racks. Some communities offer free or very low-cost trolleys, and bus systems are available throughout the county. For an overview of options, including busing, carpooling, vanpooling and cycling routes, visit www.trafficsolutions.info.

Amtrak

(800) USA-RAIL

www.amtrak.com

The Pacific Surfliner and Coast Starlight both travel through Santa Barbara County daily and offer a fun, if not inexpensive, way to get around. The train offers many their first glimpse of the coastline hidden from the general public on Vandenberg Air Force Base (p. 164). Carpinteria, Santa

Barbara, Goleta, Surf and Guadalupe all have stations, though not all trains stop at these stations.

Breeze
(805) 928-5624
www.thebreezebus.com
Commuter bus linking Santa Maria, Vandenberg and Lompoc.

City of Lompoc Transit (COLT)
(805) 736-7666
www.cityoflompoc.com/transit/colt.htm
Offering daily bus service throughout Lompoc, Vandenberg Village, Mission Hills, Buellton and Solvang with twice-weekly routes to Santa Barbara.

Coastal Express
(800) 438-1112
www.goventura.org/?q=get-there-by-bus/local-bus-services/vista
Bus service linking Goleta and UCSB with Santa Barbara, Carpinteria and points south to Oxnard and Ventura.

Easy Lift
(805) 681-1181
www.easylift.org
Provides Dial-A-Ride service throughout Southern Santa Barbara County for people with disabilities that preclude them from taking other mass transit.

Greyhound
(800) 231-2222
www.greyhound.com
Regular daily routes with stations in Santa Maria and Santa Barbara

Guadalupe Flyer
(805) 922-8476
www.smoothinc.org
Bus service linking Guadalupe and Santa Maria.

San Luis Obispo Rapid Transit (RTA)
(805) 781-4472
www.slorta.org
Daily bus service linking Santa Maria to San Luis Obispo with stops throughout southern San Luis Obispo County.

Santa Barbara Bicycle Coalition
(805) 568-3046
sbbike.org
Bike maps, rides, tours, commuting, safety – want to know about biking in Santa Barbara County? Start here.

Santa Barbara Metropolitan Transit District (MTD)
(805) 963-3366
www.sbmtd.gov
Operates daily bus service throughout southern Santa Barbara County and commuter express routes linking Solvang, Buellton, Goleta and downtown Santa Barbara. MTD also operates Santa Barbara's Downtown-Waterfront Shuttle. The shuttle is the county's best mass transportation deal at just 25

cents per rider each way serving the waterfront from Santa Barbara Zoo to the marina and Stearns Wharf up State Street and east one block to Alameda Park.

Santa Maria Area Transit (SMAT)
(805) 928-5624
www.ci.santa-maria.ca.us
Daily bus service throughout greater Santa Maria including Orcutt and Tanglewood. Dial-A-Ride service also available by reservation to those with disabilities.

Santa Ynez Valley Transit
(805) 688-5452
cityofsolvang.com/index.php/santa-ynez-valley-transit
Bus routes serving Santa Ynez Valley from Riverview Drive in Buellton to Meadowvale Road in Santa Ynez and north to Los Olivos. Monday through Saturday, 7 a.m. to 7 p.m. Also offers Dial-a-Ride service for seniors.

CLUBS, GROUPS AND OTHER GATHERINGS

While this information was up to date at publication time, please be aware that many smaller clubs and organizations tend to change leadership, and thereby contact information, regularly.

4-H
Countywide
(805) 962-1734
groups.ucanr.org/SB4H
National organization with some 16 clubs throughout Santa Barbara County aims to help youth develop citizenship, leadership and life skills through any of a number of extracurricular activities under adult volunteer supervision. Traditionally bent toward agriculture and home economics, but modernization has resulted in additional offerings. Call for info on your neighborhood club.

American Youth Soccer Organization (AYSO)
Countywide
www.ayso.org/region_locator.aspx
National competitive youth soccer program for players ages 4 to 18.

Bici Centro Youth Bike Program
La Casa de la Raza
601 E. Montecito St., Santa Barbara
bicicentro.org
(805) 617-3255
Low-cost to no-cost bicycle repair education center.

Boy Scouts of America – Los Padres Council
Countywide
(805) 967-0105
www.lpcbsa.org
Leadership program for boys ages 7 through 17 includes Cub Scouts, Boy Scouts and Venturers.

United Boys & Girls Club of Santa Barbara County
www.unitedbg.org
Youth programs including daycare and afterschool child care, field trips
and other organized activities for kids ages 6 to 18 enrolled in school.
Locations serving Carpinteria (684-1568), Goleta (967-1612), Santa Barbara
(966-2811) and Lompoc (736-4978).

Boys & Girls Club of Santa Maria Valley
(805) 922-7763
www.bgcsmv.org
Youth programs including daycare and afterschool child care, field trips
and other organized activities for kids ages 6 to 18 enrolled in school with
three locations: 901 N. Railroad Ave., Santa Maria; 200 W. Williams, Santa
Maria; and 4689 11th Street, Guadalupe.

Boys & Girls Club of Santa Barbara
632 E. Canon Perdido St., Santa Barbara
(805) 962-2382
www.boysgirls.org
Youth programs including daycare and afterschool child care, field trips
and other organized activities for kids ages 6 to 18 enrolled in school and
limited programs for kindergarten and pre-kindergarten students.

Braille Institute
2031 De La Vina Street, Santa Barbara
(805) 682-6222
www.brailleinstitute.org/santa_barbara
Non-profit agency providing classes and outings for people with visual
impairments.

Camp Fire USA
(805) 773-5126
Youth service organization serving the Central Coast.

Carpinteria High School Track & Field All-comers Meets
Carpinteria Valley Memorial Stadium
Carpinteria High School, 4810 Foothill Road, Carpinteria
(805) 684-4107
www.warriorcountry.com/track/allcomers/all_comers.htm
Each summer, the high school track program, under the direction of Coach
Van Lantham, offers a full-schedule of track and field competition for
athletes ages 7 through adult.

Central Coast Corvette Club
Santa Maria
(805) 934-3948
centralcoastcorvettes.com
Corvette owners and enthusiasts meet at 7 p.m. the first Thursday of each
month to discuss the vehicles, plan events and socialize.

Civil Air Patrol 101
Santa Maria & Vandenberg Air Force Base
cap-sq101-vafb.ucoz.com
The official civilian auxiliary of the United States Air Force for aircraft
enthusiasts ages 12 and older. Regular meetings held Wednesday evenings.

Coastal Quilters Guild of Santa Barbara & Goleta
P.O. Box 6341, Santa Barbara
(805) 967-5311
www.coastalquilters.org
Open to all quilters and quilt enthusiasts. Some 200 members gather monthly for presentations by guests and peers. Satellite groups hold additional meetings to explore similar interests such as appliqué, rotary quilts, traditional quilts and more.

Coastal Valley Orchid Society
Lompoc
www.coastalvalleyorchidsociety.com
Meets monthly to discuss orchids, hear guest speakers and view member exhibits. Affiliated with the American Orchid Society.

Dance Away Santa Barbara
Unitarian Society, 1535 Santa Barbara St., Santa Barbara
danceawaysb.com
Alcohol-free, smoke-free, drug-free setting for barefoot, freestyle dance with music that varies from New Age to World Music to Pop. No dress policy. Drummers welcome for weekly jams. Offered Fridays from 7:30 p.m. to 10:30 p.m.

Daughters of the American Revolution
Lompoc - www.geocities.com/rancho_purisima_dar
Santa Barbara - californiadar.org/chapters/missioncanyon
Santa Maria - californiadar.org/chapters/capthenrysweetser
Service organization open to women ages 18 and older who are descendants of "those who aided in achieving American Independence during the period between April 19, 1775, and November 26, 1783."

Dos Pueblos Challengers
Goleta & Carpinteria fields
(805) 681-9165
www.dpllchallengers.org
Little League baseball for physically and developmentally challenged boys and girls ages 5 through 18.

Echelon Santa Barbara
P.O. Box 1957, Goleta
www.echelonsantabarbara.org
Road cycling group with a competitive focus. Juniors rides, Saturday group rides and women's rides are among the offerings.

Elks Club
www.elks.org
Santa Maria, Lompoc, Santa Ynez Valley and Santa Barbara
This nationwide service organization provides social outlets and community service through local lodges. Santa Maria Elks Lodge, for instance, is a major funding source force in Santa Maria Valley youth recreation programs, sponsors an annual parade and rodeo event, allows use of its facilities for other rodeo events and bicycle motocross, and features Friday night Cook Your Own dinners for the 21 and over set.

Endeavours
Lompoc
endeavours.org
Offers space camps and other educational programs with a focus on space exploration.

Experimental Aircraft Association Chapter 499
Santa Maria
www.eaachapter499.org
Enthusiasts of recreational aviation and homebuilt aircraft meet at 7 p.m. on the second Tuesday of each month.

Families with Children from China's Central Coast Chapter
(805) 927-2232
fwcc.org
Provides a local resource, play groups and New Years party.

Family Homeschool Adventures
(805) 733-2692
groups.yahoo.com/group/FamilyHomeschoolAdventures
Homeschool support and event group serving Lompoc, Buellton, Solvang, Santa Maria, Santa Barbara and surrounding communities.

Friendship Club of Santa Maria Valley
(805) 937-6320
Women's social club available to residents of the Santa Maria Valley including Orcutt, Guadalupe, Sisquoc and Garey. The wide array of activities reflects members' interests, including monthly luncheons and soirees, and an annual fashion show, as well as regularly scheduled book chats, bridge, bunco, golf, pinochle, morning coffees, member-hosted potlucks and more.

GenSpan Foundation
Santa Maria
(805) 614-4968
www.genspan.org
Matches senior volunteer mentors with schools and other organizations.

Girl Scouts of California's Central Coast
Countywide
(800) 822-2427
www.girlscoutsccc.org
International leadership program for girls ages 5 to 17.

Girls Inc. of Carpinteria
5315 Foothill Road, Carpinteria
(805) 684-6364
www.girlsinc-carp.org
Offers school-age girls specialized programs including cultural arts, athletics, juvenile justice, teen programs, summer programs and after school enrichment.

Girls Inc. of Greater Santa Barbara
531 E. Ortega St., Santa Barbara (805) 963-4017
4973 Hollister Avenue, Goleta (805) 967-0319
www.girlsincsb.org

Offers school-age girls specialized activities including teen programs, gymnastics, summer programs and after school enrichment.

Goleta Valley Cycling Club
www.goletabike.org
Goleta-based, recreational cycling club focused on encouraging people new to cycling or new to the area. Families welcome.

Grunion Rugby
Elings Park, Santa Barbara
Grunionrugby.com
Amateur rugby club for players of all ages and experience levels.

Hearthstone Home Educators
Santa Maria Valley
(805) 937-7099
sites.google.com/site/hearthstonesm
This Christian support group dedicated to homeschooling families. Participants in this volunteer-driven association may organize field trips, science fairs, art programs and more. They also host the annual Central Coast Home Education Conference each spring.

International Folk Dancers
(805) 895-4885
Meets in Santa Barbara twice weekly to explore and enjoy dance from various countries. Families welcome.

Jewish Federation of Greater Santa Barbara
524 Chapala St., Santa Barbara
(805) 957-1115
www.jewishsantabarbara.org
Offers a variety of programs ranging from chess and comedy clubs to cultural education and fitness programs. No religious affiliation required to participate.

Junior Lifeguards
UCSB Junior Guards - www.ucsbjgs.org
Refugio State Beach Junior Guards - (805) 968-1760
Carpinteria Junior Guards - www.carpinteria.ca.us/parks_rec/Jr Guards.shtml
Santa Barbara Junior Guards - www.santabarbaraca.gov/SummerFun/ jr_lifeguards.htm
These competitive programs, typically for swimmers ages 8 to 17, include beach and water safety training, first aid, surf lifesaving and workouts that include swimming and running.

Leisure Time Games Groups
159 Town Center West, Santa Maria
(805) 614-GAME
This game store provides play space and direction for gamers interested in Pokemon, Magic, Warhammer, Dungeons & Dragons, Yugioh, Street Fighter, Chess and other games. Call for current schedule, tournaments and special events.

La Leche League
www.llli.org/Web/California.html

This international organization provides support, information and education for breastfeeding mothers and mothers-to-be interested in breastfeeding. Regular monthly meetings and other events are offered throughout the county, and babies are generally welcome. For information about LLL in the north county contact La Leche of Santa Maria (805-938-0789 and online at www.lllusa.org/web/SantaMariaCA.html); in the south county, contact La Leche of Santa Barbara (www.lllusa.org/web/SantaBarbaraCA.html).

Let It Go Yoga
Goleta
(800) 736-1670
LetItGoYoga.com
Offers a variety of yoga classes including "Family Yoga" and training for yoga instructors. All classes are taught by appointment and reservations are required.

Little League
www.littleleague.org
Provides competitive baseball and softball play for youth nationwide. Check website for teams in your neighborhood.

Lompoc Valley Bicycle Club
www.bikelompoc.com
Lompoc-based cycling club.

Lompoc Tsunami Swim Club
lompocaquatics.com
(805) 315-8968
Basic lessons and competitive training for swimmers of all levels ages 7 to 17.

Los Alamos Seniors
Senior Center, 690 Bell Street, Los Alamos
(805) 344-4610
Provides a social potluck for seniors on the last Friday of each month at 6 p.m. Bring a friend or find them here.

Luis OASIS Senior Center
420 Soares Ave., Orcutt
(805) 937-9750
oasisorcutt.com
This active recreation center open Monday through Friday from 8 a.m. to 4 p.m. provides year-round activities varying from silversmithing to line dancing, pilates and yoga for older adults and reflexology to HAM radio operators meetings, ukulele lessons, fiber arts guild gatherings, support groups, floral design groups, regular potlucks, guest performances and more. Call for current schedule.

Main Street Cycles Group Rides
311 E. Main St., Santa Maria
(805) 922-5577
mainstreetcycles.com
Group rides organized out of the store include beginner road rides, racing echelons, indoor training programs and mountain bike rides.

MOMS Club of Orcutt
(805) 350-3148

momscluboforcutt.yolasite.com

Support group for stay-at-home and part-time working moms with small children.

MOMS Club of Santa Maria
(805) 928-8806

Support group for stay-at-home and part-time working moms with small children.

Moms In Motion
Throughout Santa Barbara County

momsinmotion.com

International, volunteer-driven fitness training program for women and girls. At publication time, local groups were limited to the South County, but new groups may form anywhere.

Montecito Trails Foundation
(805) 969-3514

www.montecitotrailsfoundation.org

This private, non-profit organization has worked on trail acquisition and maintenance since 1964. Today, these volunteers help maintain some 300 miles of trails in the Montecito, Carpinteria and Summerland areas. Membership is open to anyone interested in lending a hand. Members receive maps, newsletters and invitations to events including monthly group hikes, an annual barbecue and an annual meeting.

MOPS (Mothers of Preschoolers)
Pacific Christian Center

3435 Santa Maria Way, Orcutt

(805) 934-3491

Support group for mothers of children ages birth to kindergarten.

Newcomers' Club of Santa Maria Valley
(805) 349-8976

This member-driven club is designed to help residents new to the area make friends, learn about their new community and feel more comfortable in their new setting. Monthly meetings include guest speakers and other activities. There are also various special interest groups that gather more frequently.

One Way Water Polo
Santa Maria

(805) 878-1285

onewaywaterpolo.com

Competitive water polo program for boys and girls of all levels, ages 7 through adult.

Orcutt Historical Society
Orcutt

(805) 934-5169

Free meetings held at 10 a.m. the third Saturday of each month feature local and guest speakers with particular expertise in Orcutt history. Meets at Luis Oasis Senior Center, 420 Soares Ave.

Orcutt Mineral Society
Santa Maria
(805) 929-3788
Rockhounds gather on the second Tuesday of each month to discuss their hunts, their finds and other news related to rocks and minerals.

Orcutt United Soccer League
Orcutt
ousl.org
Recreational soccer league for players of all abilities and ages 4 to 19. And co-ed adult soccer on Sundays.

Poison Oak Cachers
Countywide
www.poisonoakcachers.com
Family friendly group dedicated to recreational, high-tech treasure hunting involving GPS and treasure troves.

Presidio Fencing Club
Santa Barbara
(805) 403-6895
Presidiofencing.com
Lessons and open recreation for fencers of all abilities ages 7 and older. All equipment provided.

Quilters Etc.
PO Box 2507, Lompoc
(805) 733-1182
www.members.tripod.com/quiltersetc-ivil
Focuses on sharing the knowledge and appreciation of fine quilts, quilt-making and collecting, quilting techniques, patterns and history through educational meetings, travel, and friendship.

Rancho de Guadalupe Historical Society
1005 Guadalupe Street, Guadalupe
(805) 343-5901
Meets at 6 p.m. the first Wednesday of each month.

Retired Senior Volunteer Program
Countywide
(805) 922-9931
Matches volunteers aged 55 and older to nonprofit and public agencies.

Retired Active Men of Santa Maria
home.comcast.net/~atdulaney/RAMS/RAMSMainPage.html
(805) 934-2627
Meets at 8:30 a.m. the fourth Tuesday of each month. Open to retired, active men ages 54 and older.

Roots & Shoots
Countywide
www.rootsandshoots.org/findagroup
The Jane Goodall Institute's international environmental and humanitarian program for youth of all ages.

Santa Barbara Astronomical Unit
www.sbau.org

Members meet monthly to discuss astronomical events, equipment and plan a variety of events including monthly star parties.

Santa Barbara BMX
Elings Park (p. 39)
1298 Las Positas Road
Santa Barbara
(805) 564-8859
www.sbbmx.com
Weekly bicycle motocross races, practice nights and regularly scheduled training clinics.

Santa Barbara Country Dance Society
Santa Barbara
(805) 682-1877
www.sbcds.org
English country dance and contra dance for all ages in varied settings. Learn new dances, make new friends or bring your own.

Santa Barbara County Trails Council
South County
(805) 963-2779
www.sbtrails.org
Since 1969, volunteers have worked to develop and maintain trails for various uses.

Santa Barbara Foresters
Santa Barbara
(805) 684-0657
sbforesters.org
Summer college baseball league that also offers baseball camps for kids.

Santa Barbara Go Club
Santa Barbara
www.santabarbaragoclub.com
Meets weekly for recreational play of this ancient, Chinese board game.

Santa Barbara Homeschool Network
Santa Barbara
groups.yahoo.com/group/SBHN/
Homeschooling families supporting each other through social gatherings, field trips and more.

Santa Barbara Horseshoe Pitching Club
Santa Barbara
(805) 965-7710
This member of the Southern California Horseshoe Pitchers Association meets regularly at Oak Park. Call for current events schedule.

Santa Barbara Jugglers Association
Goleta
www.sbjuggle.org
Bring your toys and learn a new trick, or share your oldies.

Santa Barbara Mountain Bike Trail Volunteers
(805) 681-0048
www.sbmtv.org

Santa Barbara-based mountain biking group with an emphasis on community service.

Santa Barbara Newcomers
Santa Barbara
(805) 564-2555
www.sbnewcomers.org
With more than 400 members and dozens of committees dedicated to special interests, this social networking club helps new area residents make new friends while learning about social, cultural and civic opportunities in the area.

Santa Barbara Police Activities League
Santa Barbara
www.santabarbarapal.com
Provides various programs including arts, athletics, after-school programs and summer camps.

Santa Barbara Radio Modelers
San Lucas Ranch, near Santa Ynez, and Elings Park, Santa Barbara
www.sbrcm.org
Meets the first Thursday of each month at Santa Barbara Airport Visitors Center (p. 121) to promote the hobby of model aviation.

Santa Barbara Rose Society
(805) 652-7443
sbrose.org
Since 1959, this volunteer organization has helped to maintain the AC Postel Rose Garden (p. 47). Members meet monthly to discuss and enjoy roses.

Santa Barbara Seals Surf School
Santa Barbara & Goleta
(805) 687.9785
www.santabarbaraseals.com
Provides private surf lessons as well as afterschool, summer and independent study programs for surfers of all ages and abilities.

Santa Barbara Surfrider Foundation
(805) 966-4219
sbsurfrider.org
Local chapter of this non-profit environmental organization dedicated to the protection and enjoyment of the world's oceans, waves and beaches for all people, through conservation, activism, research and education.

Santa Barbara Swim Club
Santa Barbara
(805) 966-9757
www.sbswim.org
USA Swimming affiliated competitive team for all abilities ages 5 and older.

Santa Barbara Triathlon Club
Carpinteria to Santa Ynez
sbtriclub.com
Support, friendship and potential teammates of all ages and abilities meet

to train, socialize or compete. Monthly dinner meetings include guest speaker.

Santa Barbara Turtle Riders
(805) 687-4677
Social cycling group for the slower set typically rides dedicated bike paths once a month. Families welcome.

Santa Barbara Water Polo Club
Swimbac.com
Year-round competitive water polo program for players of all abilities ages 6 to 18.

Santa Maria 4 Wheelers
Santa Maria Valley
(805) 928-7532
www.cal4wheel.com/santamaria/santamaria.html
Meets the fourth Tuesday of each month to plan runs, volunteer efforts and special events.

Santa Maria Valley Beekeepers Association
Santa Maria
(805) 934-4453
Meets month in Santa Maria to discuss all forms of beekeeping.

Santa Maria Bridge Club
Santa Maria
Acbldistrict22.com/543
Meets weekly for recreational play.

Santa Maria Camera Club
Santa Maria
www.lightpreserve.com/smcc
Meets semi-monthly to share and discuss all things photographic.

Santa Maria Inclusive Learners (SMILe)
Northern Santa Barbara County
This inclusive, secular homeschool group coordinates regular play days, co-ops and field trips.

Santa Maria Men's Club
Santa Maria
(805) 937-1499
Meets monthly for breakfast featuring speakers of particular interest to men of all ages.

Santa Maria Police Activities League
Santa Maria
(805) 925-0951, ext. 516
santamariapal.org
Local police officers work side by side with area youth to develop discipline, positive self-image, mutual trust and respect. The free programs have included baseball, boxing, fishing and girls club, paintball, off-highway vehicle training and rides, video production and disc jockey club.

Santa Maria Valley Mothers of Twins
Santa Maria
(805) 925-6605

Support group and resource for mothers of twins with regular gatherings.

Santa Maria Orchid Society
Santa Maria
(805) 739-1934
Meets on alternating months for education and discussion promoting the orchid growing hobby. All skill levels welcome. Call for current schedule.

Santa Maria Swim Club
Santa Maria
(805) 928-9655
www.santamariaswim.com
A nationally-recognized swim program for youth ages 5-18 from novice to college and Olympic-level competition. Masters swimming for all levels ages 18 and up.

Santa Maria Valley Genealogical Society
Santa Maria
(805) 937-2388
Members are available at the Santa Maria Public Library (p. 171) every Wednesday from 1 p.m. to 4 p.m. to help people find their roots.

Santa Maria Valley Sportsmen's Association
Santa Maria
(805) 937-8622
Members of all ages meet the second Tuesday of each month at Liberty School, 1300 W. Sonia Lane, to coordinate hunting, fishing and shooting opportunities including skeet, trap and pistol ranges. Works on conservation programs and offers youth programs including fishing tournaments and junior pheasant hunt.

Santa Maria Youth Football League
www.eteamz.com/SMYFL
Provides competitive football play for pre-high school set.

Santa Ynez Summer Water Polo
(805) 709-4191
Provides youth water polo training for competitors of all abilities ages 8 through high school.

Santa Ynez Valley Bow Club
1817 Jonata Park Road, Buellton
(805) 688-8579
www.syvbowclub.org
Offers family memberships for archers of all abilities and a Junior Olympic Archery Development program.

Santa Ynez Valley Sportsmen's Association
Santa Ynez
(805) 680-7356
Outdoor shooting ranges including rifle, pistol, trap, sporting clays, skeet, and summer safety and junior sportsmen's programs.

Scrabble Players
Oak Knolls Haven
4845 S. Bradley Road, Orcutt
(805) 934-0885

Anyone interested in playing Scrabble is welcome to join in most Fridays from 1 p.m. to 4 p.m.

Special Needs Network Parent Support Group
Santa Maria
(805) 937-8756
This support group for parents of people with special needs meets monthly to share ideas, ask questions and find solutions.

Tailwinds Bicycle Club
www.tailwindsofsantamariabc.org
Santa Maria-based social road cycling club.

Team Tailwinds
www.teamtailwinds.com
Santa Maria-based competitive road bike team.

The Cutters
(805) 938-9082
Orcutt-based cycling club.

THINK! Camp
Santa Barbara
(805) 565-7247
thinkcamps.org
Westmont Institute for Liberal Arts offers several summer camp programs. Past offerings have included Spanish language immersion, science, computer, music and theatre camps.

Toastmasters International
Countywide
www.toastmasters.org
This non-profit organization aims to help people be more competent and comfortable speakers and leaders. Locations countywide. Check Web site for latest updates, meeting times and special events.

Treble Clef Chorus
Goleta
(805) 967-4009
This women's chorus for singers of all ages and abilities rehearses Wednesday evenings and offers performances throughout the year.

Village Dirtbags
Vandenberg Village
www.villagedirtbags.com
Recreational cycling group with a tendency toward community service.

Vapor Trail Vettes
Santa Maria
(805) 937-4420
vaportrailvettes.com
Club for Corvette owners and enthusiasts.

Wilderness Youth Project
5386 Hollister, Ste D
Santa Barbara
(805) 964-8096
www.wyp.org

Outdoor education for all ages including family camps, youth camps, adult workshops.

Word Wizards Writers' Group
Santa Maria
(805) 925-0098
Authors of all experience levels gather weekly to discuss their craft, swap critiques and socialize.

Santa Barbara Fencing Academy
Santa Barbara
(805) 252-2990
sbfafencing.com
Olympian Michael D'Asaro, Jr. offers group and private instruction in sabre, epee, and foil for children and adults. Seated and wheelchair fencing also taught. Basic equipment provided, including protective gear and weapons.

ANNUAL EVENTS

Santa Barbara County's events calendar is busy all year round. Here are some of the annual highlights.

February
  Winter Dressage, Santa Barbara
  West Coast Nationals Tractor Pull, Santa Maria
  Santa Barbara International Film Festival, Santa Barbara
March
  International Orchid Show, Santa Barbara
  Renaissance Festival, Lompoc
April
  Earth Day, Santa Barbara
  Santa Barbara Fair & Expo, Santa Barbara
  Santa Maria Valley Strawberry Festival, Santa Maria
  Spring Arts Festival, Lompoc
  Sea Festival, Santa Barbara
  Dance Day, Santa Barbara
  Vintners' Festival, Lompoc
May
  Cinco de Mayo, Santa Barbara
  iMadonnari, Santa Barbara
  Children's Festival, Santa Barbara
  Classic & Hot Rod Car Show, Santa Barbara
  Irish Festival, Santa Barbara
  Jewish Festival, Santa Barbara
  Vintner's Festival, Santa Barbara
  West Coast Kustoms Cruisin' Nationals, Santa Maria
June
  Summer Solstice Festival, Santa Barbara
  Santa Maria Elks Rodeo, Santa Maria
  Caribbean Festival, Santa Barbara

Lompoc Valley Flower Festival, Lompoc
Live Oak Music Festival, near Lake Cachuma
Los Olivos Jazz & Olive Festival, Los Olivos
Lompoc Kennel Club Dog Show, Lompoc

July

French Festival (Bastille Day), Santa Barbara
Greek Festival, Santa Barbara
Santa Barbara National Horseshow
Semana Nautica, Santa Barbara
Santa Barbara County Fair, Santa Maria
Bent Axles Annual Cruise & BBQ, Santa Maria
Obon Festival, Santa Maria

August

Old Spanish Days Fiesta, Santa Barbara
Greek Festival, Santa Barbara
Quick Draw Art Festival, Los Olivos
Woodies Car Show, Santa Barbara

September

Old Town Harvest Festival, September, Santa Barbara
Los Alamos Old Days, Los Alamos
California Organic Festival, Santa Barbara
Flamenco Arts Festival, Santa Barbara
West Beach Music Festival, Santa Barbara
Sandcastle & Sculpting Festival, Santa Barbara
ArtWalk, Santa Barbara
Book & Author Festival, Santa Barbara

October

Autumn Arts Grapes & Grains Festival, Santa Maria
California Lemon Festival, Goleta
California Avocado Festival, Carpinteria
Old-Time Fiddlers' Convention, Goleta
Day in the Country, Los Olivos
Avocado Festival, Carpinteria

November

Santa Barbara National Open Western Horse Show, Santa Barbara
National Amateur Horse Show, Santa Barbara
Santa Ynez Valley Vaquero Show & Sale
Solvang Julefest
Veterans Memorial Parade, Santa Barbara
Carvers' Artistry in Wood, Santa Maria

December

Holiday Parades, most cities
Holiday Boat Parade of Lights, Santa Barbara
Parade of Lights, Santa Maria
Olde Fashioned Christmas, Los Olivos

Sources

County of Santa Barbara. Office of Long-range Planning. *2nd District County Lands Inventory with Enhancement Opportunities and Recommendations Report.* March 2006.

California Dept. of Fish & Game. *Burton Mesa Ecological Reserve Final Land Management Plan and Environmental Impact Report.* 2007.

City of Lompoc. *City of Lompoc Bicycle Transportation Plan.* November 2008.

City of Guadalupe *(ci.guadalupe.ca.us)*

City of Guadalupe. *Vision for Guadalupe 2030, Background Report.* December 2008.

City of Santa Barbara *(www.santabarbaraca.gov)*

City of Goleta *(www.cityofgoleta.org)*

City of Santa Maria *(www.ci.santa-maria.ca.us)*

City of Santa Maria. *Santa Maria Bikeway Master Plan.* Alta Planning + Design. Aug. 21, 2009.

City of Solvang *(www.cityofsolvang.com)*

County of Santa Barbara. County Executive Office. *Santa Barbara County Operating Plan, Proposed Budget 2009-10 Fiscal Year.* June 2009.

County of Santa Barbara. Planning & Development Dept. *COASTAL RESOURCES ENHANCEMENT FUND STATUS REPORT OF GRANTS, 1988-2008.* April 10, 2008, Updated August 26, 2008.

DriveInMovie.com (www.driveinmovie.com)

Gaviota Coast Conservancy (www.gaviotacoastconservancy.org)

Google Maps (maps.googlecom)

John McReynolds. *Lompoc: Padres to Pinot.* Lompoc: McReynolds. 2009.

La Purisima Audubon Society *(www.lapurisimaaudubon.org)*

More Mesa Preservation Coalition. *More Mesa Handbook.* December 2008

National Parks Service. Pacific West Regional Office. *Draft Gaviota Coast Feasibility Study & Environmental Assessment.* Martha Crusius et al, April 2003.

Santa Barbara County Parks *(www.sbparks.org)*

Santa Barbara Convention & Visitors Bureau *(www.santabarbaraca.com)*

Santa Barbara Hikes.com

Santa Barbara Visual Arts Association (www.sbva.org)

Santa Ynez Visitors Association (www.syvva.com)

Thomas Guide: Santa Barbara & San Luis Obispo Counties. Rand-McNally. 2008.

U.S. Census Bureau. *2009 Boundary and Annexation Survey (BAS): Goleta city, CA*

Walker A. Tompkins. *Montecito History.* www.theziagroup.com/MontecitoHistory.php

U.S. Census Bureau (quickfacts.census.gov)

Index

G

Gaffney Park 102
gallery 12, 13, 16-19, 21-25, 30, 31
Gallup & Stribling Orchid Farm 90
Ganna Walksa Lotusland 72
garden 13, 16, 18, 19, 20- 22, 26-28, 31-33, 37, 40, 41, 44-46, 48, 51, 53, 54, 56, 57, 64-66, 72, 87, 101, 111, 120, 125, 130, 139, 142, 182, 184, 185, 243, 255
Gaviota Coast Beach Access 215
Gaviota Peak 202
Gaviota Hot Springs 218
Gaviota State Park 216
Gemini Twin Theater 147
Gibraltar Reservoir 205
Girsch Park 102
Glen Annie Golf Club 102
Goleta 5, 74, 91-123, 234-236, 241, 242, 244-248, 250, 251, 254, 255, 258, 260, 261
Goleta Beach County Park 102
Goleta Library 94
Goleta Valley Community Center 120
golf 7, 57, 101-105, 108, 112, 115, 117, 118, 130, 156, 157, 187, 189, 190, 192, 212, 226, 249
Gould Park 41
Granada Theater 18
Grant House Sewing Machines 65
Greek Park 103
Grogan Park 178
Grossman Gallery 147
Guadalupe 5, 193-198, 224, 225, 235, 245, 247, 249, 253, 261
Guadalupe Cultural Arts & Education Center 194
Guadalupe Library 194
Guadalupe-Nipomo Dunes 195
gun club 191, 232, 233
gymnasium 67, 162, 177

H

Hagerman Sports Complex 178
Hale Park 41
Hammonds 74
handball 36, 74, 197
Hans Christian Andersen Museum 126
Hans Christian Andersen Park 129
Haskell's Beach 103
Hendry's Beach 34
Hi-way Drive In 169
Hidden Oaks Golf Course 104
Hidden Valley Neighborhood Park 41
Hilda McIntyre Ray Neighborhood Park 42
Hillside Park/Honda Valley Park 42
Horse 20, 163, 260
horse 20, 29, 128, 132, 133, 163, 179, 203, 225, 226, 260
horseback riding 55, 62, 111, 179
Horseshoe Pit 254
horseshoe pit 44, 103, 114, 130, 131, 153, 156, 158, 160, 177, 180, 182, 197, 198, 224, 226, 229, 254

I

Inspiration Point 62
Isla Vista 5, 91, 93, 95, 97, 99-101, 103-105, 107, 109-111, 113, 115, 116, 117, 118, 119, 121, 235
Isla Vista County Beach 104
Isla Vista Disc Golf Course 105
Isla Vista Teen Center 121
island 28, 86, 213
Island View Distinctive Flora 86

J

Jack O'Connell Park 196
Jalama Beach 219-221
Jim May Park 178
Joe White Park 179
Johns-Manville Park 155
Judith Hale Gallery 142

Notes